Connecting Generations

Connecting Generations

Bridging the Boomer, Gen X, and Millennial Divide

Hayim Herring, PhD

ROWMAN & LITTLEFIELD
Lanham • Boulder • New York • London

Published by Rowman & Littlefield
An imprint of The Rowman & Littlefield Publishing Group, Inc.
4501 Forbes Boulevard, Suite 200, Lanham, Maryland 20706
www.rowman.com

6 Tinworth Street, London SE11 5AL, United Kingdom

British Library Cataloguing in Publication Information Available

Library of Congress Cataloging-in-Publication Data

Names: Herring, Hayim, author.
Title: Connecting generations : bridging the boomer, Gen X, and millennial
    divide / Hayim Herring, PhD.
Description: Lanham : Rowman & Littlefield, [2019] | Includes bibliographical
    references and index.
Identifiers: LCCN 2019005454 (print) | LCCN 2019007689 (ebook) | ISBN
    9781538112175 (electronic) | ISBN 9781538112168 (cloth : alk. paper)
Subjects: LCSH: Intergenerational relations. | Intergenerational
    communication. | Social isolation—Prevention.
Classification: LCC HM726 (ebook) | LCC HM726 .H47 2019 (print) | DDC
    305.2—dc23
LC record available at https://lccn.loc.gov/2019005454

∞™ The paper used in this publication meets the minimum requirements of
American National Standard for Information Sciences—Permanence of Paper
for Printed Library Materials, ANSI/NISO Z39.48-1992.

Printed in the United States of America

Contents

~

Foreword

Jonah: Dad, why did we agree to write a foreword for a book when no one reads forewords?

David: Jonah! What are you talking about? It's an honor to be asked to write someone's foreword.

Jonah: Oh, I don't doubt that at all. I think it's a huge honor. But I still don't think it's worth it when no one reads a foreword.

David: Who says that no one reads a foreword?

Jonah: C'mon! It's like an introduction or prologue. . . . blah, blah, blah . . . Just get to it with chapter 1!

David: But Jonah, a good book needs setup, explanations, introductions to the main characters. Of course, people read forewords.

Jonah: Nah. That's what a book flap is for.

Ah . . . a generational difference at its finest! To David, a Gen Xer, it makes all the sense in the world to have a linear setup that prepares the reader for what they are about to dive in to. However, to Jonah, a Gen Z'er, he's used to all of his media and entertainment being streamlined, or to having the ability to fast forward through a commercial. So naturally, anything other than starting with chapter 1 feels like a waste. Maybe ask a Millennial and the conversation could be all about whether or not the book comes in an e-version. Ask a Boomer and, who knows, the conversation could be all about the author's credentials.

For years people have analyzed factors like gender, race, ethnicity, socio-economic status, religion, educational background, thinking styles, Myers-Briggs profiles, even signs of the zodiac, to find ways to understand each other better. Yet somehow most have failed to recognize the form of diversity that affects every human being on a daily basis—*generational differences.*

When many think of a generation, they immediately think of a person's age. "Oh, he is sixty-five, he must be a Baby Boomer!" Contrary to popular belief, connections or conflicts between generations are not simply the result of differences in age. Generational differences go much deeper. The key to understanding generations and why connections and conflicts arise is to adopt an ageless attitude. You do this by looking at how each generation shares a common history. Certain events and conditions have determined a lot about who we are and how we see the world. As a result of these events and conditions, each generation has adopted its own and unique "generational personality."

Events and conditions can include all kinds of things. For example, they can be day-to-day *icons* like our heroes, sports stars, slogans, favorite products, or songs. (What Boomer wouldn't identify on some level with the slogan, "Turn on, tune in, drop out?" And what Xer doesn't remember, "Just say no?") Or they can be actual *events,* such as Richard Nixon's impeachment, the civil rights and women's rights movements, the Gulf War, or 9/11.

Conditions are the forces at work in the environment as each generation comes of age. The Cold War was a condition that permeated the youth of many Boomers, while Millennials born after 1989 will never know a world in which there were two different cities called East and West Berlin. Economic upheavals are conditions that profoundly affect the wealth and health of our citizens and permanently affect our way of looking at the world. Those who lived through the Great Depression or who were raised by parents who did were changed forever by the fear of not having a job and being able to put food on the table. Other large-scale upheavals in one's upbringing, such as major changes in the divorce rate, the marriage rate, or the number of single-parent families, can all play a role in shaping the generations.

Take something like space exploration. Ask a Boomer who witnessed a man landing on the moon as a youth and he/she will say it is very exciting. Compare that to a Gen Xer who witnessed the Challenger and he/she is likely a lot more skeptical. What about a Millennial or Gen Z'er? Who needs NASA when we have Elon Musk!

The generations' influences play out during their formative years. This results in a set of different attitudes, values, and work styles that each generation wakes up with every day.

The problem is that we definitely know the lens through which our own generation sees the world. However, we so rarely put on the lens of a different generation to understand how they see the world. We simply assume that everyone sees the world the same way. We do not take the time to understand the events and conditions that shape another generation. When is the last time you went out to lunch with someone from a different generation and said, "Say, I would really love to hear about a big event that took place during your formative years that shaped your view of the world." Again, we just assume everyone is looking through the same lens. Then, when we encounter someone who thinks a different way, we immediately judge and go into the mode of trying to figure out who is right, wrong, better, or worse.

When it comes to generations, no one is right, wrong, better, or worse. The generations are just different.

Unfortunately, too many shy away from differences and see them as obstacles rather than what they really are . . . opportunities. This book helps readers see those opportunities. It breaks down the stereotypes that we have about the different generations so that we can not only embrace what makes each generation unique but can leverage each other's strengths.

Right now, there are so many strengths to be leveraged, as never in history have we had so many living generations trying to work together and communicate with one another on a daily basis. Who do we have?

- The Traditionalists, born between the turn of the century and the end of World War II (1900–1945), are a combination of two generations who tend to believe and behave very similarly. This population is comprised of about seventy-five million people.
- The Baby Boomers (1946–1964) were the largest population at eighty million, until their children came along.
- The Generation Xers (1965–1979) are a much smaller but very influential population at forty-six million.
- The Millennials (1980–1994), who are the children of the Boomers, represent the largest demographic cohort at eighty-two million.
- Finally, we have the Gen Z'ers (1995–2012), who at seventy-eight million might not be as large as Millennials, but whose influence is already making a mark.

As we have been traveling the world to introduce Gen Z, we are met with so many leaders who will say, "Gee Jonah, Gen Z sounds very interesting, but I am going to wait until they are a little bit older to really get to know them." What that is code for is: "I am going to wait until they get older and are more like me." Unfortunately, that never happens, and the only thing created is an increase in generational gaps.

It's easy to look at the different generations and think, don't we all have to be born, be educated, find work, find partners, create families, age, retire, and eventually die? And don't we hit these life stages pretty similarly? The answer is yes, and no. Yes, we all have certain life stages in common, but no, the different generations do not approach them the same way. But again, what happens is that we run away from these differences, rather than embrace them. Whether it be retiring, parenting, or getting a job—no generation has ever done a life stage the same as others. They each put their own stamp on it.

What makes this book so important is that it not only embraces generational differences, but it shows readers how beneficial they truly are. Now, more than ever, we need to be engaged in intergenerational dialogue as there are forces at play that are keeping the generations from bridging gaps.

One area is the business world. Consider . . .

The "war for talent" is fierce. Much of the challenge has nothing to do with economics and everything to do with demographics. Because Generation X is close to half the size of the Baby Boom, as the older generations move up and out of organizations, the labor pool to draw upon is just dramatically smaller. In other words, regardless of what happens with the economy, there will always be fewer workers available from the age group that's currently poised to move into the management ranks. It is pretty scary when you consider how many Boomers are getting ready to retire in droves. At the other end of the spectrum, with the younger generations feeling like they live in a global village as well as having so many more options to pursue, they are definitely way more spread out when it comes to opportunities, making it harder to recruit.

Innovation is being redefined. So many companies have boasted about having an innovative culture to help recruit and retain a multigenerational workforce. However, most don't realize that the younger generations define "innovation" differently. Therefore, many of the conversations about looking ahead and getting ahead aren't evening resonating or on the same page.

Commerce is being turned upside down. Traditionalists, Boomers, Xers, and Millennials all witnessed retail going from brick-and-mortar to online and e-commerce. However, we now have a generation (Gen Z) that has seen retail start online and is now building brick-and-mortar. Every powerful brand in the world asks itself, "How is our customer service?" The problem is that the answer doesn't include multigenerational aspects. The real question is "What is our customer service?" because each generation has its own definition.

But of course, it's more than just business. There are also changes in society as a whole that are depriving us of intergenerational dialogues. Consider this . . .

Segregated living. When previous generations arrived in this country it was the norm to have two, if not three, generations living under one roof. Today, there are senior neighborhoods with age restrictions, and heaven forbid there is a Big Wheel in the driveway. Or there are young, urban neighborhoods with trendy restaurants and coffee shops that don't have a gray hair around for miles. With living becoming more segregated by generation, we have become one step removed from having intergenerational engagement on a daily basis.

The rate of change is so fast. Whether through differences in shared history, language, work experience, education, or even communication style, it is increasingly difficult for the generations to find common ground at work. A few decades ago, three or four generations might have gathered together to listen to *The Shadow* on the radio. Now we hear a Traditionalist complaining that radio is dead and that there's nothing decent on television, a Boomer still lamenting the loss of *Seinfeld*, an Xer explaining how she is trying a new streaming platform, a Millennial sharing that he no longer has cable TV and only downloads, and a Gen Z'er who claims YouTube is their entertainment network of choice. As a result, it's no longer possible to assume that a multigenerational group of people will have the same life experiences in common. This translates into communication challenges and a breakdown of the bonds that have traditionally been so strong.

The political landscape is so polarizing. It used to be that regardless of one's political camp, the feeling was still that we were *all* in it together to make our country a better place. Republicans and Democrats reached across aisles to make our country the best it could be. Today, if there is one topic that is polarizing, it's politics. Now, all we see are Republicans and Democrats bashing one another and doing everything to stop the other's progress. The last thing this suggests is that the generations can come together and make the world a better place.

There's a new generation and no one is paying attention. Hark back to the '90s and any Xer will tell you they remember that all the attention was on the Boomers and that Gen X was ignored. Flash forward a couple of decades and it's déjà vu. There is so much chatter about the Millennials that no one is paying attention to Jonah's generation—Gen Z. If we treat Gen Z like the Millennials, it will backfire—and it already is. While this book may focus on Boomers and Millennials, let's be clear. *All* voices are needed. One nonprofit we worked with decided to roll out their youth marketing strategy again, as it was so successful in the year 2000 with the Millennials. The problem is that they tried the same strategy and didn't realize that this was a new generation. It failed, as did their attempt to pull in a new generation.

As we have seen, each generation has its own wonderful lens through which they look at the world. Each lens provides a point of view that is not only valid, but so needed. If only we would take off our own lens and look through the lens of a different generation. The more we put on other lenses, the wider our view becomes. There is no denying that we need all the generations' voices at the table and working together. The timing of this book is critical. If we become more segregated, the business world will suffer, our communities will suffer, and most of all—we as people will pay a price. We will become more and more isolated.

Now we know there are still readers who have a skeptical eyebrow up. We meet you on a daily basis as we travel the world exploring intergenerational communication. Some of you have shared your skeptical tone during Q & A and have asked, "Hey, aren't you two just perpetuating stereotypes when you try to tell us that a member of a generation is going to think or act a certain way?"

It's a fair question, and for that person, we have two answers.

First, you can make generalizations about people. If one generation experienced a divorce rate of 15 percent during their formative years and a later generation experienced a 50 percent divorce rate, you can bet they have been impacted by divorce in different ways. Likewise, if one generation grew up during the Great Depression and another during a long economic boom, we can make some assumptions about how they view the marketplace. People can't help but be influenced as a generation by the events and conditions that have shaped who we are and how we see the world.

But the second answer is this: we expect that anyone who is interested enough in reading Hayim's book has a genuine desire to gain some new tools for dealing with the generations in thoughtful ways. And we assume that every reader has the moral sense to try earnestly not to use information to stereotype people but to become a better listener, a better observer of the human condition, a better boss, or a better friend. And those are the people for whom Hayim has written this book. His mission is not to put people in a box, but to open up the box so that we can all get a better glimpse of who and what is inside.

—David Stillman (Gen Xer)
—Jonah Stillman (Gen Z'er)

Acknowledgments

In writing my last Rowman & Littlefield publication, *Leading Congregations and Nonprofits in a Connected World: Platforms, People, and Purpose* (November 2016), coauthored with Dr. Terri Elton, I became acquainted with Linda Ganster, Editorial Director in the Academic and Professional Division of Rowman & Littlefield. I contacted her in July 2017 with an early-stage idea about a book that would be unlike my other books that Rowman & Littlefield had acquired and published. This volume would address issues of social isolation and a generalized sense of disequilibrium that people of all generations were feeling because so much of our knowledge about how relationships, employment, education, and our civic communities worked no longer seemed relevant. Linda was very encouraging and suggested that I develop the idea into a full proposal that she could discuss with her editorial team.

A few weeks later and to my delight, Linda responded that her colleagues also thought that this proposal had merit and, without mentioning any of her team members' names, told me that she had "some thoughts" about who would be an excellent choice as my executive acquisitions editor. Enter Suzanne Staszak-Silva! Suzanne is someone who reminds authors that writing and editing are two distinct skill sets through the essential questions that she asks and incisive comments that she offers. Suzanne, if this book has the broad impact that Linda, you, your team, and I hope it does, it will be in no small measure because of your thoughtful and high editorial standards.

I also had some extremely significant help from another Millennial, someone who was not afraid to be completely forthright with me while I was conducting research and sharing ideas about this book: my daughter, Tamar Krivosha. Even as a young child, I noticed that she had a gift of seeing what others often could not, which expressed itself in asking the kinds of questions that not even her clever parents had considered. Now, as a young woman with a law degree, just imagine how much deeper and more focused that talent has become! When I asked Tamar to review my initial draft interview questions that I was planning to ask Baby Boomers and Millennials, her overall response was something like, "You're not asking the right questions, and even if you were, you can't ask them that way!" Thank you, Tamar, for restraining my more academic impulses and in helping me to reframe these questions and ideas in ways that honored the many people who were willing to participate in the research that I conducted for this book. Had you not intervened, instead of being the lively people they are, these interview subjects would have come across as dusty museum portraits that had been stored in an unnumbered, locked closet.

To meet an accelerated deadline, and because editing is not my forte, I engaged Kayla Hechsel as my personal editor for this volume. I felt so confident in her editorial abilities when I first met her that I made her an offer on the spot and I'm grateful that she accepted. Kayla, thank you for enabling me to submit a manuscript that met the high expectations of Rowman & Littlefield and for graciously adapting to my compressed timetable for completing the manuscript.

My previous books and articles have primarily focused on the intersections of community, spirituality, technology, and organizational structure. I wrote them for a niche audience of readers who are active in faith-based spiritual and nonprofit communities, which is another way of saying that only two family members were able to read past the introduction of my prior books. I don't fault them, because these books straddled the worlds of theory and practice of synagogue, the Jewish community, and lately, parts of the Protestant world. I wouldn't read them either if they were not my area of interest or calling.

But as I mentioned, this volume addresses contemporary issues about what it means to be human, to be in relationships with others of all ages, and to live purposeful lives in vital communities. Although it has great application for faith-based communities, my audience is anyone who believes that people of all ages have something precious and unique to share with one another, and in the act of sharing, have the potential to enrich our families and communities. For me, being alive means to continue to grow in new directions, and this volume is what I hope will be one of the first fruits of an expanded course of life that enables me to plow territory that is new for me, with colleagues whom I had never met before and were incredibly generous with their time and expertise, while still tending my longstanding field of interest in spiritual communities.

I interviewed approximately thirty individuals for this book and spoke with many more. Ten of them are experts on intergenerational issues, and you can learn about them in appendix C. I have used fictitious names for the other approximately twenty Baby Boomers, Gen Xers, Millennials, and even several elderly active individuals whom I interviewed, but that won't affect how inspirational you'll find them. I also want to thank my neighbors, Buffy Abrams and Stephen Ziff, for sharing their feedback and helpful resources in refining several concepts and suggesting action steps that I included in this book.

I've never asked other authors if they have acquired any idiosyncrasies to help motivate them to complete a book. But I have one that is exceptionally compelling, namely, visualizing the faces of those mentioned in the dedication paragraph. Holding this visual image of the people in my life who are so important to me is something that sustains me during the process of conducting research and writing a book. Thankfully, I've been able to dedicate my prior books to my parents and my in-laws, my wife, my children and my grandson. (Sisters and brothers-in-law, I haven't forgotten about you; hopefully, more writing to come!) Having touched my most immediate family bases, I could only see a blank space for the dedication but wasn't especially concerned as I trusted that an answer would emerge.

And it did in a most joyful way. I was speaking with my senior editor one afternoon about the flow of the book's chapters and remembered that I still was uncertain about who I wanted to dedicate the book to—until my phone rang about an hour later. My son and daughter-in-law, Avi and Shaina Herring, told me that grandchild number two was on the way, and without hesitation, I could visualize that blank dedicatory paragraph writing itself. You can decide if that was serendipitous or providential, but having just spoken with my senior editor about the book and pondering to whom I would dedicate it, I was literally taken aback. Liba Amalya, *Savta* ("grandmother" in Hebrew) and I want to thank you, not only for filling in the blank space on the page, but for filling our hearts with so much joy and love. I dedicate this book to you.

I also want to dedicate it to another individual whose name recurred in thinking and writing about intergenerational issues: Rabbi Kassel Abelson. In the Jewish tradition, we're taught that we have biological parents and spiritual parents, teachers who shape our souls and character. We recognize that while we may not be able to accomplish as much as our spiritual parents, they inspire us to do more than we think we're capable of achieving. The path that we pursue will invariably differ from our spiritual parents. But they also endow us with confidence because their values strengthen us to live with purpose, develop enriching relationships, and strive to make our communities better. Since 1985, Rabbi Abelson has been my mentor, teacher, and spiritual parent, and when I read about ancient rabbinic sages from the past, whose humility masked their dedication and service to their communities, I realize that some of them still live among us today. I also dedicate this book to my spiritual parent, Rabbi Kass Abelson.

Liba, you're now about nine months old, and Rabbi Abelson is ninety-four years old. Rabbi Abelson is a member of the Greatest Generation, which means that he was born prior to 1928. Liba, you're so young that, alas, your generational cohort has not yet been given a name! But the two of you make a perfect pairing in a dedication for a book about intergenerational communities and locating the common tasks of each generation, independent of the generational labels that sociologists give you. In addition to the many positive attributes you'll gain from being a part of a wonderful family, my prayer is that I will be able to transmit in some measure Rabbi Abelson's kindness and goodness in relating to all people, regardless of background, as reflections of God's image.

~

Introduction

Some people greatly enjoy jigsaw puzzles. I'm not one of them, but for the past several years, I've grappled with what has felt like a kind of jigsaw puzzle that involves people and trends instead of pictures and words. Here are four stories that I'll metaphorically call "jigsaw puzzle pieces" because they initially appeared to look random, the way that puzzle pieces do when first opening a new puzzle box filled with pieces. But I've intuitively felt that these "pieces" or stories were somehow connected. I imagined that if I could envision how they fit together, they would create a compelling picture that could especially inspire Baby Boomers, Gen Xers and Millennials to think about their lives and relationships with their peers, and with those who are younger and older.

Puzzle Piece 1:
The Short Life of My New Winter Coat

Last year, after noticing several holes in my fifteen-year-old winter coat, my wife and a few friends gently suggested that it was time to buy a new one. As a Sabbath-observing Jew in Minnesota, purchasing a heavy winter coat is no trifling matter. Although I only have a ten-minute walk to synagogue, when it's minus twenty degrees Fahrenheit, being covered from hood to toe with a long coat can be a literal lifesaver. My coat was so bulky that one of my friends in New York once described it as a tent with a zipper, while another said that I looked like I was wearing a space suit. (When I first moved to Minnesota, I was so shocked by the tundra that I now call home, I even purchased ski goggles to protect the area around my eyes, although I didn't ski!) The problem was that in the fifteen years since I had purchased that brand of coat, I was unsure if I could find a model with the specs that would really protect me from the cold. Newer technologies and fabrics guaranteed the same warmth with less bulk, but I was skeptical. Nonetheless, I decided to search on Amazon and within a few minutes I found what was advertised as a "slim men's long down coat and attached hood." Having a hood with faux fur trim was not exactly my style, but I was cold and desperate, so I used my "One Click" option and bought it.

I was grateful to see the box with my new coat on my doorstep in just a few days, but mildly appalled when I opened it. Not only did it have fake fur trim on the hood, but it also had leather epaulets on the shoulders that I didn't notice when I viewed it on my computer screen. Still, I reasoned, I wouldn't be wearing it that frequently and as a non-native Minnesotan, I had decided long ago that my motto during winters would be "function over fashion." When I tried it on for size and saw that it covered me as promised, I decided to keep it.

In the several days that passed since I ordered it, I noticed that when I logged on to Amazon for some books, advertisements for women's coats kept popping up on my screen. I didn't pay much attention to them, or perhaps I was intentionally in denial that some foreign manufacturer had passed off an overstock of long down coats for women as "slim men's coats." I had some upcoming travel and was flying into cold weather, so I braved the mild embarrassment of wearing my new coat. When I was waiting at the airport for my plane, I did a double take when I saw a tall woman who was wearing the exact same coat as mine—faux fur trim around the hood, leather epaulets, and all. The next week when I had to fly again, it was still chilly (by Minnesota standards, about ten degrees Fahrenheit) so with determination, I zippered my coat, drove to the airport and, while waiting for my plane, saw another person wearing the same coat—only this time it was a man. When I returned to Minneapolis, I promptly donated my coat to a clothing drive and reached for my old, tattered, winter coat that I hadn't yet discarded. I was taken aback at the sight of a woman wearing the identical coat that I had purchased, but when I saw a man wearing it, I realized how utterly ridiculous I must have looked. (I mean no disrespect to anyone else's fashion tastes, but that coat was definitely not me!) In retrospect, some Amazon algorithm had indeed determined that I had purchased a woman's coat, and that's why advertisements kept appearing on my Amazon home screen for several weeks promoting "great deals on women's winter coats."

Puzzle Piece 2:
Lunch at Perkins and Panera

Throughout much of my life, I have been fortunate in having older friends and mentors. Coincidentally, about six years ago, I scheduled a time to meet separately with several of them within a six-week period. I learned over time that "having a cup of coffee together" was not as meaningful as having breakfast or lunch at Perkins or Panera, the two clear favorite restaurants for these seniors. Setting a time for lunch rather than just meeting for a "cup of coffee" signaled to them that we could have more time together. As I had no "agenda" other than wanting to spend time with them, I stopped asking my mentors if they wanted to meet over coffee and invited them to lunch. My mentors were then between the ages of seventy and eighty-five, in relatively good health, living independently and married except for one recently wid-owed individual. At some point during each lunch, unprompted, they made similar observations about their stage of life, which I would paraphrase as: "I still feel that I have something to offer to those who are younger, but I can't find a way to connect with them. There aren't any places for me to naturally interact with people of different generations. Don't misunderstand me, when I encounter younger people, they are polite and inquire about my health. But the conversations never go any further."

These older individuals were not interested in creating a new initiative or leading a program. They were bright, social, and altruistic people who were eager to engage with younger individuals about contemporary issues, curious about how they were living life today, and interested in hearing about how they saw their future. They did not want to spend much time with people who were living independently, but whom they considered "old," replaying yesterday's experiences. They preferred to spend more time looking ahead, drawing upon the past for insights, but looking at life through the front wind-shield and not the rearview mirror. What made their observation about not knowing how to contribute to others more poignant was that they had family members nearby with whom they regularly spent time. But they still felt like they had "too much time on their hands," and "more to give," which sounded to me like they were also lonely and unsure of how to find more organic ways for intergenerational interactions.

Puzzle Piece 3:
Disequilibrium Does Not Discriminate

My wife is an accomplished corporate attorney. Over the years, I noticed how she had participated in various "women's only" professional groups. These were not support or self-help groups, but a group of peers who seemed to energize one another by connecting regularly. As a member of the emotionally less intelligent gender, I finally realized that meeting informally with a group of male peers could be valuable. A few years ago, one of my very best friends, Bill, said to me, "It's too bad that you don't know Jim and Jon.[1] I get together with each of you individually, and I really think that the four of us would have fun." My friend had retired from work many years ago and is one of those all-around great guys who is a full-time volunteer. As he had more discretionary time than the other three of us, I replied, "Well, you're retired. Why don't you organize a time for us to get together and we'll see how it goes?" Within a few weeks, we were sipping Scotch together at his home, and testing the waters and spirits for potential future get-togethers. While we don't meet as frequently as we would like, we have been meeting ever since and greatly value the times when we're able to schmooze.

Our discussions have been wide-ranging, from issues relating to the decline in health and eventual death of parents in some cases, to our adult children, who must have read about the concept of "delayed adulthood" based on our opinions about how long it was taking some of them to grow up. We also listened to one another's career struggles, transitions, and triumphs. We helped each other through some difficult crises and marveled at the joyful milestones that we celebrated individually and in our families: college and graduate school graduations, weddings, grandchildren, crossing into a new decade of life, and changing career directions.

In retrospect, I realized that the experience of "meeting with the guys" enabled me to understand that I wasn't alone in feeling like the ground beneath my feet was unsteady. In different ways, we were all experiencing a sense of disequilibrium. Unanticipated changes in our work, coaching our children into young adulthood more than we expected, fine-tuning our relationships with our marriage partners, and feeling like we just couldn't find the sweet spot between balancing concern for our parents' well-being with equal care for their dignity left us feeling like our internal gyroscopes were malfunctioning. They could not keep us on the course of how we expected our lives to unfold. It wasn't the Scotch that made us wobbly; the cause was living in an intergenerational world characterized by ever-accelerating changes in many areas of our lives.

The Final Piece to the Puzzle:
More Connected and More Lonely

For decades, I've also engaged in volunteer work with teenagers. From that experience, and some formal training in adolescent development, I knew that teens can enjoy the presence of older adults who create space to discuss issues of importance to them—provided that these adults are not their own parents! Like my older mentors, they also wanted to be heard, respected, and engaged in thinking about pressing issues. However, they often felt that adults did not value their opinions and disempowered them from self-initiating action. Many had caring high school teachers, but teachers are often mired in mastering the latest state curricular standards or adjusting to the newest school principal's idea on "reinventing education,"[2] leaving them with little time to be available for teens who could benefit from a trusted adult outside of classroom hours.

Youth group leaders typically range in age from students in their college years to young adults in their mid-thirties. But youth group participation is less popular than it used to be, so many teens have lost another channel for connecting with young adults. And if teens even encounter an older neighbor, they may judge that older neighbor as "nice" but not of much value. They do not understand that while Google is phenomenal for facts, it cannot offer the lived experience, empathy, and inventiveness that someone older has acquired. They're feeling pressure at an earlier age to think "strategically" about how to advance their educational goals and can't imagine how someone a generation or two older may be of use to them. (I've heard this anecdotally from parents whose children are only in ninth grade.) Today's Millennials have been weaned on technology, and the generation behind them, even more so. As they live so much of their lives online and lack ongoing interactions with adults who are not their parents,[3] they cannot remember a time when intergenerational interactions were the norm, nor can they appreciate how this absence of connectivity compounds their feelings of social isolation.

Puzzled Solved: My Coat, My Lunches,
My Friends, and Youth Work

What do these stories and observations have to do with one another? Together, they illustrate three truths that form the foundation and integrated framework for this book:

1. We need fulfilling relationships with people our own age and across the generations to lead lives that are rich in meaning and purpose.

2. Social and technological revolutions create powerful waves of isolation that disconnect us from one another.
3. Regardless of age, we're all experiencing a feeling of ongoing disequilibrium, as if we can never adapt quickly enough to the changes swirling around us. Whether you're eighty or twenty-eight years old, if you consider how you're living many aspects of your life today, they are probably different than only a few years ago and are likely to be different a few years from now.

My hunch that these seemingly random "puzzle pieces" were related has led me on the most fascinating investigative journey that I've ever undertaken and deepened my understanding of how critically important it is to intentionally foster more intergenerational communities. I'll introduce you to others who have been doing this work and the stories and insights of about thirty diverse individuals[4] whom I interviewed for this book. While my journey is only beginning, I hope that this work will create a new paradigm that integrates the realities of having six generations of people alive today, the hunger for greater social connection within and across generations, and the velocity of change in so many areas of our lives into an urgent call for us to think and act intergenerationally. Knowing the tremendous value of intergenerational relationships, my question now is, "Are we ready to recover and reprioritize intergenerational relationships as a societal good that we can't afford to lose? Will we reorient our inner attitudes and external social environments so that intergenerational relationships and communities will flourish again?"

Sociologists give names that differentiate generations from one another,[5] based on the most formative events that shape their view of the world when they are young and persist throughout their lifetimes. These labels are helpful as they provide insights into differing attributes and attitudes that need to be navigated in our families, workplaces, and communities. Yet, what I heard from others and read about suggested that individuals across the generational spectrum were attuned to the unpredictably rapid turns that their lives could take without warning, were feeling less connected with those in their own generational cohorts, and had few if any friends from different generations. Young and old, although sometimes for different reasons, were feeling more lonely and isolated. Perhaps underneath the distinctive generational labels that we use—Gen Z or post-Millennials (that is, individuals born after the year 2000; think "today's 'teens,' the oldest of the youngest generation alive today"), Millennials, Gen Xers, Baby Boomers, the Silent Generation and the Greatest Generations—there was some inflection point that individuals of all ages were experiencing that called for conversations. But there aren't many organic venues to share, name, and learn from one another about how to navigate these changes. Clearly, generational labels are useful for underscoring what is unique about people born at a given time, but I began to wonder if they also obscured what we shared, and inhibited possibilities for reconnecting people across the generations. Fostering intergenerational relationships is something that we will need more experience in, as having six generations alive at one time is an unprecedented norm.

While there are six distinct generations alive today—Gen Z, Millennials, Gen Xers, Baby Boomers, and the very elderly members of the Silent and Greatest Generations—telling the stories and researching the unique attributes of all these generations could be an ambitious project better suited for academics and a legion of research assistants. While my observations rest upon research, my goals in writing this book are not academic. Rather, I've written this book for those who are eager to learn from others' real-world experience in navigating family, professional, and volunteer issues that frequently involve people from multiple generations. I also decided at the wise recommendation of my editor, Suzanne Staszak-Silva, to focus more deeply on two generations, Baby Boomers and Millennials, rather than broadly on all six generations, for several reasons.

First, their stories and perceptions of one another are also relevant for upcoming generations as well. They provide some concepts for making sense of life across the generational spectrum as it continues to emerge in the twenty-first century. Second, as a younger Baby Boomer, I am intimately familiar with the issues that I'll be exploring but can still maintain some objectivity as a researcher. Additionally, Baby Boomers and Millennials are currently roughly equivalent in number—approximately seventy-five million each.[6] Issues, experiences, and experiments surrounding intergenerational interactions are therefore abundant and easily accessible.

Although separated by only one generation, changes in societal values and technological revolutions have reinvented almost every aspect of how we experience daily life—from education to entertainment, from doctor-patient relationships to membership in civic or faith communities. The ways that these two generations are responding to these significant changes are often radically different at first blush, creating the potential for serious misunderstanding between Baby Boomers and Millennials. With the proliferation of social apps, we seem to have decreased our ability to openly and empathetically discuss differences in how our respective generations are trying to make sense of our world.

With a tighter focus on these two numerically significant generations, I aspire to build better bridges of mutual understanding and collaboration between them and provide a window through which upcoming generations can peer to learn more about themselves and their intergenerational interactions. Many Gen Xers are likely to find aspects of their lives and relationships with parents, children, colleagues, and neighbors in this book. By interviewing a diverse group of experts who have vast experience in intergenerational issues, I have also been able to expand the discussion about intergenerational relationships and communities beyond Baby Boomers and Millennials. Regardless of your age, you'll hopefully find this volume of interest and value, as currently no other book examines the impacts of increasing social isolation and accelerating societal and technological forces of change through an intergenerational lens.

In researching this book, I have learned how important it is to distinguish between the terms "multigenerational" and "intergenerational." "Multigenerational" is a demographic reality, signifying the number of generations alive at one time. As noted, that number is six, an unprecedented phenomenon in human history that's here to stay. "Intergenerational" means the intentional fostering of relationships across the generations that provide mutual meaning and purpose. "Multigenerational" is a number; "intergenerational" is a value. Therefore, I use both terms with their unique meanings and not interchangeably.

Overview

Are we on the verge of an epidemic of loneliness, or is the "loneliness crisis" just another hot topic that will soon be replaced by the next big issue? There is convincing evidence that increased loneliness and social isolation are real issues, with devastating costs for people of all generations and our broader society. While it's wise to be cautious about prognostications, there are alarming indications that social isolation and loneliness are only likely to increase without intentional interventions that community leaders can take now to mitigate their damaging impacts. In chapter 1, I set the context for understanding the multifaceted reasons for this epidemic of loneliness, and why intergenerational relationships have the potential to restore individuals' feelings of purpose and self-worth.

In chapter 2, I introduce a broad framework for contrasting Boomer and Millennial worldviews that emerged from my primary and secondary research. This framework helps to illuminate the stereotypes that Boomers and Millennials hold of one another. It also provides the context for the book's remaining chapters on how these two generations think about the nature and value of community, participation in community (civic, sectarian, or faith-based), education, and work. I conclude this chapter with an examination of how Baby Boomers and Millennials view the impact of social media and digital technologies on their relationships with family and friends, and share a hopeful research finding that can contribute to restoring critical conversations between these generations.

Building upon the framework in chapter 2, I'll explore new relational ground among Baby Boomers, their elderly parents, and their Millennial children in greater depth in chapter 3. What separates today from the past is that we lack inherited wisdom in addressing some unprecedented family issues that result from having so many different generations alive at one time. For example, some Baby Boomers could recall "the talk" that their Greatest or Silent Generation parents had with them when they were adolescents: there was "the talk" about "safe driving" and "the talk" about "responsible relationships." When Baby Boomers' children, who are Millennials, approached adolescence, Boomers could update and apply some inherited wisdom to guide them in their discussions with their adolescent children. But for Boomers who have aging or elderly parents, we lack inherited precedents to help us sensitively raise delicate questions about their capacity for driving, or inquire about their sexual activity if they find romance again after the death of a spouse.

These are just some of the new issues that will create further distance across generations unless we learn how to talk with one another about them. In this chapter, I'll suggest healthy, alternative strategies for initiating these conversations that replace the stereotyping and "distort and divide" tactics commonly in use that compound generational misunderstandings. Gen Xers and Millennials are witnessing Boomers' interactions with the most elderly in our communities. Whether they learn to adopt an intergenerational approach to relating to others will depend in part on how they see Boomers encounter unprecedented situations with elderly parents and their own children.

In chapter 4, I'll explore the value that different generations attach to the concept of "community." By community, I am referring to a group of people who gather voluntarily and regularly with nonrelatives to pursue an interest or cause. A "community" might be a church, a civic organization, or neighborhood sports league. The constant, common elements of community have been an ongoing commitment to being in relationships with a core group of people and experiencing a feeling of meaning that transcends self and family by engaging in shared, purposeful work.

I'll also examine mental models that individuals from different generations have of "community." Does participating in a community require at least some face-to-face time with others in the same room physically, as Boomers claim, or does ongoing participation in a network through FaceTime or other digital platforms also constitute an alternative but equally valid experience of community? As augmented, virtual, and holographic reality technologies simulate an even greater feeling of intimacy, bringing our subconscious mental models about "community" into the light of our awareness is a pressing task to undertake.

No discussion about "community" is complete without exploring how past housing policies and more promising future trends in housing influence greater or lesser generational segregation. As America has become a more polarized nation, the sustainability of diverse communities is becoming more challenging.[7] That is why understanding the values that individuals attach to community, their implicit mental constructs of community, and how they physically live in community is critical for advancing the creation of intergenerational relationships and communities.

Education: how complicated can this topic be from a generational perspective? Extremely! Members of the Silent Generation, born between 1928 and 1945, had more neatly defined educational choices, typically intertwined with gender. Men who graduated from high school could easily enter the workforce, especially if they had vocational training, joined a union and became an apprentice at a trade, entered the military for a period of years and acquired training in fields like electronics if they didn't want to become "career military," or find work in manufacturing. Those who could afford it furthered their education and entered lucrative professions like medicine, law, and accounting. Women had far fewer options. Some went to college and became teachers or nurses, but many entered the workforce after high school for a brief time as secretaries. They may have worked for several years, had children and devoted the rest of their lives to raising a family, or resumed working or pursuing an advanced degree once their children were older.

Beginning with Baby Boomers, when educational options became more accessible to both men and women, and continuing with Gen Xers and Millennials, the percentage of individuals who earned a college degree has increased.[8] The trajectory of those completing at least a bachelor's degree has been on a consistent upward climb for five generations—the Greatest Generation, the Silent Generation, Baby Boomers, Gen Xers, and Millennials—and the gap between men and women who were college-educated has not only narrowed but has become inverted with more Millennial women than men earning a bachelor's degree.[9]

Today, the educational landscape is more like a maze of unclear options than a clear trajectory for younger and older generations. Think about the different calculations that members of each generation must consider. If you're a post-Millennial, you're trying to understand how to prepare educationally today for a job that may not exist three or five years from now. If you're a Millennial or Gen Xer, you may be weighing options for upgrading your skills and educational credentials without incurring additional debt because you hadn't been forewarned about how school loans could damage your overall financial health for the rest of your life. And if you're a Baby Boomer who is still in the workforce, you may have to hire a high school or college student to help you master a new technology that your work now demands to remain competitive.

Older adult workers who no longer need additional educational credentials, and those who have retired from the workforce or are close to retirement, often engage in learning opportunities because they view learning as an important source of growth. On the local level, community centers, libraries, and college campuses market classes to Boomers, and Boomers can also take advantage of a plethora of online learning formats, including TED talks, podcasts, graduate-level courses on platforms like Coursera or edX, or workshops on a range of skills and interests at little cost on platforms like Udemy or LinkedIn. Employers have expectations that their employees will engage in formal or experiential education, and many retired or semi-retired Boomers are engaged in learning, so I have subtitled chapter 5 on education, "anything, anyone, anytime anywhere," reflecting the vast array of educational options now available for those who need it for employment and for those who voluntarily engage in learning.

A typical first meeting between two Baby Boomers who haven't met before might go something like, "Hi, my name is Sam. I'm an attorney. What's your name and what do you do?" The response might be, "Hi, I'm Suzanne and I'm a writer." For many Boomers, disentangling their work and professional identities is challenging. However, Millennials seem to have an easier ability to express multiple facets of themselves and do not automatically default to their primary identity of how they earn a living. Sometimes, Baby Boomers interpret that separation between work and other identities as a sign of "laziness" or "lack of passion." And Millennials may interpret Baby Boomers' obsession with work as self-absorption with power, status, and authority. Of course, these are generalizations, and I know Baby Boomers, Gen Xers, and Millennials who sell mortgages or work as administrative assistants during the day and play or sing in a band on the weekends. When asked "What do you do," they answer, "I'm a singer" or "I'm a musician." It's their passion that defines their identity and not the number of hours that they spend on the job. The meaning that people of different generations ascribe to work and its impact on their identity often varies by generation, and we'll explore that and related issues in chapter 6.

In the concluding chapter, I'll challenge readers to empower themselves as agents for change in creating intergenerational communities. Having been fellow travelers with me in listening to the stories primarily of Baby Boomers, Millennials, experts on intergenerational issues, and a few Gen Xers and the very elderly, I hope that you'll also have learned to appreciate the different but equally valid views that members of various generations have of institutions like family, education, and community. My agenda is not to persuade members of one generation that their views on any issue are superior to those of another. But, I believe that understanding difference will help to reduce stereotyping and contribute to greater mutual empathy. With greater understanding and empathy, together we can work on turning the reality of living in a multigenerational world into an intergenerational world. You'll have unraveled a perennial paradox, namely that by expanding our concern for the well-being of all generations, our respective individual generations have a better chance to prosper.

Baby Boomers are only the first generational wave to experience the full weight of this great intergenerational disequilibrium that we find ourselves in today. As a generation, Boomers have prided themselves on leading social change, and many are thinking more urgently about legacy for future generations. (When you peer into the mirror and realize that the reflection in the glass increasingly looks more like one of your parents and not that youthful self-image that you carry in your head, you'd be surprised at how urgently you want to act upon issues that matter!) The generations that follow will face their own set of intergenerational issues. But I hope that with *Connecting Generations: Bridging the Boomer, Gen X, and Millennial Divide* as a guide, Boomers can help pave the way for the generational waves that follow to create their own intergenerational conversations and communities and show that we can navigate ongoing societal disequilibrium by reclaiming intergenerational interactions as the norm.

~

CHAPTER ONE

An Epidemic of Loneliness?

I increasingly began to think that the connections we have or think we have, are like a kind of parody of human connection. If you have a crisis in your life, you'll notice something. It won't be your Twitter followers who come to sit with you. It won't be your Facebook friends who help you turn it round. It'll be your flesh and blood friends who you have deep and nuanced and textured, face-to-face relationships with.[1]

—Johann Hari (TED Global London 2015)

A Loneliness Epidemic: True or False?

Are we on the verge of an epidemic of loneliness, or is the "loneliness crisis" just another manufactured fad that savvy people will leverage for new business opportunities? This is a complicated and highly important question to answer. An epidemic is "the occurrence of more cases of a disease than would be expected in a community or region during a given time period."[2] When applied to infectious diseases like meningitis or avian flu, there are epidemiological thresholds for determining when a disease reaches epidemic proportions.[3] But there are no definitive medical metrics for labeling detrimental psychosocial behaviors as "epidemic."

Lacking agreed upon metrics makes the question of whether we are experiencing a "loneliness crisis" complex. But it's extremely important because of the correlations between social isolation and a host of medical health risks associated with it. A phrase like "social isolation epidemic" can become a sticky social meme in the media, causing the general public to view it as the latest "hot topic." And we know what happens to a "hot topic." Even if it is significant, its importance is fleeting because it is soon displaced in the public's consciousness by the next "hot topic."

Donna Butts, executive director of Generations United, expressed another caution about well-intentioned efforts to decrease loneliness across the generations. While she is gratified at the growing public awareness of the issue of social isolation, Butts is concerned about "people jumping into the intergenerational space poorly, because I think it can be as detrimental as it can be powerful if it's not well thought out, well prepared, or planned. I [am concerned about] people thinking that they're experts in how to connect generations or feeling like they should jump in and start a program, mixing old and young, and everything's [automatically] going to be great. It's kind of dangerous because if people have bad experiences, that becomes their lens and it can be more harmful if not done well."[4] Speaking to her concern about unqualified opportunists capitalizing on issues, the prestigious Harvard Business Review compiled a series of articles by distinguished scholars on loneliness in the workplace,[5] suggesting that there is a market for workplace solutions to the loneliness crisis.

I've spent some time on the complexities of labeling increased rates in social isolation as an "epidemic" because the stakes are so high. But, even lacking medical agreement, the weight of expert opinion from a variety of disciplines is that social isolation and loneliness are rampant and have been dramatically increasing, especially since the early to mid-2000s. Even more alarming, the reported rate of increase of these feelings is most pronounced in younger generations. In the past, self-perceptions and realities of social isolation were associated more with those who were elderly or infirm and lacked the ability to lead active lives that brought them into ongoing contact with others. Now, it's the post-Millennial generation—the youngest generation today—that seems to be the most vulnerable to feelings of social isolation and loneliness.[6] We possess multiple, independent sources of information on this topic, enabling us to 1) reasonably conclude that when it comes to having close relationships, we're in critical condition, 2) understand the origins of these issues, and 3) thoughtfully and responsibly begin to address them.

Let's briefly review some key data points about social isolation at a top level. Those who wish to delve more deeply into these studies and findings will find references to them in the endnotes. "Strikingly, in a recent Generations United/Eisner Foundation survey of adults nationwide, more than half of respondents—53 percent—said that aside from family members, few of the people they regularly spend time with are much older or much younger than they are. Young adults between the ages of 18 and 34 appear to be the most isolated from other generations, with 61 percent reporting a limited number of much older or much younger acquaintances."[7] This finding about younger adults appearing to be the most socially isolated from other generations is consistent with a report recently issued by Search Institute. "We've known for decades that high-quality relationships are essential to young people's growth, learning, and thriving—including for those young people who face serious challenges in their lives and in the world around them. Yet, as many as 40 percent of young people feel lonely."[8]

And matters are no different at the other end of the generational spectrum. In 2012, researchers at the University of California, San Francisco's Division of Geriatrics analyzed data from a nationally representative study of older adults conducted by the National Institute on Aging. One of their findings was that 43 percent of Americans over the age of sixty reported feeling lonely.[9] That was lower than a study conducted more recently by linkAges, involving a much smaller sample of older adults involved in a pilot program to create generational connections, in which 55 percent of respondents reported feeling lonely.[10] Compare those statistics with some studies from the 1980s in which 20 percent of older adults reported feelings of loneliness, and it's easy to understand why the word "epidemic" comes to mind so quickly.[11] Simply stated, in study after study conducted in different Western countries emanating from an array of disciplines, levels of loneliness are on the rise.[12]

Rounding out the picture, there is consensus among social scientists and respected health journalists that the number of individuals whom we describe as "close confidantes"[13] has declined dramatically from three to only one (or in some studies, none) since the mid-1980s.[14] The number of close friends that people have today compared to a few decades ago has dropped, people generally don't have relationships with those born in other generations, and feelings of social isolation are more widespread than before. Not long ago, suicide was more common among the elderly population but, "suicide in the United States has surged to the highest levels in nearly 30 years, a federal data analysis has found, with increases in every age group except older adults."[15] With this large, diverse body of consistent findings from researchers and health practitioners, which include longitudinal data that enable us to track trends, it certainly feels like we're in "epidemic" territory.

Behind every one of these statistics is a human being who is in pain, and when you translate those statistics into the numbers of individuals who are suffering, there are real consequences for all communities. Mitch Prinstein, a professor of psychology and neuroscience at the University of North

Carolina at Chapel Hill, is an expert on topics including peer networks and popularity. In a recent New York Times Opinion piece,[16] he cited a remarkable study by another psychologist, Julianne Holt-Lunstad at Brigham Young University. This study caught his attention for several reasons. Most relevant among them is the finding that she "consolidated data from 148 investigations published over 28 years on the effects of social relationships, collectively including over 308,000 participants between the ages of 6 and 92 from all over the world. In each study, investigators measured the size of participants' networks, the number of their friends, whether they lived alone, and the extent to which they participated in social activities. Then they followed each participant for months, years and even decades to track his or her mortality rate."[17] Her conclusion, as reported by Prinstein, is that social isolation, feeling lonely and disconnected from others, predicts our lifespan.

We also know that loneliness can accelerate cognitive decline in older adults,[18] and isolated individuals are twice as likely to die prematurely as those with more robust social interactions.[19] These effects start early: Socially isolated children have significantly poorer health twenty years later, even after controlling for other factors.[20] All told, loneliness is as important a risk factor for early death as obesity and smoking.[21] In reviewing the effects of social isolation, even at first blush, we can understand the urgency of need to address this issue. As Jane E. Brody, long-time personal health columnist for the New York Times simply and powerfully stated, "Social interaction is a critically important contributor to good health and longevity."[22] Social isolation, loneliness, and a decline in the number of close friends have economic costs, and I can't even imagine how to calculate the magnitude of misery for individuals who are alone, and the emotional impact on their friends and families.

I've provided this background information about social isolation because it's tempting to pinpoint a singular change that has created this environment; for example, the rise of social media. But if there were only one cause, we would only look for one "solution." The fact that so many people of different generations are feeling these painful effects means that social isolation is more like a large river fed by many tributaries. There are many mutually interactive factors that have contributed to this retreat away from others and into the self, and that explain why we have tended to stop looking to those who are older than us for guidance in troubled times, as we used to in the recent past.

The Economy

Baby Boomers have experienced multiple economic recessions. For example, during the economic recessions of 1975, 1992, and 2002, unemployment rates respectively were 8.5 percent, 7.4 percent, and 6 percent, but were then followed by periods of growth. But nothing prepared us for the impact of the Great Recession that began in 2007 and peaked in 2009 when the unemployment rate reached almost 10 percent of the population. This economic recovery has been slow, it depleted the savings of many Baby Boomers, left many Millennial college graduates with a significant educational debt load coupled with fewer decent employment prospects, and further decimated a shrinking number of blue-collar jobs. Unlike other past recessions, people continue to feel much more financially vulnerable and wonder if they can hope for even some economic gains given the widening income inequality gap that currently exists.[23]

What are some of the technological tectonic plates that shifted in 2007 that affected workers of all ages? As Thomas L. Friedman writes in his book, *Thank You for Being Late: An Optimist's Guide to Thriving in the Age of Accelerations*, a cluster of companies emerged that changed how we interact with one another in all spheres of life: business, family and other social relationships, and community.[24] Here are a few of the better-known developments that Friedman writes about: the release of the first iPhone, Google's purchase of YouTube and its public launch of Android, an open mobile operating system, Airbnb, Twitter, the opening of Facebook beyond college campuses, Amazon's Kindle, the building of IBM's "Watson," which represented a significant breakthrough in combining machine learning with artificial intelligence, renewable and more efficient energy sources, and a dramatic drop in the cost of DNA sequencing. Basically, 2007 was the year in which human interactions started to become less necessary, as a new infrastructure that used big data began to direct how we do our shopping, reading, banking, health care, and education. We started to gain greater accessibility and connectivity to the world, but with fewer human interactions. We could do more alone and were needed less because initial advances in artificial intelligence and machine learning began to eliminate work that people used to do.

To illustrate just how significant this emerging infrastructure was only over a decade ago, let's look at a company called 99designs. 99designs describes itself as "the world's largest online graphic design marketplace." It connects designers from around the world with individuals who have graphic design needs. If you worked at a graphic design company, potential customers could now drive the price of your bids down because they knew that you were competing for their business on a global scale. As 99designs clearly boasts on its website, "Today, a new design is uploaded to our platform every 1.5 seconds. . . . Having offices located around the world is a pretty sweet deal, but we think it's even more amazing that any designer—from Sydney to Serbia—can succeed on our platform."[25]

The pitch behind 99designs sounds very exciting, doesn't it? And indeed, someone young just starting a career in design may be attracted to an opportunity to compete on his or her own merit. But a Baby Boomer who had been working at a design firm for decades and became a casualty in a "reduction of force" action because of global competition, may not have felt as excited. As a younger Baby Boomer, I didn't only read statistics about my peers being right-sized, downsized, turned into contract employees and accepting financial concessions in return for flat or decreased earnings to maintain health care benefits. I also personally witnessed how they struggled to reinvent themselves so that they could remain employed or even under-employed. Despite many efforts at plying their social networks, I could periodically sense their feelings of failure and humiliation, and their understandable reluctance to share their experiences openly. Some even became isolated and depressed as they realized that the story of their lives in their middle years was unfolding very differently from the one they had subconsciously written.

Millennials faced a different set of economic challenges. For those who attended college, many graduated with a school debt load that they expected to repay after working at a middle-class or higher-paying job for a period of years. But the new conventional wisdom was that employers viewed a bachelor's degree as the equivalent of a high school degree and a master's degree as equivalent to a bachelor's degree. When Baby Boomers graduated from college, a four-year degree in the humanities or sciences virtually guaranteed them a decent job. However, for Millennials, a four-year college degree in the humanities might earn them an unpaid internship. While those who graduated with engineering and computer science degrees had better employment prospects, the Boomer dream of college as an automatic ticket to upward mobility died with many Millennials. Additionally, many traditional blue-collar jobs in manufacturing that had paid a decent wage were being replaced by more sophisticated automation and robots.

As a result, homeownership also receded and Millennial children boomeranged back to their childhood homes because they could not achieve financial independence at the age that their parents had. "As of 2016, 15 percent of 25- to 35-year-old Millennials were living in their parents' home. This is 5 percentage points higher than the share of Generation Xers who lived in their parents' home in 2000 when they were the same age (10 percent), and nearly double the share of the Silent Generation who lived at home in 1964 (8 percent)."[26]

This remains a frustrating experience both for Baby Boomers and Millennials. Although they are at very different stages of life, each of these generations may not have the freedom and independence that they had anticipated, often for reasons that are beyond their control. A Boomer parent who was terminated from a job and a Millennial who is searching for a first job might be living under the same roof. Those are ingredients that can create a very combustible home life, especially when there is an unwillingness or inability to openly dialogue about this kind of situation.

Housing Inhibits Intergenerational Relationships

The first time that I heard the phrase "gated community" was about twenty years ago when my in-laws decided that they had enough of cold, snowy Nebraska winters and were ready for a warmer climate all year long. Now that I'm older, I'm able to identify more with the attraction of being able to walk outside, unafraid of the perils of icy sidewalks from November through March. The attraction of a snow-free climate became even more clear to me when I fell on a sidewalk on an icy January day several years ago, resulting in a concussion. (While concussions are serious and require immediate medical attention, as an ordained rabbi I wondered if there was some divine irony in landing squarely on my temple!) Like many of their generation who relocated to sunnier climates, they lived in a "gated community." In fact, in some parts of Florida, Arizona, and California, it's difficult to find a community that isn't "gated!" Some gated communities have clear age-related rules (you must be at least fifty-five years old, children under age eighteen may not stay for a more than one night, etc.). But the phrase "gated community" was jarring when I first heard it because it contradicted my understanding of community. While the people who live in these communities may be very open (and they don't come more open than my in-laws), community implies openness to all, while a gate publicly signals selective openness.

Gated communities are only one manifestation of how housing developments contribute to age segregation. Approximately in the early 1980s, a "continuum of care" model of housing for seniors began to emerge. Today, many variations of these kinds of housing options for the elderly exist, that often include independent, assisted, and full-time care facilities, with special "memory units" for residents with Alzheimer's disease co-located on the same site.[27] For those who are healthier but whose driving is limited, or who may no longer drive anymore, regularly scheduled transportation is provided so that those who are independent do not remain homebound. For even greater convenience, many facilities offer some basic amenities onsite including small mini-markets, hair stylists, restaurants, fitness, and educational classes. Often, to make it easier for elderly residents to maintain independence for as long as possible, different types of housing are provided on the same campus. For example, an indoor corridor may lead directly from an independent living apartment building to an adjacent building that has a memory care floor for people with dementia. That way, if one spouse can live independently but has a spouse who must live in a memory care facility, the healthy person can simply walk a short distance to be with his or her partner.

Clearly, the motivation behind this concept was compassionate—make it as easy as possible for an individual to live independently and to be near a lifelong partner. These models strive to help individuals remain independent by removing barriers like transportation and offering shuttle bus services for outings. Some also integrate basic medical and mental health services into the places where people live. However, many of these facilities are far removed from residential neighborhoods and discourage intergenerational interaction.

When elderly people must move from a home in which they've lived for decades, they don't only lose intergenerational interactions. The social and emotional disruption of upheaval can also contribute to cognitive difficulties and can be much costlier to taxpayers. So, an alternative concept of helping people transition into older adulthood, "aging in place," began to emerge several decades ago. One pioneering model of aging in place, PACE (Programs of All-Inclusive Care of the Elderly), traces its roots to the early 1970s.[28] The philosophy behind PACE was to extend the ability of individuals to live in their apartments or homes by bringing a range of medical and other therapeutic services to them as their mobility became limited or, when that was not possible, to provide free or very inexpensive round trip transportation for them to receive services outside of their homes.

Beginning in the 1980s, another organic model of supporting seniors who wanted to remain in their homes was developed. This model was called NORC, an acronym that stood for "Naturally Occurring Retirement Communities." A NORC, "is a demographic term used to describe a community that was not originally built for seniors, but that now has a significant proportion of older residents."[29] NORC programs are designed to keep seniors engaged in their communities, and the kinds of services that they offer, both those that are for free to residents and those that require residents to pay, vary greatly by state. "The (NORC) model draws its strength from multidisciplinary, public-private partnerships that unite social service and health care providers, housing managers or representatives of neighborhood associations, and community residents, especially older adults. Government agencies and philanthropic organizations provide essential funding."[30]

Again, there is wisdom and compassion in these models, but recent research has shown that the "aging in place" paradigm can turn people's dwellings into an unintended experience of near-solitary confinement. According to one study in the Journal of the American Medical Association (JAMA), almost two million people over age sixty-five, or nearly 6 percent of those Americans are "homebound" (defined as those who in the past month had not left their homes at all or had gone out no more than once a week), and another six million people are "semi-homebound" (able to leave home only with difficulty or with another's assistance).[31] While helping elderly people stay in their homes was motivated by thinking about what is in their best interests, an unanticipated consequence of "aging in place" has been to create a larger elderly homebound population.

Millennials face a different set of housing issues that still often produce isolation from other generations. Millennials who can afford to rent or even own a home want to be located near their generational peers. Some Boomers were happy to purchase a first home that required renovations, but many Millennials prefer turnkey, move-in ready homes. Some even expect "smart homes" in which appliances, heating and cooling systems, and home security systems communicate with one another and inform their owners about needed maintenance or groceries that are running low. These digital amenities are increasingly becoming necessities for Millennials but can be intimidating to Baby Boomers who do not understand what the acronym IoT (Internet of Things) stands for and may prefer digital simplicity to "state-of-the-art" smart homes. Marc Freedman, CEO of Encore, summarized the impact between social isolation and housing when he said, "I think that housing did more than anything else to separate the generations."[32] Much of his work has been focused on "how we went from the nineteenth century being an incredibly well-integrated society by age to being one of the most age-segregated societies."[33] On the positive side, there are a multitude of experiments in housing that are being designed around a core value: that individuals and communities thrive when older and younger generations are in close proximity with one another, and where there are intentional, sustained efforts to foster intergenerational interactions. Later in the book, we'll examine some of these developments because becoming involved in existing ones in your community or helping to create additional options are some ways that you can lead change in your community.

Social Media: Easier to Connect But More Lonely

I intentionally left the topic of digital media for last in this chapter because of a rush to judgment to name them as the primary cause for generational disconnections.[34] I've identified several significant trends (housing, employment, etc.) that have contributed to our deteriorating interpersonal and intergenerational relationships, but we do need to reckon especially with digital media and their known positive and negative impacts. Doing so means that we'll need to look more deeply inward at ourselves to understand how they are changing us, and collectively look outward to anticipate their potential impacts on our collective selves and communities.

I vividly remember one technology moment that gave me a sense of dread about the future of working environments, although I greatly underestimated how radically it would transform how we work. It was in 1995 when the nonprofit for which I was working at the time installed Windows 95 on everyone's computer. Windows 95 was a major leap forward in personal computing in the workplace. Items like the "start menu," the "taskbar," email for computer networks, word processing, and database management broke through many barriers that had made computers costly, frustrating, and not worth the expense for many employers. With the introduction of Windows 95 almost all employees who had refused to learn how to use a computer in my organization finally had to part with their cherished typewriters and attend mandatory training sessions on a keyboard and screen.

At my first training, "booting up" Windows 95 stunned me when I saw the opening display screen of a lush green field and billowing clouds. Judging by 1995 standards, its graphics were dazzling, and suggested the freedom of outdoor exploration and the promise of entering new, unimagined worlds. But I also had this creepy feeling that Microsoft was making an intentional effort to misdirect the user away from the reality of the office layouts that were then in vogue, for many companies at that time had replaced offices with drab modular cubicles with high walls and no windows. In retrospect, the Microsoft screen image of the field and clouds were an omen of the increased demands for worker productivity. Better to enjoy the artificial view of the outside through Microsoft Windows, because fewer people could peer through a glass office window or door or even chat with coworkers a few feet away, whose view was blocked by a dreary cubicle wall that discouraged "unproductive" social interaction. Instead, we would be taking in our view of the outside world through an Internet browser on a computer screen, because only a few weeks later, Microsoft also introduced its enhanced web browser, Internet Explorer. I truly remember feeling that personal computing might lead to impersonal social interaction.

Now, with small, powerful, handheld smart devices, social media sites, content creation tools, 24-7 connectivity to the world, and the predominance of social networks, we are more intimately connected to our devices than to one another. With all the many enabling benefits of connections that social media platforms have fostered, they have also unintentionally made face-to-face interactions less frequent at work, in social settings with friends, and even at home. For example, how many colleagues who work in the same office building could have avoided a simple misunderstanding if they had walked a few feet into another colleague's office and briefly conversed instead of generating a tangled chain of emails? How much confusion could have been preempted by having a face-to-face conversation or a phone call because the tone of a text message was misunderstood? Although even the sacred word was rendered into emojis with the release of "Bible Emoji: Scripture 4 Millennials" in May 2016,[35] it so often feels like human communications have become cheapened, making it easier to retreat into a device than to expand our personalities through direct personal contact. Is it healthy in the long run to text a family member under the same roof when we have a question, rather than descend a flight of stairs to ask it in person? As of March 2017, there were over five million apps available between the Google Play and Apple App Store.[36] We have more apps available, but are we becoming more socially inept? Has the creation of more social apps afflicted us with "social in-app-titude," something that I would describe as our ability to be adept with our thumbs but awkward with fundamental emotional intelligence used in forming human relationships?

Still, you may be asking, "Could such a small device as a smartphone create such large damage to relationships?" Sherry Turkle, professor of the Social Studies of Science and Technology at MIT, is a world-renowned expert on the impact of digital technology on the human personality. In her most recent book, *Reclaiming Conversation: The Power of Talk in a Digital Age*, she writes, "so it is not surprising that in the past 20 years we've seen a 40 percent decline in the markers for empathy among college students, most of it within the past 10 years. It is a trend that researchers link to the new presence of digital communications."[37] Turkle reaches this conclusion based on the rich stories of the behaviors of young people who are unable to part with their smartphones and how their mere presence fundamentally changes the nature of empathetic conversation. She adds, "human relationships are rich, messy, and demanding. When we clean them up with technology, *we move from conversation to the efficiencies of mere connection*. I fear we forget the difference. And we forget that children who grow up in a world of digital devices don't know that there is a difference or that things were ever different."[38] Turkle doesn't exaggerate: 100 percent of eighteen- to twenty-nine-year-old young adults now own smartphones,[39] and by the end of 2017, children under age eight were spending an average of forty-eight minutes per day on a mobile device.[40]

In other words, staring into a screen—whether it's a tablet, a smartwatch or smartphone, television or computer—diminishes our capacity for empathy. Empathy is the foundation that makes a deep relationship with another human being possible. Being able to converse with someone while making eye contact enables us to experience another person differently than reflexively sending a text. In a face-to-face conversation, we grow to understand that our words affect others' feelings and that we are accountable for their impact, just as the other person experiences how their words make us feel when they are looking at us. When more people intentionally avoid an opportunity to have face-to-face conversations, we diminish our ability to acquire empathy. Indeed, there may be some physiological truth to the proverb, "The eye is the window to the soul."[41]

Jean M. Twenge, professor of psychology at San Diego State University, has been studying generational differences for twenty-five years and was more accustomed to seeing generational differences represented by graphs in behaviors and attitudes as "modest hills and valleys."[42] But in 2012, she noticed alarming increases in rates of teen depression and suicide and stated that in the United States, we are "on the brink of the worst mental health crisis in decades."[43] She wanted to know why members of the iGen, the term that she coined to describe individuals born between 1995 and 2012, were behaving so differently from prior generations of teens, even Millennials, the generation that immediately preceded them.

For example, "12th graders in 2015 were going out less often than *eighth graders* did as recently as 2009."[44] In addition to staying at home more or choosing to go out more with their parents—not typical teen behavior—she also observed that other teen behaviors like getting a driver's license, dating, and sexual activity, all markers of social behavior, were sharply declining. Her conclusion about the roots of these changes? "The more I pored over yearly surveys of teen attitudes and behaviors, and the more I talked with young people . . . the clearer it became that theirs is a generation shaped by the smartphone and by the concomitant rise of social media."[45] Indeed, as of February 2018, over 75 percent of Americans owned smartphones[46] and a survey of over five thousand teens revealed that three out of four teens owned an iPhone,[47] so researchers rightfully can point to the correlation between social media sites and their ready accessibility, and the rise in mental health issues for members of the youngest generation.

Turkle is a Baby Boomer and a pioneer in studying the evolution of digital technologies and their effects on our personalities. As a digital immigrant, she was among the first to raise concerns about technology and cautions about some of their potential negative implications. Twenge is a Gen Xer, which makes her an early digital native, and like Turkle, she has witnessed and participated in the digital revolution. Like so many other researchers and practitioners, these two veteran researchers, from different generations, have drawn the same conclusions and expressed them with a special eloquence and power. They are not opposed to digital technologies but challenge parents and educators to become more mindful of the potential negative impacts of screen time.

Small Talk, Large Value

I asked Dr. Keith Wilbert, one of my Boomer interview subjects for this book and a pediatrician, about how he responds to parents who are on their smartphones when they enter his office with their children. After all, one of the issues that he discusses with families is the amount of screen time that they permit their children to have. His response to their behavior is, "You know, I have an app where I can make myself pop up on your screen if you prefer that."[48] They quickly get his message and put away their smart devices, but he wonders if the message sticks. With an abundance of data on the use of smart devices on children and teens, it's time for us to really consider more deeply how a silver screen can damage the prospects for raising children with golden hearts.

For us to do so, we're going to have to strengthen relationships across generations and have ongoing discussions that enable us to use our collective wisdom to better anticipate both the positive and harmful effects of existing technologies and new ones as they emerge. Those who remember what life was like when current technologies either didn't exist or weren't so relentlessly intrusive, and those who have grown up with these technologies but recognize their potential to damage relationships, can play a role in "reclaiming conversation," to borrow a phrase from Turkle's book, titled *Reclaiming Conversation: The Power of Talk in a Digital Age*.[49] In fact, we don't even have to be that ambitious. We can take a first step and reclaim "small talk."

I was reminded of how significant small talk with a stranger can be when I interviewed Linda Archer, a Millennial participant in my study. When I asked her for a suggestion about how she would initiate greater intergenerational connections, she offered a compelling recommendation: "I think that there's a lot of power in conversation, and I think a lot of times we tend to stick [to] talking and creating friendships with the people we feel most comfortable, whether that's demographics or in a variety of ways. But I think that if people step more outside of their comfort zone and have conversations with someone that was different than their own age range, like a Millennial talking to a Baby Boomer or a Baby Boomer talking to a Millennial, we can bring generations together."[50]

I persisted and asked, "But how do you do that?" She wisely answered,

For people to do something, they have to feel like what they're doing is actu-ally going to make a difference or it's actually of importance, and so I don't know, but I wonder if somehow we could convey the message that conversa-tions are important... and that [when] you're sitting next to someone on a bus, or if you're [in a store] checking out [an item standing] next to someone in a really long line, and you say to someone older [standing] behind you who is wearing a really cool jacket, and you say, "that's a really nice jacket," or [you learn that they swim regularly and say] "I didn't know that you go swimming every weekend, that's cool." You just start having a conversation. And I feel like it's through those [kinds of] conversations where you're able to really break down the stereotypes, because you actually get to talk to a person and begin thinking, "Oh wow, you're actually really cool and you're old!"[51]

Again, I asked her if she really believed that if more people were intentional about taking a risk and simply starting a friendly conversation, could the impact be so great? To that Linda responded, "Yeah, it could be pretty im-pactful, because I think our world needs more empathy and I think through conversations and understanding different people from different walks of life that are different from yours, that's how we grow as individuals and that's how we grow as a country and a world."[52]

About one week before my conversation with Linda, a Millennial, I had interviewed Dr. David Alter, a licensed psychologist with expertise in how the mind, brain, and body interact. My reason for interviewing him was that his practice with individuals, couples, and families of all ages is integrative, helping people probe the relationship between mind, body, emotion and, from my conversations with him, I would also add spirituality when his cli-ents are open to that dimension of life. Having developed this integrative approach over many years, which overlapped with my curiosity about better integrating generations, I wondered if he had any suggestions on how to in-crease the experiences of intergenerational conversations.

Dr. Alter echoed Linda's observations:

One of the points that you're making is that this [bringing together people of different generations into conversation with one another] is not an easy process. But I think, as an example—if you and I were to think about people who we know well enough, but not too well, who probably don't agree with us [on some important issues]—if the two of us invited a few people that we know disagree with us, now we have between four and eight people, and [if we keep asking other people to repeat the process] the exponential growth curve goes from there. If the conversation is respectful, and if the conversation is led by risk-taking where it's not about each person defending his or her position, and the goal is for you to better understand someone else's position and [you accept that] if nobody understands your position, too bad . . . if respect and understanding are the [non-negotiable] criteria, we can have more intergenerational conversations.[53]

What You Can Do

1. Test the advice of Linda, push yourself out of your comfort zone, and make small talk with an adult who is a generation older or younger than you while waiting in a long line.
2. Take an even greater risk and experiment with Dr. Alter's suggestion of inviting a few people who are one step removed from your inner circle of friends and learn about their views on an issue which differs from yours. Or, invite just one person. Be transparent about what you hope to accomplish, and be committed to learning and understanding, rather than influencing someone else to believe like you.
3. Search online for existing "conversation projects" that aim to reduce political polarization and increase broader citizen engagement in your local community.[54] After vetting them to ensure that they are bipartisan, try participating in a session.

On a personal note, about six months before the 2016 United States presidential election, I decided to take my own small risk and get to know a few people in my new coworking space. Rather than just silently acknowledging a familiar face with a head nod or a mumbled "hello," I introduced myself to several people, and explained why I hoped that we could now greet one another by name. I haven't been as consistent as I could have been, but I now have about five people from different generations with whom I can make small talk, and among those five, several with whom I regularly have serious conversations. With those friends, we each know where we stand on certain issues and although in some cases we hold significantly different views, we listen to one another without interruption and try to gain insight into one another's perspectives. Personally, this has been a very rewarding experience. It is also empowering because I don't need to wait for an act of Congress to begin connecting with others across the generations and help to make some of the changes that I aspire to see in our world. I only have to choose to take a few minutes each day and start a conversation.

CHAPTER TWO

~

Generational Stereotypes

Definition of entitled: "Believing oneself to be inherently deserving of privileges or special treatment."[1]

"When I hear the phrase 'Baby Boomer,' an adjective that comes to mind is entitled." "When I hear the word 'Millennial,' an adjective that comes to mind is entitled." Both comments are responses from participants in the research that I conducted for this book.

—Author's note

Stereotypes Reinforce Social Isolation across Generations

In conducting research for this book, I interviewed thirteen experts who work or have worked in the field of intergenerational issues. They are all exceptional in different ways, and you'll learn more about them later. I also consumed a significant number of books, articles, TED Talks, and podcasts that you'll find in the Works Cited at the end of this book. Reading about differences in values and attitudes between Baby Boomers and Millennials in academic journals, reports, and books is one essential part of the research process.

But I was most captivated by the formal interviews of the nine Baby Boomers and eight Millennials that I conducted.[2] Listening to them respond to questions that they seemed to have been thinking about in some quiet place of their minds and sensing some of their emotions was like alchemy.

Their stories made the objective, definitive findings on some smartly designed academic and organizational reports somewhat fuzzy because they were filled with turmoil and certainty, curiosity and affirmation, love and fear. They provided the kind of nuance and emotional authenticity of lived experience that statistical findings and analyses can't capture. Their candor and thought expanded my own capacity for empathy and I'm sure that their experiences will be teachers to the many others who are grappling with similar issues.

As my research sample was relatively small, I strove to have diversity among Baby Boomer and Millennial participants. I included straight and gay men and women, white people and people of color, married and partnered couples, unmarried individuals, individuals or couples with children and without children and, in the case of Baby Boomers, with grandchildren and without grandchildren, and individuals who had varying levels of formal education, from those who had opted not to attend college to those who had graduate degrees. This diversity enabled me to capture a potentially wide range of views. What surprised me was how consistently members of the same generational cohort responded. As a researcher, that gave me greater confidence in my analyses and interpretations of their stories.

An underlying assumption of this book is that social isolation is a significant societal issue and that fostering organic relationships across generations is one way that people of all ages can ease their feelings of loneliness.[3] Stereotypes are barriers that prevent people from developing relationships with one another. Scrutinizing stereotypes and giving voice to people in their own words opens greater possibilities for us to develop relationships with those who differ from us in fundamental ways. After all, it's easy to dislike a stereotype of a person because stereotypes turn people into impersonal objects that misrepresent their perceived negative attributes and obscure their positive ones. But once you take time to get to know the real person underneath the stereotype, your views tend to evolve. Perhaps you won't become best friends with that person, but you're likely to change your views both of that individual and the group that he or she represents to you.

With that goal in mind, I generally asked the same or similar questions of both Millennials and Baby Boomers to better understand the landscape of generational stereotypes. By asking mirror-image questions, I hoped to locate either misconceptions that each had of the other or to identify their mutual understanding of their respective differences. This strategy proved successful.

Here are the primary categories of questions that I asked Baby Boomers and Millennials:

1. The meaning of adulthood and if they believe it has evolved both in its early and later stages;
2. For Baby Boomers, perceptions and phrases that came to mind when they heard the term "Millennial," and for Millennials, perceptions and phrases that came to mind when they heard the term "Baby Boomer";
3. The meaning of work and how defining it is or was to their personal identities;
4. The value of college education relative to its cost, and expectations about continuing education and lifelong learning;
5. Friendships and the number of close friends they have;
6. The importance they attach to participating regularly in a voluntary community (for example, a faith-based community, a community service group, etc.) and having at least one mentor who is from an older generation;
7. The average amount of time they spent in front of a screen after work hours during the week and on the weekends, and how much of their screen time was interactive, for example, texting friends or talking with a friend or partner during a television show, and how much of their screen time was not interactive. A "screen" included everything from a television to a smartwatch;
8. Their perceptions about the overall value of social media and its impact on relationships with family and friends;
9. Their perceived value of committing a year of national service either after high school or college in a structured program with older mentors in programs like Teach for America, AmeriCorps, or serving in the military; and for Baby Boomers, questions about volunteer engagement; and
10. Caring for older relatives or anticipating that they will be caring for older family members.

In this chapter, I'll introduce the broad framework for contrasting Boomer and Millennial worldviews that emerged from my research, which helps to explain the stereotypes that Boomers and Millennials hold of one another. This framework provides the context for the book's remaining chapters on how these two generations think about the nature and value of community, participation in community (civic, sectarian, or faith-based), education, and work. I'll also conclude with a surprising observation that illustrates how generational cohort labels, which condition us to think about difference, also obscure similarities that can potentially reconnect the generations.

Millennials and Boomers: Pathways Verses Ladders

I wouldn't be surprised if someday an archeologist found that the earliest recorded words in human history were, "You just don't understand what I'm going through!" written by a frustrated child to his or her parents. In my faith tradition, while we're taught that having children is a blessing filled with joyful moments, we also have an ancient Talmudic expression that captures the emotionally fraught challenges of being a parent: "the anguish of raising children" (*tza'ar gidul banim*).[4] One of my colleagues once quipped that there should be a parallel expression from a child's point of view, "the agony of raising parents" (*tza'ar gidul horim*).[5]

In broad strokes, a framework for thinking about many differences between Millennials and Boomers can be summed up in the phrase, "pathways and ladders" (no, I'm not confused with the children's board game, Chutes and Ladders). "Pathways and ladders" captures a fundamental difference in the worldview of Millennials and Baby Boomers and provides context for understanding their divergent views about relationships, work, community, and institutions. Baby Boomers generally had a more predictable linear progression that they could expect to follow: graduation from high school; then to a vocational school, an apprenticeship, college or directly to a first job, often in manufacturing; marriage, employment, first home, first child; continuation up the ladder of milestones of achievement (more children, advancement at work, a larger home); and finally, retirement.

On average, "in 1965, the typical American woman first married at age 21 and the typical man wed at 23,"[6] and a significant percentage of Baby Boomers already owned homes in young adulthood.[7] In other words, they were ready at an earlier age to begin their ascent up a Boomer ladder of achievement, whose rungs were represented by marriage, children, homeownership, and career advancement.[8] By age sixty-five, or more recently, at age sixty-seven, many older Baby Boomers also retired with a gold watch from "the company," signifying that they had "put in their time" at work and now time was theirs to control. With retirement came relaxation every day, not only on weekends. The company pension, post-retirement health care benefits or Medicare, and Social Security were the perks of hard work that provided financial and medical peace of mind, now that a regularly scheduled paycheck ceased. While the level of Boomer achievement varied, and members of minority communities often encountered additional hurdles to, or outright exclusion from, this ladder to upward achievement, these were the generally recognizable contours of this linear progression for many Boomers.

When I interviewed Millennials and asked them if they had a "ladder of Millennial milestones" signifying adult achievement, the answer was a resounding, "No!" with only one exception. While the image of a ladder of progressive steps up into adulthood did not resonate with Millennials, the analogy of multiple pathways into adulthood did. For Millennials, each "rung of achievement" of the prior generation's ladder had to be removed and evaluated on its own merits, based on their situation in life at that given moment. For example, homeownership was not an automatic aspiration but needed to be assessed as a potential financial investment or liability. It might make sense to purchase a home in early adulthood or it might never make sense. The cost of a college education also needed to be weighed against accumulated debt which they knew could have lifelong consequences, and Millennials had access to alternative options to college for advancing their education. Most of the Millennials in this study did not view employment at the same place or even in the same field for an extended time as likely or desirable because the job that they have three years from now may not even exist today. Marriage and children—maybe, maybe not—these choices also had to be freely chosen and not automatically made based on the expectations of prior generations.

Millennials were clearly not following a linear ascent up a ladder that "society" had predetermined for them but were forging their own idiosyncratic pathways into adulthood. In hindsight, Boomers should have expected significant variation and variety of Millennials' passage into adulthood. Many Millennials had watched their Baby Boomer parents and were implicitly critiquing what they perceived as the negative toll of hard work on their parents' relationships, enjoyment of life, and opportunities to explore options while they were young. The Millennials whom I interviewed loved their parents and appreciated the childhood experiences that they provided for them. But they were convinced that they did not want their parents' lifestyle.

Without being aware, Millennials were living more like some of their Boomer parents had when they were young, who had also rejected preassigned roles and expectations that their own Silent Generation and Greatest Generation parents had of them! Speaking as a Baby Boomer, didn't many of our parents initially have difficulties with some of our choices? But a rejection of a lifestyle is not the same as a wholesale rejection of values, and while generational differences are real, those of us who are Boomers periodically forget our own rebellious attitudes toward our parents' conventions and expectations. Many of us either took or were given the freedom to first "follow our bliss"[9] and our generation's motto was, "Don't trust anyone over

30."[10] We started the process of overturning inherited wisdom before transitioning to a more conventional, linear ladder of adult achievement. Perhaps those recollections can help us view Millennials' aimless meanderings into adulthood as more purposeful nonlinear pathways that they needed to create because our conventional wisdom of entering adulthood no longer worked.

Boomers Became Adults, But Millennials Practiced Adulting

One area in which this difference between a linear entrance into adulthood contrasted with a more ambiguous and wandering pathway toward becoming an adult is reflected in the word, "adulting," a term that I encountered during my research several times. One Millennial, Linda Archer,[11] explained how what I thought was a noun, "adult," had morphed into a verb, "adulting." For Boomers, sometime between the ages of eighteen and twenty-one, society looked upon you as an adult (noun) and you had entered a new stage of life, "adulthood." But Millennials did not identify age as a criterion for perceiving themselves as adults. Rather, this Millennial explained, she and her friends would play at "adulting," which she described as engaging in adult-like behaviors over an extended stretch of time.[12]

Taking on adult responsibilities gradually and episodically enabled Millennials to internalize their self-perception of having permanently entered adulthood. Reaching "adulthood" in their early twenties for Boomers, versus "adulting," moving into adulthood more slowly for Millennials, led me to ask Boomer and Millennial participants in this study the following questions: "What does it mean to you to be an adult today?", "When do you think that you became an adult?", "Are there any defining events or moments in your life when you had that 'aha' moment when you realized, 'I'm a real adult now'?"

Both Baby Boomers and Millennials identified adulthood with "responsibility," that is, being responsible for making and owning your own choices. For example, that meant not relying upon others to provide financial support for them and for their families if they had partners or children (although we'll later see that there is some tension and difference in expectations around how much support Boomers believe they should be providing their Millennial children, and how much support Millennial children expect from their Boomer parents). They also believed that responsibility extended beyond one's immediate self, family, and circle of friends, and required being more aware that "the world doesn't just revolve around you," as Rachel Nunez, one Millennial, said.[13] Millennials and Boomers were generally in agreement with the belief that "adulthood" also included having responsibility for one's neighborhood or even broader community.

But the shift in self-perception concerning when a person became an adult, and the process of becoming an adult, were clearly different for Baby Boomers and Millennials. Of the Baby Boomers whom I interviewed for this book, only one could identify a three-month timeframe in which he felt like he became an adult, because he married, graduated from college, and started a job within those few months. The other Baby Boomers believed that they had reached adulthood between their late teenage years and early twenties. For some, leaving home, enlisting in the military, beginning college, or moving into a first apartment, signified that they were adults, and these events occurred between the time of high school graduation and their early twenties. That was when both they and their parents understood that they were now responsible for themselves. That didn't mean that their parents were unavailable to them, but regardless of parental feelings about their choices, they no longer needed their approval. It was time to begin living their lives on their own terms.

Among the Millennials whom I interviewed, some thought of themselves as adults, while others were still adulting. Was age a factor in this change in self-perception? Not for the sample of Millennials with whom I spoke. Interestingly, Sharri Bear, a younger Millennial manager of a co-working space, explained that she first felt like an adult at age twenty-one, when she was responsible for making medical appointments on her own. Sharri and several older Millennials viewed choosing a health care plan without the help of a parent as a significant milestone for them on the road to adulthood.[14] Health care in the United States is much more complicated today than it was for Baby Boomers. If they are employed and their workplace offers health care benefits, or if they receive them through a state program, Millennials must make decisions about health care options that change annually. As health care plans are not portable, when Millennials "job hop," they trigger another round of confusing health care decision-making. These choices involve gambling on their risk of being healthy and paying a lower annual premium with fewer benefits, versus a higher annual premium that diminishes their take-home pay but provides them with greater protections against a catastrophic event. Several Millennials whom I interviewed mentioned that making decisions about their health care plans without the advice of a parent was a significant indicator that they had entered squarely into adulthood. Being unsure about other factors that might have influenced Millennials' owning their self-perception as adults led to my next question: who decided that Millennials get to sing the refrain "I won't grow up" for a longer time than Baby Boomers did?[15]

Does It Take Longer Today to Reach Adulthood?

Generally, Boomers and Millennials agreed that becoming an adult took longer today than it did in the past. Those Boomers who had Millennial children described them as "late," "slow," or "taking longer" to become an adult in comparison to their younger Boomer selves. In comparing themselves with their parents, Millennials were often astonished at what their parents had accomplished by their late twenties. Sandra Petrowski, a Boomer, said about her children, "Relative to where [my children] are at when I was their age, I feel that they are 'behind the eight ball.' They are doing well, but when I look at what I had accomplished by age thirty-five—four kids, marriage, work—and then look at my children, sometimes I want to shake them. Some have college degrees, and some do not. They have had jobs, like bartending and playing hockey, but they are late to adulthood."[16] Boomers and Millennials offered varying explanations as to the reasons for this developmental change, and social scientists also have theorized about it.

Ellen Roos, an older Millennial, conjectured that Millennials lumbered into adulthood because they needed time to develop the emotional security to resist the expectations of those who had played a significant role in their lives, especially a parent. Ellen had been a premedicine undergraduate major. Her parents made significant sacrifices for her education, and she internalized the messages that she should choose the most difficult major and one that would enable her to help others. Ellen then described an epiphany that she experienced that broke through those messages and enabled her to hear her own voice. "I was in chemistry lab [one day] and I realized it was my life, and that I had signed myself up for that chemistry lab, and I was in the chemistry lab to make my dad proud. Nobody cared if I was there or not. And that was a huge moment where I very acutely realized this is actually my life and I'm not doing anything for other people. I'm the only person I have to answer to."[17] Today, this Millennial is still driven by a desire to help people, but does so as a church youth worker and an author of books that will have a positive influence on young women—just to name a few areas of her interest.

Another Millennial, Sam Baglioni, said, "Unequivocally it takes longer to reach adulthood for a multitude of reasons."[18] One significant reason that he and others expressed was that the economic "trappings of adulthood—the house, the dog, the fence"—took longer to obtain for them than for Baby Boomers. Allan Sherman, another Millennial, observed that "technology advancements have made accessing information, doing tasks that used to be difficult—like physically having to go to a library to research information in a book, so much faster. Because things are so much easier today, it takes longer to grow up."[19] Gary Harper, a Baby Boomer, also identified technology as a culprit for slowing the maturation process of adulthood: "With the advent of technology, things seem to only get easier, contributing to delayed adulthood."[20] And Harper was not a Boomer Luddite. He served in the Navy for over twenty years with increasingly sophisticated electronic systems, and later worked in the corporate world in digital communications. He personally witnessed the impact of technology on younger generations. Another Millennial, Angela Krintz, wondered if the abundance of options in all walks of life sowed confusion and created pressure about making optimal choices, contributing to delayed adulthood.[21]

What is delayed adulthood? Some social scientists and brain researchers have introduced the concept of "delayed adulthood" or "emerging adulthood," a new developmental stage that covers the ages between approximately eighteen and twenty-five years old. They note that the human brain and executive decision-making functions do not mature until about age twenty-five and that when we add a few years of experience, individuals don't really become adults until their late twenties or early thirties.[22] However, this newly identified stage of emerging adulthood is controversial as other researchers claim that this is a manufactured rationale for enabling young people to delay maturation because of the leniencies that parents and educators granted children.[23] They believe that promoting a belief in emerging adulthood deprived Millennials of critical life experiences that could have contributed to their adult growth sooner.

And not all the Boomer and Millennial participants in this study were convinced of the developmental theories of delayed adulthood. Some of them acknowledged that it had become more socially acceptable to take longer to "settle into adulthood." Sam, the Millennial whom I quoted earlier, was convinced that it took longer today to become an adult. He said later in our interview that, "it seems more acceptable these days to NOT know what the heck you're doing for a significant portion of your life."[24] Rachel Nunez, a Millennial whom I also cited previously, recalled a conversation that she had with her then-boyfriend when she was twenty-one years old. "I would say when I met my boyfriend [who was four years older than Rachel], I felt very much still as a kid—because I had just graduated college and was still, in my mind at least, not an adult. And I remember we were having a conversation, and I said something like 'Oh, grown-ups can figure that out,' and he said, 'We are the grown-ups' and that struck me at that time."[25]

Keith Wilbert, a Baby Boomer pediatrician, alluded to the issue of self-perception and adulthood that Rachel expressed. Wilbert suggested that it doesn't take longer for young people to reach adulthood, but that it takes longer for them to realize that they are adults. I asked him to elaborate on the distinction between "taking longer to reach adulthood," and "taking longer to realize that they are adults," as I was curious if his practice of pediatric medicine had led him to this insight. He explained that he has watched over the approximately thirty years of practice how some parents hinder their children's maturation into adulthood. The mistakes that adolescents make are typically more consequential than those of younger children, so it's better if parents let their younger children's mistakes become teachers of lessons about responsibility, lessons that will help them in their adolescent years. "What happens—I think I have seen this with a lot of parents—is they're continuing to bail their kids out, which enables them to [persistently] make these silly decisions. You realize you're an adult when you can say, 'I messed this up and I better fix it, and I can't just expect everything will be handed to me. I have to go out here and earn it.'"[26]

He then shared a recent anecdote describing how some parents had enabled their adolescent child to avoid serious consequences yet again. His adolescent patient had started using drugs and missing classes in school. What did his parents do? They bought him an expensive car that he drove while he was drunk and he caused an accident. His parents called Dr. Wilbert in a panic and after ascertaining that their son wasn't seriously injured, the first thing that he asked was if their son still had his car keys. They answered, "Yes." He then replied, "The first thing that you have to do is take the car away, impound it, let the air out of the tires, do whatever you have to." He and the parents then arranged for this adolescent to receive substance abuse treatment. On a follow-up visit a few weeks later, his parents said that their son's situation had improved and that he was planning a car trip.

Dr. Wilbert was incredulous and having seen variations of this story, knew that it was unlikely to end well. When adolescents reach the age of legal majority their parents cannot so easily "bail them out." At that point, these young adults who had been accustomed to being saved by their parents since they were young children may find themselves in prison because of unlawful behavior. Not having learned to pay the less steep consequences of prior mistakes when they were minors, regardless of their self-perception as "not yet being adults," the law shocks them into realizing that they are.

Observationally, we can conclude that a variety of factors interact with one another in ways that cause a delay in Millennials reaching adulthood compared with Baby Boomers. An abundance of choices, an unsettled economy, greater social acceptance of taking longer to "find oneself," parental behaviors that hindered their children's maturity, and an understanding that while state laws determine when young people are treated legally as adults, their brains continue to develop well into their twenties. Baby Boomers had identifiable steps of progression into adulthood, and society had less tolerance for delays, but Millennials wind through more ambiguous and numerous pathways into adulthood over a longer time.

Regardless of the existence or proposed causes of delayed adulthood for Millennials, I don't think that Baby Boomers should be let off the hook so quickly for this change. In fairness, we didn't grasp how radically different the world into which Millennials were born was from ours, and how the velocity of change was rapidly increasing. I asked earlier, "Who decided that Millennials got to sing the refrain 'I won't grow up' for a longer time than Baby Boomers did?" To a degree, the answer is Boomer parents, educators, community leaders, and others who raised Millennials. We were the generation that did away with competition at summer camp and after-school activities because "everyone was a winner." We promoted the self-esteem of Millennial children in our homes, classrooms and youth groups, and generously handed them verbal or material accolades regardless of their abilities. We also gave them "options" in determining how they would spend time off from school during summer or winter break.

It's only when I take the time to reflect on my childhood and adolescent years that I realize how different they were from those of my children. When I was a child, my family would take a long "car trip" from Philadelphia, where we lived, to some exotic states far from home. Once, we even traveled as far west as Iowa! But my parents never asked for input from my siblings or me about our destination vacation. We were just thankful to have one, although with six of us in our unair-conditioned car, we did experience a few dicey moments.

With these contrasting images of ladders and pathways into adulthood, we have laid the groundwork to examine some stereotypes that Boomers and Millennials hold of one another. Time to buckle up again!

What Images or Phrases Come to Mind When You Hear The Word . . . ?

I asked study participants to share their immediate responses in brief phrases or images upon hearing of the other's generational cohort name. For Baby Boomers, I asked, "When you hear the word, 'Millennial,' what adjectives or images come to mind," and for Millennials, I asked, "When you hear the word, 'Baby Boomer,' what adjectives or images come to mind?" One response that surprised me was, "entitled," because Baby Boomers believed that the adjective "entitled" described Millennials accurately, and Millennials also believed that

Baby Boomers acted with a sense of entitlement. However, while each viewed the other as "entitled," their understanding of the meaning of entitlement was not identical.

When Baby Boomers describe Millennials as "entitled," that word was often paired with additional words including "snowflake," "late bloomers," "pleasure seekers," "instant gratification," "impatient," "pampered," "soft," "lacking in clarity of thought and verbal and writing abilities," "walking with their heads down, eyes glued to a screen," "socially isolated," "able to connect very broadly through social media but without realizing the consequences of using social media, like an inability to have deep positive [in-person] interactions," and "unable to have a [serious or lasting] conversation." These are all direct quotations from the Boomers in my study.

Baby Boomers did appreciate that Millennials were sophisticated in certain ways. Millennials were able to navigate the world of technology, unlike Boomers. Some Millennials had spent time in college studying abroad in another culture or had taken a year after college to serve in programs like Teach for America and were fluent in other cultures. But even when recognizing positive attributes of Millennials, Boomers often complained that Millennials lacked "grit," the ability to persevere at an entry-level job without excessively complaining about the drudgery of their work that seemed beneath their abilities. That's why I believe that when Baby Boomers referred to Millennials as "entitled," what they were saying is that simply because Millennials were savvy and urbane, their expectations about salary, position, or title in an organization were highly inflated. They also felt that their communication skills were lacking.

In contrast to themselves, Boomers believed that Millennials were "more pleasure driven than goal driven," according to Jack Jones, a Boomer who had devoted his life to medicine.[27] He believed that they were "not as concerned about where the next paycheck is coming from because they live for the moment." In a similar vein, Keith Wilbert, the pediatrician whom I quoted earlier, stated his belief that "in the U.S., in American culture, we definitely don't look at history. So anything that happened a couple days ago is already forgotten and has no bearing on anything [in the present]."[28] I asked Keith how the lack of appreciation of history, or as Jack said, of "living in the moment," affected Millennials. He said that by only looking forward "to the next week," Millennials [and Americans in general] lose the ability to form a vision of a better future. "To understand where you are [now], you need to know where you've been, and [only] then you can see where you're going, and you need to take all that [history] into account. [And if we were better at doing that] we would not repeat a lot of the things that didn't work in the past and form a vision as to what you [a Millennial] might want, and how that vision relates to reality."[29] Both of these Boomers, one white and one African American, expressed in different ways how Millennials had no interest in learning from the past. As a result, they believed Millennials were unable to form longer-term goals, a vision of what they wanted out of life, and what they wanted to contribute to their communities. While their observations are not novel, it is important to evaluate them considering how frequently we're notified about "breaking news" on our handheld smart devices, and whether the incessant bombardment of news flashes decreases our overall interest in the past.

Gary Harper, the retired naval officer and former corporate businessman whom I quoted earlier, echoed another comment that Keith and Jack made to me about the absence of older adult mentors in many Millennials' lives. Keith and Gary noted how especially in the African American community, there were people a generation older who were not necessarily your parents but took an interest in your well-being (as was true in the Jewish community, the one in which Jack was involved at a young age). They would offer advice, admonishment, and encouragement that helped younger people like themselves develop into responsible, dedicated professionals. But because Millennials believed that Boomers were out of touch with current-day realities, Gary bemoaned his experience in trying to share some lived wisdom with Millennials. He learned that Millennials will continue to listen to their peers' bad advice, and only when a Millennial peer offers the good advice that a Boomer has already given will they accept it. Gary summed up this lack of generational connection by saying, "It just feels like to me, there's a huge generational wall between Millennials and Boomers that I didn't feel between me and my parents, and people my parents' age."[30]

Millennials were not shy about their opinions of Baby Boomers. I asked them, "When you hear the word, 'Baby Boomer,' what adjectives or images come to mind?" Their responses included: "they're not fun to be with," "they're rigid," "they're conservative," "they're traditional," "narrow-minded," "they're clueless about our work, because so much of it involves technology," and "they're stuck in their ways." As I look younger than my age, or at least am willing to believe people who tell me that I do, I felt that these Millennial interview subjects forgot that they were aiming their critique of Boomers to a Boomer! But I stayed in role as researcher, listened to and probed their observations without judgment, and learned from them.

If you're a Boomer reading these words, don't worry—you also have some redeeming qualities which I will share in a moment. But first, we have to be ready to listen empathetically to these Millennial insights. By unearthing the meaning under the stereotypes that Boomers and Millennials hold of one another, we'll find greater opportunities for reclaiming understanding of our differences with mutual respect, leading to more possibilities for joint work on the local level.

Sam, a Millennial attorney whom I mentioned earlier, works with some financially successful clients who are Millennials and Gen Xers. He spoke about the sense of "entitlement" that he perceives in Boomers. "I think certain Boomers feel entitled because they've worked for so long, worked so hard, they're at a position in their life where they feel that they should be treated with a certain level of deference or a certain level of just taking what is said as gospel—which doesn't work. I think gone are the days where the sort of generational hierarchy determines the value of the advice you're giving or how successful you are. So in the world in which we live in, those sort of hierarchies with respect to the gravitas that somebody's word has—I think those are misplaced or ill-received."[31] He wasn't dismissing the experience and hard work of Boomers. Rather, his point was that some of his Gen X and Millennial clients were clearly bright and successful, so why are Boomer workplace norms like hierarchy and seniority still assumed as givens? By extension, shouldn't the opinions of Millennial associates and partners matter just as much as those of his Boomer counterparts?

Ellen, the author and church youth worker whom I wrote about before, didn't have a phrase or specific image that immediately came to mind, but she alluded to Boomers as setting a standard against which Millennials felt they had to respond. "Baby Boomers are the norm and we're responding to it [that is, their norm]. So there aren't any words popping up, except the standard, that norm, the rule creators—you created the world that we're living in, and we're responding to it."[32]

Rachel, a Millennial who works in city government, echoed Ellen's general view but added a more specific and pointed critique of the values of Boomers that she believes have wreaked havoc upon her generation. "The first thing [that I think of when I hear Boomer] is a big house with a big yard and vacations—taking a lot of space in the world. Not just because there's so many of them, but also because they really have been a generation that was able to expand in what I think is an unsustainable way for the planet, beyond all previous generations' experience of wealth and opportunity." She believed that they gave little forethought to the implications of their excessive choices for future generations and added, "I think there was sort of an abandon [to their lavish lifestyle]."[33]

Linda, another Millennial whom I referenced earlier, greatly appreciated her upbringing and educational opportunities that her parents provided her and her siblings, but she wondered at what cost? Her impression was that they made "safe and secure choices that came with the sacrifice of enjoyment, fun, meaning, and purpose."[34] For example, she said that her father worked at a job that he hated for twenty years, something that was unimaginable to her.

While these Millennials had some decisive negative views of Boomers, several also referred to their positive qualities and contributions. Just because Millennials could not see themselves chained to a job that they disliked, they did appreciate how hardworking Baby Boomers were and how they benefitted from the grind of work that their parents didn't always enjoy. Billy Thane, a successful Millennial business owner, also had "positive stereotypes" of Boomers. "I will say some of the good stereotypes—and some of these I've talked about with my Dad—are challenging the status quo, being able to have better critical thinking, thinking outside the box, being a little bit more tolerant, and those types of things."[35] Perhaps it was the willingness of Boomers to challenge the status quo that Rachel meant when she associated Boomers with the "free love and protests of the youth of the 1960s and 1970s."[36] Some of the Millennials quietly granted that Boomers might have earned some deference after all because they had paved the way for the freedoms that Millennials enjoy.

Social Media: A Help or Hindrance for Relationships?

Baby Boomers are "digital migrants," while Millennials are "digital natives." As these terms imply, for Baby Boomers entering the digital world was like moving to a new country that required a naturalization process over time, while Millennials already held a passport to it. Or think of it this way: many Millennials were using computers in their classrooms while their Boomer working parents were using typewriters. The youngest Millennials, born in 1996, were only ten years old when Facebook was opened to the public in 2006 and they may also remember its competitor, Myspace. Older Millennials didn't grow up with Facebook and other social media sites but were in their late teen years when the World Wide Web went live, and some may have had Facebook accounts that were initially restricted to a handful of elite college campuses prior to 2006. On the other hand, many of us who are Boomers can remember how efficient and advanced a Dictaphone, microcassette, and an excellent secretary were. The point is that it was a natural for even the oldest Millennials to have facility with computer and digital technologies because it was "native" to them, in contrast to Baby Boomers who had to migrate to a world of unfamiliar terms and technologies when it came to the Web, computing, and social media.

Anecdotally, I've heard stories about how some of the oldest Baby Boomers were "grandfathered" into continuing to perform work as they always had with paper and pen. While most Baby Boomers will always be slower at adopting new technologies, the digital divide between Millennials and Boomers continues to narrow. For example, Millennial smartphone ownership is nearly universal today. In only seven years (since 2011), the percentage of Boomers who own a smartphone has risen from 25 percent to 67 percent.[37]

As Baby Boomers are digital migrants and Millennials are digital natives, I was able to ask individuals from both cohorts questions about relationships with friends and family, and their perceived impact of social media on those relationships. I wanted to hear if their number of close friends had decreased as the studies that I cited in chapter 1 had found, and the extent to which they attributed any changes in their relationships to the Internet and social media. But first, I needed them to define friendship.

A friend is "someone who will accept you for who you are, [and] will be there no matter what happens, unconditionally;" or, "With a friend you can pick up [any] conversation;" or, "You can talk to [a genuine friend] about anything and ideally you can really be yourself, [as it's] someone who knows your history and where you come from." All participants agreed that "friendship meant having someone with whom you have a close emotional connection, who will be there for you" for help and emotional support. Millennials and Baby Boomers universally shared these sentiments and the presence of social media did not appear to influence their ideal of a close friend.

But there was no agreement on whether a friend was someone with whom you had to have regular, frequent contact. Some of those interviewed for the book believed that being a friend meant that having a deep, prior shared history exempted you from regular contact. That was a part of the beauty of a friendship. No matter how long ago you had been in contact with a friend, the boundaries of time and place melted when you reconnected. For others, being friends meant having ongoing contact with people and nurturing those relationships, especially for those who had made an effort to make close friends later in life. Among those who believed that friendship meant intentionally choosing to remain in touch, some believed that meant primarily in person, while others believed that regularly being in "touch" could include meeting in person, texting, or calling by phone or video platforms like Skype or FaceTime.

I was unable to conclude with confidence from this small sample of people if differences in age influenced ideas about the necessity for being in regular contact with individuals to claim them as "friends." For some, the existence of a strong emotional connection from the past, or more recently acquired through an intense, formative period together (like military service or college), was enough to create a lasting bond even if their relationship lacked ongoing contact. For others, it was remaining in a relationship that was a non-negotiable element of authentic friendship.

"How many close friends do you have?" I asked people who participated in this study to use their personal definition of a friend in answering this question. As many studies would suggest, did they have very few friends and feel like that number was declining? How did their lives stack up against the data? It's difficult to argue against the overwhelming amount of research that originated from the abundant and diverse sources of research that I cited in the prior chapter. While I still trust the conclusion that the number of close friends that people have has declined, the Millennials and Boomers in my study gave me a more nuanced understanding of why that might be so, which wasn't as apparent in researchers' interpretations.

For example, several Baby Boomers said that they had only two close friends. But one of these Boomers was still providing different kinds of support to older and younger family members. Those responsibilities might have accounted for not having the time or energy to maintain more friendships. As he reflected further on the topic of friendships, he also wondered if "the price" of being someone who was unafraid to speak his mind and challenge conventional wisdom may have lost him some friends. In another case, a Boomer had relocated to a part of the country where he had no roots and seemed content to remain in periodic contact with several of his "buddies" from his high school days. Was it coincidental that these two individuals were males, and does gender play a role in the number of friends a person has? These are some of the questions that my interviews stimulated, but generally, Baby Boomers in my study had between three and five close friends.

Some of the Millennials whom I interviewed had a greater number of friends. They were almost evenly divided between those who had three and five close friends (like some Boomers), and those who had between eight and ten close friends. The personal status of the Millennials in my study ran the gamut from "not in a relationship" to "married with children." Yet, none of them felt like the number of close friends that they had was declining.

This discrepancy between my expectations of a declining number of friendships that Boomer and Millennials would express, and my general sense that they were content with the number of close friends they had, made me more sensitive to the importance of how we interpret research on the "epidemic of social isolation." To what extent does stage of life make maintaining relationships with a larger number of people more feasible and a greater priority? As people age, they become more selective about their choice of friends, as one of my favorite Seinfeld episodes so artfully captures. In this Seinfeld episode, cast members decide to try and be altruistic by volunteering to visit "senior citizens." George Costanza's elder soon fires him because he finds George too depressing and pessimistic. George, incredulous that he has been fired for volunteering to do good, asks his elder why he is not interested in his company. His elder exclaims with exasperation, "Life's too short to waste on you."[38]

Many of us who are Boomers have watched the circle of our elderly family members' friends grow smaller as they experience illness and ultimately death. But for Baby Boomers who are still relatively healthy and vital, it could be that we have learned at an earlier age that life is too short to be friends with people who have a talent for finding the gray cloud in every silver lining. I also wonder if we're beginning to see a pendulum swing back toward greater connectedness, or if I simply interviewed Boomer and Millennial outliers who generally did not express feelings of social isolation or a desire for more friends.

Probing further, I asked them how much time they spent in front of a screen (smartphone, iPad, television, etc.) after work hours. I expected that there would be differences for Boomers who were retired or semi-retired and had more available time to spend online, and Millennials who were working and had less discretionary time. I also wanted to know how much of their screen time was spent individually and how much was spent interacting with others. I thought that these questions might help me better understand generational differences between those who desired greater social connection and those who were being seduced into isolation by their digital devices. In a related vein, I also wanted to hear if they thought that social media overall had been more detrimental or more beneficial for their relationships.

Once again, their responses raised more questions about some of the studies that I had read. Generally, Millennials spent more time than Boomers in front of a screen. But there were exceptions even within the group of the approximately twenty interview subjects for my study. During the work week, Millennials tried not to spend more than between ninety minutes and two hours after work, and further tried to limit their time during the weekends when they preferred to interact with friends or family more directly. That was true even of those who were spending between three and five hours on the weekends in front of a screen but were interacting with someone else by texting a friend or discussing a movie or show that they were watching with someone near them.

Also, surprisingly, there were several Baby Boomers who spent more time than Millennials on social media sites. They found that Facebook was a good place to reconnect with people from earlier years, and at least learn superficially about their lives today. In other cases, Baby Boomers spent the same or less amount of time than Millennials on social media sites and watching television. But generally, Millennials and Boomers were clear or becoming clearer about both the positive and negative impacts of 24-7 connectivity.

On the positive side, they appreciated the ability to remain easily linked with family members and friends when they were traveling, especially for extended periods of time. Some Baby Boomers also were grateful that as their aging parents' physical world became smaller, an iPad reopened windows to a world that they could at least inhabit virtually. For example, one expert interview subject told me about her eighty-something-year-old mother who had recently moved into her home. Her mother was from India, and one of the bright spots of her day was connecting with friends from her birthplace, which eased the pain of her move to greater dependence and social isolation.

Gary Harper, whom I referred to earlier, was a technologically savvy Boomer who was career Navy and then entered the telecommunications industry after retirement from military service. He saw more of the shadowy side of social media and felt strongly that social media was much more detrimental than beneficial for relationships. He explained that when you're on social media, "you only see the best of someone's life; communications can be very messy, misconstrued, and misunderstood; and, social media were distracting us from focusing on things in life that are ultimately significant." He further elaborated, "I think that while technological advances are necessary, that doesn't mean they're always productive, and we're not necessarily getting that much more of the important things done. We're getting more of the minor things that don't really matter. I've always been a 'big rock guy' and not 'a little rock guy,' so e-mail was just like, 'Yeah, to find the one big rock that you actually need you have to go through all of these little rocks.' So from my perspective, I think social media and cell phones could be seen as a bad use of technology." He then concluded our interview by advising, "If you have a significant other, get off of Facebook. It will ruin your relationship, and I think that it contributes to isolation."[39]

The pervasiveness of screens, whether they were television, tablet, computer, or smartwatches, was of greater concern to Baby Boomers than to Millennials, and understandably so. Boomers could remember a time when it was possible to take a cab (remember, Lyft and Uber were not yet options), be in an elevator, or even in a hotel lobby or restaurant when there were no screens. As a result, they conversed with people more easily. Moreover, all of the Boomers I interviewed were very concerned about the lack of understanding that Millennials had of the impact of their words in cyberspace. Online, they could not see or experience how a negative comment could wound someone's feelings and self-esteem. They admired the facility that their younger family members had in swiping across geographic and cultural boundaries but were worried about how much time they spent alone. They also were worried about the potential risk to which their children and grandchildren were being exposed.

The pediatrician whom I mentioned several times already, Keith Wilbert, made an excellent point about the danger of leaving children unsupervised with a smartphone. He said, "You have to really supervise them. [Smartphones] are very powerful tools . . . very powerful computers and you cannot give that much power unsupervised to a kid."[40]

Another Boomer, John Jolet, contrasted his childhood and adolescent years, which were filled with human peers and mentors, to the childhood and teen years of today's Millennials, who sometimes seemed closer to their devices than to other people. He was clearly ambivalent about the ability to always be digitally connected. He said, "On one hand, they're [Millennials] isolated as far as personal contact. On the other hand, you start to understand that the world is level and they're reaching out to everybody, but there's no consequence to what they're reaching out to. It is just energy that flows back and forth, but there's no responsibility to anyone, other than they might feel bad. Somehow, they believe, or we've given them a license to say whatever they feel like. And at the same time, they believe everything they hear too, because it comes to them [from the Internet]. There's this blur between reality and what they envision as reality."[41]

But more Millennials may be gaining greater awareness of the negative impacts of social media and had recently begun to cut back on their amount of screen time. They were making a more conscious effort to interact with friends in person, or by audio or video telephone calls. Angela Krintz, a Millennial whom I mentioned earlier, said that initially she enjoyed spending time on Facebook and Instagram, but added, "whereas now I feel like it almost hurts a little bit. You look on Facebook and you see, 'Oh this person's life is so perfect.' You look on Instagram and see that they're [her friends are] traveling and think, 'Should I be traveling, should I do this when I'm in a relationship?' And then sometimes I ask myself if I want to travel right now or do I think I want to because so many other people are. So for me [social media sites] make me second guess what is my life like. Am I making the most out of it? Do I have enough hobbies? It [a social media site] pulls on your insecurities wherever they are and it just highlights them."[42]

The individual who best expressed both the light and the shadows cast by a screen was a Millennial, Billy Thane, quoted earlier in this chapter. With great insight, he explained, "Overall, it [social media] has definitely improved your outer ring of connections of friends and family but may hurt the inner core [of your relationships]. Your outer ring—the people that you don't necessarily see all the time—it's kind of cool to be able to stay in touch with them because you get to see the marriages, the Halloween costumes, the births, stuff like that that you probably never get to see otherwise. But now you get to feel like you're a little bit a part of them and you get to break down the location barrier and are able to have a relationship with them. Where I think we've suffered internally is—with my aunts or uncles, even with my parents—sometimes you feel like, 'Just go look them up on Facebook'—you don't have the quality phone time anymore. I text my parents a lot more than I used to, where [in the past] we used to have phone conversations. The outer ring has definitely been improved, but that quality-type of your inner core has been polluted or poisoned by the outer ring."[43]

Normalizing Intergenerational Relationships

One finding in my study was crystal clear: the vast majority of the thirty people whom I interviewed—about twenty Boomers and Millennials, and thirteen experts in intergenerational issues—only have friends who are approximately their own age. A few Baby Boomers had returned to college or graduate school and found themselves in classrooms with Millennials. Of those who did, some were happy about that, while others found it difficult to relate to Millennials. Also, some Boomers were supervised by Gen Xers or Millennials. In those cases, with one exception, the experience of having younger supervisors was supremely negative.

Only a few Millennials made an intentional choice to have friends who were older. Rachel Nunez, a very perceptive Millennial quoted earlier, explained why she valued having relationships with people from older demographic cohorts. She observed, "I always appreciate talking to people who are older because we're all on the same escalator, and I'm kind of curious what the next rungs up for me are going to be like, when my stair gets a little bit higher up, and to get their perspective on how they look back on the age that I'm at now. And it's just not possible to put your life into context without having contact with people who are at different places at the same time as you, because you hold the place in time constant, and the only dependent variable is the age, so you can really figure out what that means."[44] But her intentional effort to have friends in her life who were older was the exception, not the rule.

The reality that members of each cohort tended to maintain friends within their own peer cohort did not surprise me. In fact, it was one of the motivations for writing this book—namely, my belief that collective generational wisdom and perspectives are untapped assets that we need more than ever. When was the last time you didn't have a conversation with someone about how rapidly so many aspects of our lives were changing?! Often, these changes are related to disruptive technologies that upend entertainment, business, education, health, personal finances—pretty much every aspect of life. These technologies also come with a set of underlying values that reward immediacy of choice, maximum autonomy, the pursuit of personal profit, and productivity that is measured only in terms of economic output. But they discourage other values that favor opportunities for members of all generations to succeed, they inhibit self-reflection, collective action, and collaboration, and narrow the multiple ways in which productivity can be measured (for example, through volunteer engagement and mentoring initiatives). These new values often pit one generation against another, instead of creating an alternative framework in which each generation feels invested in the other's success.

A Concluding Question for Baby Boomers

I began this chapter by introducing a framework for helping Baby Boomers and Millennials make more sense of one another's respective worldviews on relationships and their perceptions of one another's life choices. I promised to conclude with a surprising observation that can open more conversation between Baby Boomers and Millennials, and the generations immediately following. Baby Boomers have often stereotyped Millennials as lacking in direction and have difficulty in understanding why they can't seem to "settle down" and demonstrate more grit in remaining in a job or career. Millennials rightfully resent this critique because Baby Boomers show little empathy for the overwhelming choices that they have, the accelerating pace of change that spawns new industries, and their uncertainty about the most efficient and cost-effective post–high school education that will land them a job with meaning and the ability to move toward financial independence. If they needed to create a new word, "adulting," it's because there are legitimate reasons for their delay in reaching adulthood.

In that way, I view Millennials as the literal and metaphorical offspring of Baby Boomers. Baby Boomers—remember that we entered adulthood with a commitment to questioning conventions and institutions. With great advances in medical care, we have the potential for decades of purposeful living that was inconceivable only a generation ago. That's why when I asked the Baby Boomer participants in my study if the term "retirement" reflected their description of their post-employment lives, almost all of them recoiled. Retirement evoked images of their own elderly parents and grandparents, but not their vital and productive selves.

What I learned from their reaction to the term "retirement" was that in the same way Millennials are redefining their entry into adulthood, Baby Boomers are redefining their exit from the workforce. Adult development is much more fluid than it used to be along the entire adult lifespan. So here is my question for Boomers: if we are the generation renowned for redefining life on our terms and even now in our older years feel entitled to remake "retirement," why do we begrudge Gen Xers and Millennials the same right to redefine adulthood on their terms? Wouldn't we create some amazing opportunities for intergenerational learning if we understood that they've internalized our values but are rightfully taking them in new directions?

What You Can Do

1. One goal that many religions share is to help individuals slow down, pause, and gain perspective on things in life that are of ultimate importance. Whether you self-identify as religious, spiritual, agnostic, or atheist, you can likely appreciate this goal because of the relentless rapidity of change. Regardless of your religious orientation, visit the website http://www.sabbathmanifesto.org for ways in which you can build opportunities into your life to unplug and renew your relationships: with yourself, with friends, and with family.

2. If you're ready to listen and believe that you have the skills to have a challenging but constructive conversation, if you're a Boomer, ask a Millennial at work what stereotypes come to mind when a Millennial hears the phrase "Baby Boomer." And if you're a Millennial who works with Baby Boomers, ask a Boomer what stereotypes come to mind upon hearing the word "Millennial." Of course, make sure that you're in compliance with any human resource policies in your workplace, and explain your goal of increasing understanding of your coworkers if you have a human resources director. If you don't, find out in advance if your colleague is willing to have this conversation

and again, explain that you want to understand better how someone from another generation views the world. Then, make a measurable commitment to yourself to try and improve that relationship based on what you have learned.

3. Finally, for Baby Boomers, think of several occasions decades ago when you urgently felt that you had to do things your way, against the wishes of parents or mentors. Jot those times down, close your eyes, and try to recreate those scenes in your mind. You were the rebel then, the one who was accused of foolishly ignoring sage advice. Now, look at the Millennials around you and try to reframe some of their actions as a continuation of your boldness in challenging the status quo. How do you understand their choices when you're able to step back and say, "same values, different context"?

CHAPTER THREE

~

Meet the Family

At a certain point, if you still have your marbles and are not faced with serious financial challenges, you have a chance to put your house in order. It's a cliché, but it's underestimated as an analgesic on all levels. Putting your house in order, if you can do it, is one of the most comforting activities, and the benefits of it are incalculable.

—Leonard Cohen,[1] poet and musician

The House Is Disorderly

Today, "putting your house in order" is a challenge because adulthood is a much more fluid state. Regardless of age, adults may find themselves in various states of dependence and independence at different times throughout their lives. That's why the norms of responsibilities between parents and children and, more generally, between younger and older generations that held through the last century no longer serve us well. Those norms presumed that one entered adulthood sometime between the ages of eighteen and twenty-three years old and progressed upward in a linear fashion toward greater levels of independence until a person retired and faded out of sight.

But as I described in chapter 2, that model doesn't fit the realities of younger or older generations as it once neatly did. Social isolation, rapidly changing technologies and social values, generational silos in our neighborhoods and institutions, and geographic distance that separates family members from one another, make it easy to avoid substantive conversations about the challenges that each generation faces. The result? It often takes some negative event to trigger these difficult conversations, like older adult children suddenly needing to care for elderly parents or, at the other end of the age spectrum, older adults unexpectedly finding themselves emotionally and financially supporting their younger adult children.

But there are better alternatives to deferring conversations about the uncertainties of living in a world where our communities are increasingly comprised of six generations. One that I've become a more vocal advocate of through the process of researching this book is having intergenerational conversations. These conversations potentially enable us to understand that each generation has a stake in the other's well-being. In this chapter, we're going to "meet families," that is, better understand the challenges that Millennials and Baby Boomers face in their family relationships, and then broaden that knowledge to our neighborhoods and communities. Gen Xers are likely to preview versions of their future selves, and decisions and discussions, in these stories. Today's families and communities look like impressionistic paintings. With the many changes that occurred, especially within the past decade, they seem fuzzy when we're too close to them. If we want to understand them, we'll need to take a few steps back to gain the perspective that we need to appreciate the changes that have occurred within and across the generations, and that's what we're going to do now.

Growing Up Boomer

Baby Boomers, the generation born between 1946 and 1964,[2] are sometimes subdivided into early and late Boomers.[3] Early Boomers (born between 1946 and 1954) were the ones who led the Vietnam protests, took over college campuses, and reveled at Woodstock listening to powerful social change musicians. Late Boomers (born between 1955 and 1964) were a tamer bunch. Speaking as a late Boomer, I remember some protests on college campuses against apartheid in South Africa and others about the growing ecological damage that we were doing to our planet, but life on college campuses had settled down after the prior tumultuous decade. Our great ballad singers' lyrics were less edgy and more introspective about their personal lives. They included artists like Carole King, James Taylor, Carly Simon, John Denver, and Harry Chapin.

In reflecting on how to tell the story of individuals who may be part of a family that spans five or six generations living in different geographic locations, I was drawn back to Chapin's 1974 hit song, "Cat's in the Cradle."[4] He wistfully sang about a father who made the undoable error of prioritizing work over spending time with his young son who pleads for his attention. By the end of the song, it's heartbreakingly clear that this father realizes that he has bartered badly. The father has retired and craves a relationship with his now adult child and with his grandchildren. But how can he retrieve a relationship that he never had when he didn't invest time with his son between the years of diapers and driving? Those are the most precious years for a parent to lay the foundation for an enriching relationship later in life—if a parent is able and willing to make time when the child needs it and not just when it's "convenient" for the parent.

Many early and late Boomers likely recall this song as it climbed to number 1 on the "Billboard Hot 100" list in 1974, meaning that you couldn't escape hearing it on the radio. This ballad tracked the growth of the child with milestones like returning home on college break, leaving home permanently, and starting his own career and family. But its greatest personal appeal was one line about the son asking to borrow his father's car keys. When "Cat's in the Cradle" was released, I already had my driver's permit. I frequently imagined the day when I turned sixteen, passed my driver's test, and watched the thick barrier of time between holding a permit and having a license melt away so that I could ask my dad to borrow his car keys. Those keys symbolized the ability to unlock new freedoms: from double-dating with an older friend who already had his driver's license to solo dating, from a sixty-minute high school commute by public transportation to a twenty-five-minute carpool drive with friends, and from parental dependence to an overall feeling of greater independence. Gaining the ability to drive felt like a spontaneous transformation from childhood into early adulthood. Time lumbered along and decades later, I had the experience of teaching my children how to drive when they were high school adolescents.[5] Even later, when it was now their turn to ask if they could use my car when they were home on their respective college breaks, I did just as my father had done and turned my keys over to them.

As I'm close with my parents and children, I haven't personally felt the regret that Chapin soulfully sang about in his own parent and child relationship, but I can identify with the stages of a family's development to which he alludes in this song. Many Boomers had "informal scripts" when adolescents approached their sixteenth birthday. They had inherited some experiences from their parents about the conversations they needed to have with their soon-to-be drivers about driving safely and soberly, and how much of the cost of car insurance and fuel was fair for them to bear. Additionally, high schools offered Boomers driver education classes, and states legislated eligibility requirements for when teenagers could receive a driver's permit and license. (These courses have been updated to include the dangers of texting and making phone calls while driving).

Likewise, by sixth grade and continuing into middle and high school, public school teachers of Boomers began offering sex education classes, which was a relief because I couldn't have handled my parents discussing my sexual activity. By unlucky coincidence, my son contracted mononucleosis when he was thirteen years old in 1999, during the time of the impeachment trial of President Bill Clinton. When he began to feel better but wasn't yet well enough to return to school, he watched the trial on CNN during the day. When he asked me what "oral sex" was, I bravely asked myself, "Why deny my wife the opportunity to provide an explanation?" "Wait until your mother gets home from work" became a handy phrase at that time. We knew that gaps in our (okay, her) initial discussions about sexuality and relationships would be filled by our children's health education classes which now included issues like substance abuse, and care for one's emotional and physical health. They also had refresher seminars during their respective freshman orientation weeks in college on these sensitive topics, and they were comfortable calling us with mundane and existential questions through their college years. (And as the universe has a way of recalibrating justice, I was the one to have those discussions with my daughter! Talk about awkward . . .) In fact, my wife and I jokingly recall thinking about how some of the questions that our children asked us without embarrassment when they were in high school and college would still make us blush today if we were to ask our parents. But we were able to guide them through adolescence because we had parents and educators who transmitted their experiences that we could adapt for our children.

Meet the New Family

As I was outlining this chapter, I listened to Chapin's recording of "Cat's in the Cradle." It activated my nostalgic memories but unexpectedly left me feeling that its lyrics were not as timeless as I had remembered. They didn't allude to some new realities, including Millennial boomerang children,[6] grandfamilies,[7] and many individuals who were still driving at ninety-plus years old. These realities, that Chapin and my Boomer peers couldn't anticipate, are firmly embedded into today's families. Let me explain . . .

Driving
A November 2017 briefing paper from the United States Department of Transportation reported that "almost one in five [licensed drivers] . . . are

65 years or older. This age group is growing faster than any other, and is far outpacing their teenage counterparts. The largest single-year percentage increase in licensed drivers that year was among those who are between seventy-five and seventy-nine years old, increasing by 4.98 percent over the previous year."[8] In fact, on one morning when I was drafting this chapter, I had plans to attend the birthday party of a one-hundred-year-old man later in the afternoon who, by the way, is still driving. If Harry Chapin were alive today and rewriting his song, how would he sing about a seventy-something-year-old child initiating conversations about "borrowing" the car keys of a one-hundred-year-old parent—permanently. That's one conversation that we must improvise because we have no inherited wisdom to guide us. Discussing alternative options like state-sponsored transportation services for medical appointments, and private companies like Uber and Lyft that are less costly than traditional cabs, does not diminish the symbolic meaning of that conversation with our elderly parents: losing their independence. Autonomous vehicles and more state legislation regulating elderly drivers might soon reshape these conversations, but they won't eliminate other situations that raise the same symbolic issues of elderly parents feeling like their older adult children are insulting and assaulting their judgment and independence.

Boomerang Living Arrangements

In the last chapter, I asked when adulthood begins for Millennials. In Chapin's song, the definition is traditional: graduation from college and moving away from home. Writing as a Boomer, based on informal discussions with my peers, my new definition of Millennial adulthood is when Millennial children leave their parents' family cell phone plan![9] More seriously, how do Boomers respond when a Millennial child asks to move into a parent's home during transitions between careers or personal relationships? Do you ask your child to pay for a portion of household expenses and share in household tasks? And if your Millennial child is also a parent and moving back to your home with young children, what experience from the past do Boomers have in balancing how to support their grandchildren while also promoting their Millennial children to assume the responsibilities of parenthood and reclaim independence from their Boomer parents? These are not theoretical but real questions: "As of 2016, 15 percent of 25- to 35-year-old Millennials were living in their parents' home. This is 5 percentage points higher than the share of Generation Xers who lived in their parents' home in 2000 when they were the same age (10 percent)."[10]

Gary Harper, a Baby Boomer whom we met earlier, had to set limits with his Millennial children when they needed his help. For example, he explained that he was initially happy to help his son and granddaughter live with him while they needed support in regaining their footing. "My son and my granddaughter came to live with me for a little while. He was working in the evenings and would not come back at night. Then, I started to feel like he was taking advantage of me. I told my son, 'I'm not raising your daughter. You need to either find someone to take care of her, or be home to take care of her because I'm not doing it.' Then I told him that he had to pay rent."[11] Shortly after that, his son and granddaughter moved out of his home. These situations can be emotionally and physically challenging for all involved, but Gary believed that "By being clear with my kids, I can help them and still have a relationship with them."[12] While Gary's situation ended successfully, a recent article in the *Atlantic* magazine noted, "More grandparents than ever are being put in a position like Barb and Fran [two grandmothers profiled in the story]—becoming full-time parents again, often with fewer resources and more health problems than they had the first time around."[13]

On the other hand, some Boomer children are building an "Accessory Dwelling Unit (ADU),"[14] colloquially known as an "in-law unit" or "granny flat" for elderly parents, as an alternative to having them downsize to a smaller apartment or home or move into an independent living facility. Unlike what we hear in Chapin's lyrics where a child moves away, some Boomer children are moving elderly parents into or near their homes to try and prevent health issues that their aging parents are starting to have from becoming more serious problems. Sometimes these arrangements are successful, while other times they are overwhelming and frustrating for all involved.

Regardless of the family dynamic, the scenario of an elderly parent living within 24-7 view of Boomer children adds urgency to a new and delicate question: does an elderly parent have any unofficial obligations toward a Boomer child? Jack Jones, a seventy-two-year-old Boomer, pondered this question during our interview. He observed that many faith traditions are filled with teachings about responsibilities that children have toward their parents and the respect that younger generations are expected to show toward "the elderly" in general. But Jack also commented that when religious norms of "respect for elders" evolved, "the elderly" were not living well into their nineties and beyond. Moreover, elderly individuals lived within the proximity of the family, clan, and tribe, which provided a more comprehensive support system for families with elderly and often infirm parents.[15]

These religious traditions established a range of the emotional, financial, and physical actions that children were expected to provide for their elderly parents. But, given the increasing longevity of elderly parents, Jack wondered if it was time to begin asking questions about the ethical responsibilities that aged parents have toward their aging sixty-something-year-old children, who themselves may be trying to balance other family- and work-related responsibilities. And, are those responsibilities the same or different when an elderly parent lives with an older adult child year-round, or divides time between a residence in a warmer climate during winters and returns to a child's home for the rest of the year? Our legal system offers certain protections for elderly individuals and criminalizes elder abuse. But it can't legislate morally caring conversations and relationships between older adult children and their elderly parents that arouse profound feelings about mutual respect, physical and emotional well-being, and individual agency in making lifestyle and end-of-life choices.

One of my Baby Boomer friends has told me on several occasions that he frequently thanks his parents for having died so long ago. That's his response to watching some of his Boomer friends struggle with the anxiety and anguish of having very elderly parents. While I don't share his sentiment, I understand what he means, just as I'm sure that some Boomers who are reading this chapter do. There's no playbook that provides precise cues for understanding when it's time for older adults and their elderly parents to move in and out of their long-accustomed roles, with child playing the role of part-parent, and parent the role of part-child, each a reluctant actor in a movie with no director.

Even when children and parents have successfully evolved their relationships over decades, and enjoy mutual love and respect, the weight of life's changes at these late stages of adulthood can place tremendous stresses on healthy relationships. While our parents are alive, no matter how old we are, we still desire their approval and do not want to engage with them in heated conversations about their life choices. Those kinds of conversations can cause our elderly parents to resent our unwanted involvement in their lives. And when relationships between elderly parents and older adult children have remained frozen at the stage of adolescence, and a pattern of communications persists in which a child always feels belittled by a parent and a parent always feels insufficiently appreciated, lifelong simmering resentments can cause searing pain to an elderly parent and an older adult child, with younger generations (grandchildren or great nieces and great nephews) as "audience members" to this family drama. I'd like to think that Harry Chapin would find some emotionally evocative words to help us understand that what we need most at these times is conversations, because we're touching upon issues that involve such deep feelings and unspoken fears of legacy and mortality—theirs and ours.

Grandfamilies

One of the experts whom I interviewed was Susan Link, a trust and estates attorney with over thirty years of experience. In addition to her practice, Susan also launched Minnesota's Wills for Heroes (WFH) program, "[which] provides first responders and their spouse with a volunteer attorney to assist in preparing wills and other estate planning documents at no charge."[16] Between her private practice and her pro bono work with WFH, I was curious to know if she had felt the impact of having so many generations alive at one time.

Susan told me that during her early years of practice, siblings would often name one another as legal guardians of their children in case a catastrophic event occurred. But now, "Gen X and Millennial children are naming their parents as the initial set of guardians for their children, not grandparents who are in their eighties, but certainly in their sixties and seventies, and not their siblings. Many are very comfortable with how they were raised and what their parents did, and they don't have to worry if something happens to them and they can't raise their own children."[17] Or grandparents will try to legally adopt their grandchildren in the event of the death of their child when they feel that it's in the best interest of the grandchildren. These changes have led to a new category of families called "grandfamilies."

Generations United, a nonprofit organizational leader in intergenerational work, is a leading expert and advocate for grandfamilies. Generations United's website explains that "grandfamilies or kinship families are families in which children reside with and are being raised by grandparents, other extended family members, and adults with whom they have a close family-like relationship such as godparents and close family friends. About 7.8 million children across the country live in households headed by grandparents or other relatives."[18] It further notes that "about 2.5 million grandparents report they are responsible for their grandchildren's needs. In about a third of these homes neither of the children's parents are in the home."[19]

Imagine that you're a sixty-five-year-old Boomer who has reached that stage in life where after decades of hard work and taking care of others, you're finally ready to create your encore act. You've been planning and dreaming for the past several years about how you hope to develop new facets of yourself and spiral forward to others that you had placed on hold. You're feeling energized about thoughts of traveling more, becoming an avocational expert at your favorite hobby, painting, and spending more time with family. As you're imagining your future, you receive a call with the dreaded nightmare news that a parent never wants to hear. It's from an emergency room doctor. "Your daughter has died. We did everything we could to revive her." The doctor then continues, "It was an opioid overdose." You're barely able to breathe, let alone think coherently, but as you're weeping, you see a picture of your grandchild, Jesse. You're hit by a second shock wave as you realize that your grandchild has no other parent. Jesse's father disappeared immediately after he was born, and no one has been able to locate him. Without yet realizing it, you're about to join the growing ranks of grandfamilies.

This tragic scenario has become increasingly common according to a study conducted by Generations United in 2016, in which it notes that "with the rise in heroin and other opioid use, more relatives are raising children because the parents have died, are incarcerated, are using drugs, are in treatment or are otherwise unable to care for their children."[20] For grandchildren, the good news is that children in the care of relatives thrive in comparison to children in non-relative care.[21] But when grandparents or other relatives are suddenly thrust into the role of parenthood, in addition to the overwhelming emotional changes that they experience, they must also try and become experts in learning what support services are available to them, and then wind their way through a maze of state and federal laws in order to access them. If you've had any experience with governmental bureaucracy, you can imagine how utterly frustrating it can be to claim eligibility for available supports even when you have proper legal documentation. That frustration can become a second nightmare when you must fight for legal guardianship or even visitation rights because the other parent in the picture is unreliable or also an addict.

Virtual Assisted Parenting

As any marital therapist will tell a young couple contemplating a lifetime together, each person in the relationship also brings a complete cast of characters from their respective families into their home. They may not physically be in the room with you, but they are always present in your subconscious and influence your relationship in profound ways. If you're raising children today, there's likely to be a new "cast member" who is literally in the room and responds to a name like Alexa, Cortana, Siri, Bixby, or Google Voice (which clearly needs a warmer name). True, personal digital assistants don't only live in homes where there are young children. But they present unique challenges that are especially pertinent for parenting.

Rachel Botsman describes her experience of bringing Alexa into her home and watching how quickly her three-year-old daughter begins to form a relationship with "her" (that is, Alexa). The title of her opinion piece, "Co-Parenting with Alexa," brilliantly captures the moral dilemmas of raising children in an age of digital assistants. She asks the kinds of questions that are becoming more pressing than we may realize as the trifecta of big data, artificial intelligence, and machine learning gain greater potential to make decisions for us, with or often without our awareness and permission. "The Alexas of the world will make a raft of decisions for my kids and others like them as they proceed through life—everything from whether to have mac and cheese or a green bowl for dinner to the perfect gift for a friend's birthday to what to do to improve their mood or energy and even advice on whom they should date. In time, the question for them won't be, 'Should we trust robots?' but 'Do we trust them too much?'"[22] After watching her daughter, Grace, become too cozy with Alexa, Rachel decides to store Alexa in the closet, concluding with another question. "There are few checks and balances to deter children from doing just that [trusting digital assistants], not to mention very few tools to help them make informed decisions about A.I. advice. And isn't helping Gracie learn how to make decisions about what to wear—and many more even important things in life—my job?"[23]

I'm not sure if Rachel is thinking far enough ahead into the future, as is another reporter, Anya Kamenetz, who investigates technology and education issues. Kamenetz writes about the imminent reality of the day when kids will be interacting with nonhuman physical objects that create an even stronger perception, or perhaps deception, of being human.

> If the forecasters are to be believed, we'll all soon be plunged into a gently glowing alphabet soup of AR, VR, AI, MR, and IoT—augmented reality, virtual reality, artificial intelligence, "mixed reality," and the Internet of Things. We'll be inhabiting the bodies of avatars 24-7, exchanging GIFs with our sentient refrigerators, and using virtual assistants to ward off telemarketing bots. Digital experiences will be so immersive and pervasive that Yellowstone National Park will look like today's Times Square. By then, the existence of screens as separate entities, with borders and off buttons, will be a quaint, half-remembered state of affairs.
>
> The current scientific advice on digital media for children is based on the concept of "screen time." This exists in opposition to a concept of "screenless time." "Online" imagines that there is such a thing as "offline." Those are exactly the boundaries that may melt with the next generation of technology.[24]

So is parenting more complicated today than in past generations? I turned to Rhonda Hauser, an expert in child development and family relationships, for her opinion. Hauser believes that while the context of parenting has changed, the underlying issues have not. She elaborated, "[Healthy parenting] still centers around communications, clarity of expectations, clarity of boundaries, and the understanding that parents will rise to the occasion and be parents for their children [and not try to be their 'friends']. Children will have to explore and navigate through the challenges of having boundaries placed upon them, but that's all part of [a child's] learning how to feel confident and have a strong sense of self."[25]

I don't have young children, but I'm often around them because many of my friends have grandchildren in town, and my wife and I frequently visit our young grandchildren who live out of town. Based on what I was seeing, it appeared to me that raising children in a digital environment was more complicated today than only a short time ago, so I pressed Hauser further on that question. She replied, "I think people say parenting is more complicated because it's different. If you would ask our grandparents [who were born around the turn of the century] if raising their children was more complicated than the generation before them, they would probably say, 'yes,' just like if you asked our parents [members of the Greatest and the Silent Generations, born before 1946] if raising their children [Baby Boomers] was more complicated than a generation ago, they would also probably say, 'yes.' Every generation feels like they are faced with more difficulties and complications but that's just a function of living in a different context. But 'complicated' to me is just another phrase for different, unfamiliar, or uncomfortable. It's a word that helps us alleviate some of our fears and our trepidations [about parenting], but [can be used also to] relieve us of some of the responsibility that we have because our context is different from a generation ago. So yes, there are things that make parenting more challenging, but I wouldn't say that it's necessarily more complicated."[26]

What has changed in her opinion? Hauser cited four factors that have changed the context of parenting. One is the velocity of technological change that young minds cannot adapt to, especially without parental guidance. A second is the unrealistic expectations of academic success that educators and parents have of children at increasingly younger ages. The homework of a child in kindergarten today looks more like assignments that a second grader used to receive, and four-year-old preschoolers are now doing the work that children in kindergarten classes were doing. According to Hauser, "that's why children in third grade [in Texas, where Hauser is based] are being put on medication, because their anxiety level is so high in anticipation of having to take their first set of standardized exams."[27] A third factor is easy access to an overwhelming amount of information on parenting, without parents knowing how to assess its quality and reliability. And, according to Hauser, the fourth and most crucial factor is parents themselves. She has observed that "Millennial parents don't like to admit that they need support or that they don't have all the answers."[28]

From Sandwich to Hoagie

In 1981, Dorothy Miller, a social worker, introduced the phrase "sandwich generation" to describe the challenges primarily of women in their thirties and forties. These were the women who were sandwiched between raising children and caring for parents, while also in some cases pursuing careers outside of the home. The phrase, "the sandwich generation," took root in popular culture because it was an incredibly apt metaphor. Without diminishing the challenges of that generation, a sandwich is small, digestible, and something that didn't take too long to eat relative to a full meal. While the pressures that these women faced from younger children and older parents were significant, they occurred over a more compressed period because children reached independence sooner and parents didn't live as long.[29]

Thinking intergenerationally, if we're seeking a metaphor that captures the reality of six generations of people alive today, I would suggest a hoagie (or hero, depending upon your geographic region). Why? The standard-sized sandwich bread is approximately a four-inch square, and sandwiches are vertical, implying that the middle section is the essential part. In contrast, hoagies are about a foot long and horizontal. As they're horizontal, there is no implied priority of one part being more essential than another. By analogy, in our intergenerational world, we're all in the metaphoric "middle." Regardless of age and generation, we've heard experts and subjects who were interviewed for this book all along the lifespan acknowledge a feeling of disequilibrium and a recognition that roles and responsibilities can reverse at a moment's notice. The only part of this metaphor that I haven't quite completed is that today's "hoagies" would have to come not only with a side of potato chips but also computer chips, because technology plays such an important role in intergenerational relationships.

Priscilla Quentin, a Boomer, is a recently retired expert in palliative care. My conversation with her captures some of the flavor of what it means to think of all generations as one big "hoagie," as her story involves an evolution of how multiple generations learned to work together intergenerationally. My hunch was that she had learned a lot over the decades about the importance of intergenerational communications through the most significant conversations that we have, those about life and death, mortality and meaning, letting go and leaving a legacy. A friend of mine had recommended that I meet with Priscilla, both for her professional wisdom and personal experiences.

It immediately became clear within the first few minutes of my interview why my friend thought that I should meet with Priscilla. As a first-wave

Boomer, she believed that regardless of conventions in the medical field, she should be the one to decide her own career trajectory. Her intrepid spirit and entrepreneurial temperament enabled her to spot opportunities in the medical profession, which over the past several decades has been its own petri dish for experimentations in the delivery of health care.

Priscilla earned a master's degree in psychiatric nursing, a doctorate in educational administration, and acquired start-up experience in academia. She developed a master's degree program in nursing at a major state university, later became dean of a master's degree program in nursing in another state, in which she launched a rural state-wide Bachelor's of Nursing program. But the pace at which academia moved was too slow for her, so she became director of the health education department at a large Health Maintenance Organization (HMO), which entailed developing educational materials for the organization's health professionals and educational classes for patients. As Priscilla described her experience, "They kept throwing more things at me that didn't fit anywhere in the system, so I worked on chronic disease management, the mental health center, and senior home care."[30] Priscilla helped to establish many of the palliative care programs in a large metropolitan area in the Midwest before starting her own business as a health care consultant. With this vast experience, I was certain that she would contribute significantly to the overall topic of opening conversations across generations, and she did not disappoint me. In fact, her own personal experience in caring for her elderly parents was as valuable for this book as her distinguished professional accomplishments.

Several years ago, the time came to transition her mother into a palliative care program. In a gratifying way, she felt that her professional life had come full circle and that she would know how to tap into the palliative care services that she had created to keep her mother comfortably and safely at home. Her initial contact with those administering the program was positive, and they told her that they would help to arrange for whatever her mother needed. But even with the excellent private medical insurance that supplemented her mother's Medicare plan, Priscilla was surprised at the level of family support needed once a family member enrolled in a palliative care program. Yes, the program provided medical equipment, medication, nursing visits, bathing and other professional services. But, in her professional judgment, Priscilla knew that these services were disturbingly insufficient for the quality of care that she believed any person in palliative care needed, and soon realized that greater family involvement and financial contributions would be required.

Additionally, in her professional role, she had witnessed how frustrating for families the lack of communication and coordination of care could be as patients transitioned in and out of different settings: hospitals, transitional care facilities, and back home for palliative care. Now, she was no longer witness, but recipient of the challenges created by a siloed medical establishment. She had to bridge the process of enabling her mother to transition from a hospital setting to home. As she said, "I am a PhD nurse and I still do not understand how the system works. I helped to create the field and I've worked in the system and in the end, I was lost. It's like, 'Who is going to do this [that is, take care of a need] for her?' There are a lot of resources out there, and there are organizations that somewhat pull research together, and say that they will fill that gap in palliative care where more hands-on care is needed, but we can only perform x, y, and z services. So these services and organizations wind up butting up against one another."[31]

How did Priscilla's story unfold? A Millennial nephew moved into her mother's finished basement so that someone would be available if a night-time emergency occurred. With some coaching from his aunt, her nephew really stepped up to the plate. For example, she explained to him that elderly individuals often do not hear clearly and that when he returned from work, he needed to let her know that the television sounds coming from the base-ment were not the noise of a burglar trying to break into her home. After all, why would a younger Millennial know this without being coached by a family member? She also hired help from an organization that advertises nonmedical services provided by bonded and insured individuals for people in her mother's situation. But as Priscilla learned, even under watchful eyes, these organizations are imperfect. Her mother was assigned a fluent but non-native English-speaking Millennial to regularly visit her. That was problem-atic because sending someone who spoke English with a thick accent can create a language barrier with an elderly, hard of hearing person.

Priscilla, who was still working full-time, called her mother every day to see how she was feeling until she could visit her after work. During one con-versation, her mother explained that her helper [from this organization] and her helper's friend were taking her to the doctor. Priscilla thought that her mother was confused as she had only hired one aide. Her mother explained that her helper had been speaking with a friend named Surrey, who sounded very kind. Surrey explained to her helper how to write a check and which route to take to the doctor, so she assumed that Surrey would also accompany the two of them to her appointment.

Priscilla left her office immediately after the call, drove to her mother's home, fired her mother's helper on the spot and then revealed who Surrey was to her mother. Holding her iPhone, she explained that Surrey was a digi-tal assistant who "lived" inside her iPhone, to which her mother responded,

"Oh, well, I couldn't really hear her." Eventually, Priscilla made the choice to retire and take the lead role in caring for her mother, one that she was best suited for personally and professionally. She also wanted to keep the promise that she and other family members had made to their father before he died that they would "take care of Mom at home."[32]

I've included Priscilla's story because it illustrates that even those who are well-steeped in the medical establishment can find themselves frustrated at the time they need it most. Priscilla, whose father had been a physician, came from a family that openly spoke about death and dying, and family members had spoken in advance about their parents' medical and end-of-life needs. She was able to piece together a plan that worked. So, what can those of us who lack her background and frequently are unwilling to discuss issues related to end-of-life care learn about the importance of conversation around difficult issues from Priscilla?

Replacing Just-In-Time
Talks with Advance Discussions

One of the themes that I heard from the experts whom I interviewed for this book is the need for greater conversation and advance preparation for life's transitions across the generational spectrum. That includes conversations with young adults experiencing a tumultuous time because of economic difficulties or elderly adults clinging to independence, unwilling to accept that they are putting themselves and others at risk. But that need for open discussions runs counter to a reality that emerged in my interviews of Boomers and Millennials, one that Priscilla stated succinctly: "Palliative care is about the ability to have conversations about big issues based on our relationships, and if we can't converse beyond trivialities, we'll never get to the big things."[33] Because of the velocity of change that we're all experiencing, her comments about the need to converse about "big things" encompass more than end-of-life issues, but let's start there just to illustrate some of the advantages to advancing these kinds of discussions before a catastrophic trigger event makes them unavoidable.

The Millennials whom I interviewed ranged in age from their late twenties to their mid-thirties. Several of them had already assumed limited or episodic care-taking roles for their parents, and while most of their parents were in good health, a number of these Millennials who had older parents observed that they were beginning to "slow down." With one exception, these Millennials had not had substantive discussions about their parents' long-term well-being.

It's easy to understand why Millennials want to avoid this topic. Millennial children don't often think about the reality that their parents will one day die, or consider if death will arrive suddenly or be a long journey intermingled with periods of illness and wellness. Unless you grow up in a household where a parent or some other older adult comes into regular contact with death because of his or her profession, a parent's mortality or even serious illness seems so far off in the future, especially if Millennials' parents are active and healthy. In several cases, the Millennial children whom I interviewed for my book had witnessed or were watching their Boomer parents' struggles with age-related issues of their own elderly parents (that is, their grandparents), which enabled me to ask if they had contemplated the time when they might be involved in caring for their own parents as they aged.

In general, while they had all considered that possibility, they did not see the need to initiate those discussions unless they had already had some experience in that role. One Millennial, Sam Baglioni, said that when the time came to have discussions with his parents about lifestyle and medical decisions when they were old, "I hope[d] they would be reasonable."[34] Another Millennial, Linda Archer, believed that it will take a trigger event to have difficult conversations about her parents' living arrangements and wasn't sure if her parents had advance medical directives.[35] In several interviews with Millennials, they and their siblings had quietly begun discussing among themselves the likelihood that they may be involved in caring for their parents when they become elderly. However, they also believed that if they began to initiate these conversations now, their parents were likely to "brush them off." They seemed resigned to wait until the inevitable happened.

But there were several Millennials who had begun taking on the role of caretaker for a parent and had begun to formulate a plan for sharing those responsibilities with siblings. Another Millennial suffered the loss of a sibling. That tragedy motivated him to purchase a life insurance policy and opened the door for discussions with his parents about life insurance, wills, and power of attorney. However, they have not yet spoken about what care for them will look like when their health declines with age.

Since 1985, whenever I've needed a dose of wisdom (wisdom = experience + knowledge + empathy), I've turned to my rabbinic mentor, Rabbi Kass Abelson, who is a member of the Greatest Generation. Although he is exceptionally humble and does not like accolades, he truly is one of the greatest people whom I've been privileged to know. Over the years, I've spoken with him about the complexities of living in an intergenerational world. With his permission, I'd like to invite you into our dialogue which took place about a year ago when he was *only* ninety-two years old. I've polished the direct transcript of our interview and you're now invited to listen in on our conversation, informed by his over seventy years of rabbinic experience. "KA" stands for (Rabbi) Kass Abelson and "HH" is yours truly.

HH: What was it that enabled you to make decisions [like moving into an independent living facility, and limiting and later completely stopping to drive] without having your children try to make them for you?

KA: I have been an independent person throughout the years and I have made decisions that would keep me independent. I tried to anticipate what my children might be thinking and came up with the decision to stop driving on my own before the pressure began and tensions arose. Many of my age mates had waited too long and there was tension between them and their children. I decided I would make the decisions before pressure began.

HH: In other words, you made those choices so that you could keep control over your own life?

KA: That's almost accurate—I would pick up signals from my age mates, anticipate what my children might be thinking, and act on my own.

HH: What advice would you give to your peers so that they don't have to make decisions under pressure from family members?

KA: You have to keep an open mind and not stubbornly adhere to a position that may prove inadvisable over a period of time. Anticipate, be sensitive and pick up signals. I think that children should drop hints and raise questions like, "Have you thought about . . . [not driving on highways]?" without applying pressure. Pressure may work but it brings both parties through a very difficult and angry period. Kids should be sensitive to their parents' feelings and try to work at it without pressure. Sometimes pressure might prove necessary because of exposure to potential danger to parents and to other people who might be caught in an accident caused by an elder who should have known that the time had come to stop.

HH: In other words, children should initiate conversations with questions and not make demands unless there is an imminent danger. But sometimes parents don't want to have these conversations with their children. What do you suggest in that situation?

KA: I haven't thought that question fully through. In most of the cases that I have dealt with, the parent has been subjected to quite a bit of pressure. The parent will concede to the pressure after a while, hopefully not after the anticipated fear materializes. I guess what I would respond is that a relationship exists between parents and children, and we should not subject it to unnecessary tension. It should be a warm, loving relationship where both parties act reasonably.

HH: Maybe a way to preserve that relationship is for older adult children and their parents to begin these conversations much earlier, before they are live issues.

KA: I would expand it so that they talk not only about these issues, but issues in the family and in the community, including financial issues, so that they become accustomed to discussing things that are important and developing methods of resolving the issues. Develop the practice of conversations around meaning and legacy and matters of importance and not just issues around change and loss.

HH: What about grandchildren? They're paying attention to two generations: their parents, who may be "seniors" or approaching that stage, and their elderly grandparents. What roles do they have in these conversations?

KA: They are family, and as a part of the family, should be open to these discussions. In fact, that interest should work in reverse and grandparents may open the issues that they see as being important with grandchildren. That doesn't mean judging a grandchild's response by saying, "You're wrong," but by asking clarifying questions and respectfully offering an idea, without pushing it where there is a bit of difference. All members of the family should have a sense of responsibility and a desire to be helpful and do it in a way that doesn't create hostility. And grandparents should pull back if there is an angry response from grandchildren.

HH: So, tread lightly, test the waters, don't go too far, try to be a coach and ask questions that they may not have thought about.

KA: I think it's a very good summary of what we've talked about.

HH: I've noticed that when people reach a very old age, one way that they prepare themselves emotionally for death is to start using phrases like, "After I'm gone . . . " when speaking with family members. They're not being morbid, but realistically accepting the eventuality of death. We're rabbis, so we're used to discussing mortality. But many people don't deal with death and dying on a regular basis, and I've found that older adult children are sometimes quick to dismiss their parents' need to refer to the "time after" with phrases like, "Mom, don't talk that way," or, "Dad, you know that I don't like to hear you say that." So we have situations where elderly parents are trying to prepare themselves and their families for the time when they will no longer be alive, while older adult children may not want to have these conversations.

KA: The subject of mortality is difficult. Parents should tackle it with sensitivity and thoughtfulness and it should not come out of the blue. But if older adult children and their parents have been having conversations about life changes in advance of a crisis, and if they are talking about the meaning of their lives and their values, then they are already having discussions indirectly about mortality.

HH: "Honor and respect for parents" are deeply held values in Judaism and, in fact, many faith traditions. Because these kinds of conversations are difficult for older children to initiate with their elderly parents, do elderly parents have to respect their children's feelings and take the lead in initiating them?

KA: Yes, elderly parents can be helpful to older adult children by initiating these discussions at a time when it isn't a crisis. Families can bring in legal, medical, and accounting advice so that the parent doesn't lose total control and so that families can lay out an agreed upon path. Bringing in someone neutral is very helpful to diffuse tensions and keep discussions respectful. Family members may only have to make difficult decisions once or twice. But having professionals—not as intermediaries but as people who can call upon deep experience—can remove some of the difficulties. It's a way for elderly parents to maintain their independence and choice, and for their children to have peace of mind.

HH: Kass, thank you for allowing me to share your wisdom publicly. I know that my contemporaries will find your insights helpful, and I have a feeling that they'll be forwarding your words to other family members.[36]

What You Can Do

"Just-in-time" is a great manufacturing process pioneered by the carmaker, Toyota, to improve productivity. "Just-in-time" means making "only what is needed, when it is needed, and in the amount needed."[37] But people aren't widgets, and the goal in having these conversations isn't to make them more efficient. Rather, it's to make them more valuable and caring, something that only develops with practice and won't happen in a crisis when, paraphrasing the opening quote to this chapter from Leonard Cohen, we don't feel like we've lost our marbles.

1. If you're raising young children, have confidence that by learning how to set age-appropriate limits with new technologies, you're teaching your children to thrive later in life because they'll learn how to self-regulate their behavior. Be sure to explain why these limits are important, listen empathetically to their responses, and as they mature, help them become navigators of their lives by making them aware that if they don't control technology, technology will control them. Most importantly, model unmediated, face-to-face conversation with

them. You can also visit websites like Zero to Three, Common Sense Media, and National Association for the Education of Young Children for hands-on resources and guidance, in addition to speaking with pediatricians and developmental therapists who are there to help.[38] And talk with those who have raised children. True, they didn't have to consider how to integrate smartphones into their lives, but our most elderly members of society can remember bringing their first television set into their homes, and Boomers can remember lugging a large desktop into their homes. As Hauser noted earlier, the context has changed, but you might learn something about how they responded to issues that are similar to ones that you may be experiencing with a small screen. Hauser has generously offered a Family Technology Education Plan as a practical guide for families with children ages two and older (see appendix A). It's also helpful for Boomers who spend time with children, either in family roles or as volunteers, to help understand the changed context of working with children today.

2. As a general rule of thumb, advance the timetable for discussing transitional issues along the adult lifespan. Whether it's a young adult struggling financially who may need to temporarily move back to a parental home, or an elderly parent who is still driving but has had a couple of "fender benders," initiate conversation and planning before an issue turns into a crisis. In a related vein, as the wise rabbi recommended, vet a few neutral, third-party individuals who can help mediate difficult discussions among family members if needed. In many cases, if parents and children had strained relationships in earlier years, they are likely to repeat that pattern without the intervention of someone who mediates these discussions professionally and has perspectives and experience that families don't.

3. Become literate with the various kinds of legal and financial tools that are available to you and family members and have values-based discussions as a family about them when you're not under duress. Consult with an attorney, financial planner, and other trusted and knowledgeable professionals about the various kinds of legal powers that you want to codify now, and which ones you want to have conversations about with other family members in the future. For example, you may be paying for your young adult child's health care premiums if they are under age twenty-six, but that does not mean that you have immediate and sole determination of your child's medical care unless you have a notarized advance medical care directive. As Susan Link, whom I cited earlier, said, "Everyone should have an advance medical direc-

tive."[39] Dr. Sherrill Zehr, another expert whom I interviewed, created a Health Care Transition Discussion Guide specifically for this volume (see appendix B) to ideally help families initiate difficult discussions prior to a health emergency, although it can also be used when a serious health event occurs. This guide can help family members initiate intergenerational discussions about the needs of aging family members and the roles that other family members may expect to assume in providing support.

4. Become familiar and help support grandfamilies. Generations United has abundant resources on its website to help educate you about challenges of this hidden community, and how you can advocate for policies that support them.[40] If your heart lies in volunteering to help teenagers or connect younger and older generations, be sure to visit the websites of organizations like Search Institute, Encore, Help-Full and Dorot.[41] You'll be reading more about them in later chapters, but these are a few of the organizations that might just get you hungry enough to swap the sandwich metaphor for the hoagie.

CHAPTER FOUR

~

Understanding Community

FaceTime or Face-to-Face Time?

An intergenerational community is one where young people feel like they can contribute, be challenged, and there's a future for them, and where older people feel like they can be engaged, challenged, and there's a future for them. It's one that realizes that they can use their resources to connect generations rather than separate them, [one] where people see connecting with other generations as a normal part of life.[1]

—Donna Butts, executive director, Generations United

What Is Community?

"Community" is one of those words that is used loosely and, as a result, people understand it differently. We're accustomed to seeing civic, religious, and neighborhood associations include the word "community" in their descriptions. More recently, manufacturers, sports leagues, and corporations have gotten into the community business. For example, you can join the Lexus or NASCAR community Facebook pages. But once you've become a member of one of those "communities," what does it mean? Are you obligated to take or refrain from certain actions, or participate online or in person in Lexus or NASCAR-sponsored events? Are you expected to adhere to a certain set of values or behaviors that bind you to others in the group? If we want to foster more intergenerational communities, for the purposes of this book, first we're going to define more precisely what we mean by "community," and include how the concept of community is evolving because of the existence of "on-line communities."

At its most basic level, the pull for participation in a community is what summons a group of people to meet regularly and primarily in person (that is, face-to-face) around a shared purpose for which they reciprocally care. For example, individuals who are committed to environmental conservation may hike, bike, and raise funds for environmental causes together. Art enthusiasts may connect regularly with other art lovers to ensure that their community maintains a robust artistic community. High school and college students may experience community by belonging to a group or club, and profession-als through their involvement in their respective professional associations, or through associations related to their profession when they seek to extend their influence, either within or beyond their profession more broadly (for example, attorneys who volunteer time to their local chapter of the Legal Aid Society, or doctors who participate in Doctors Without Borders mis-sions). What makes these professionals a community in these cases is not merely a shared professional credential, but a desire to extend their impact for some greater good with a subset of like-minded colleagues.

What do these very different kinds of communities have in common? They provide individuals with opportunities to express, explore, and con-tribute a positive change to the world through their active participation, something that only a group of like-minded individuals can hope to achieve.[2] As the motivational speaker Norman Vincent Peale said about the potential for even a small group to change the world, "[It's] a demonstration of an age-old principle: That you can change your life, that I can change mine and that together we can change the world around us."[3] When individuals opt to participate in a community, they expect it to make some demands upon them and in return provide them with a group identity and a collective purpose. At their best, participants in a community experience a feeling of well-being, a by-product of doing good work with others. Members of an authentic com-munity know that they have others whom they can count upon in times of need and celebrate with in times of joy.

I don't own a Lexus and I'm not a NASCAR fan, but I have a feeling that Lexus owners and NASCAR fans are brand enthusiasts but not part of a community as I've described it. They may own a similar product or share a similar passion, and they may even participate in periodic face-to-face altruistic events sponsored by their respective brands. But I think that most people can distinguish between belonging to a community based upon a branded product and belonging to a community whose DNA is designed to contribute greater purpose and meaning to the world.

Having worked in the nonprofit sector for several decades, there was something else that I noticed about belonging to a community. When people were in face-to-face communities, they had a better understanding of the impact that their words and actions could have on others. Often, they came to understand that they were accountable for what they did and said, and realized how a word spoken directly to someone's face could change a life for the better or for the worse. If people wanted to maintain their community, they had to become more aware of another person's perspectives and more empathetic to others' positions on issues so that they could continue to engage together in purposeful work. A community can only be sustained with mutual empathy.

With the Internet, the value of community as we've known it has become murkier. Here is a question that I've frequently heard from both Gen Xers and Millennials about community well before I began working on this book: "If I can select a cause that matters to me, use digital tools to mobilize people around it, fundraise for it, and have much more immediate impact, explain why should I pay membership to a community organization, join one of its committees that doesn't really interest me and meets at an inconvenient time, and volunteer for a number of years before I can rise to a position of leadership where I then realize that those who promoted me really only wanted incremental change?" Boomers who have more experience with physical communities may first react defensively to such comments. Although they're not naïve about the frustrations of a traditional type of community, they've also experienced its more enduring benefits. But because Boomers and not Millennials have that experience, it's up to Boomers to make the case to younger generations about the greater value of face-to-face interactions that root a person in a structured community, versus contributing time or money to a worthy online cause and then moving on to the next. And that case is increasingly more difficult to make because community organizations have been slow to adapt to the multiple expressions of community and to respond to the legitimate critiques of Gen Xers and Millennials.

Meaning doesn't exist without structure and, prior to the Internet, personal participation with others in civic and nonprofit organizations provided the organizational structure that supported communities of purpose. But with the rise of online communities, "community" now exists in three dimensions: old-fashioned face-to-face communities, online communities, and a hybrid in which people meet regularly in person and online. As I've written elsewhere, traditionally structured face-to-face communities and communities that are designed to live primarily online each have a different value set and "rules" of engagement.[4] Gen Xers and Millennials helped to construct online communities, while Boomers are more accustomed to brick-and-mortar organizations that supported communities of purpose. That led me to wonder how Baby Boomers and Millennials perceive community and if generational differences would again surface. Let's listen to their respective perceptions on the value and shape of "community," beginning with some good news.

With only two exceptions, one a Baby Boomer and one a Millennial, everyone else whom I interviewed agreed that participating in a face-to-face community is important. Naturally, retired Baby Boomers were more heavily involved in face-to-face communities, but even Millennials, who had much less discretionary time, were involved in some regular face-to-face community activity unrelated to their work. Additionally, members of both generations believed that individuals should ideally be involved in a year of national service in a structured program with participants from diverse backgrounds,[5] either after high school or college. They thought that serving their larger community with people from different walks of life would strengthen the overall state of community of today.

That might come as a surprise given the headlines that Robert D. Putnam's book, *Bowling Alone: The Collapse and Revival of American Community*, made in 2000, in which he chronicled the steep decline in participation in civic community and its supporting institutions. Putnam saw a glimmer of hope in a greater trend toward volunteer engagement of youth but was not overly optimistic that it would translate into significantly increased civic engagement of Millennials, absent some national emergency.[6] Then 9/11 occurred, and in a subsequent study that Putnam and his colleague, Thomas H. Sander, conducted, they found that "the years since 9/11 have brought an unmistakable expansion of youth interest in politics and public affairs."[7]

These more recent findings of Sander and Putnam are consistent with the sentiments of the Boomers and Millennials who expressed how much they valued community. Their motivations for involvement overlapped but weren't identical, as they're at different stages of life. Some Boomers traced their desire for strengthening community to their teen or college years, when a mentor took an interest, inspired, or gave them a boost of confidence that set them on a life-changing trajectory of belief in their abilities. John Jolet, an older Boomer, had that experience. John was born into a working-class community in which attending college was not an expectation. John joined the Boy Scouts, and he and his scout leader shared the same ethnicity. Unlike his working-class contemporaries, his scout leader was an engineer. During our interview, John rhetorically asked, "Who knew anybody who was an engineer [then]? I didn't know what an engineer was. But this scout leader said to me, 'You know, John, I think you should go to college. I think you have the opportunity to be whoever you want to be,' and [those words] changed my life."[8] Another Boomer, Celia Dent, founded and owns a business in home renovation. She began working in construction in her college years where she connected with an engineering professor. "He [her college professor] ended up being the Chief Engineer of one of the largest construction companies in the country, which I worked [at for some time]. That man taught me a ton along the way in my career."[9]

Several other Boomers were active in their respective faith communities, where they were taught and saw members enact their values of community service. While volunteering had become integral to their way of life while they were relatively young, they had a foundation on which to build when they had reduced their hours at work or retired. Hunter Weiss, who worked at a demanding profession in New York City, voluntarily retired at age fifty-five to pursue community and philanthropic activities full-time, which he has been doing for about ten years. He started volunteering for an organization whose mission is to help children, teens, and adults with certain neurological conditions while he was in his early twenties. Today, over forty years later, he is still involved. What was his connection to this organization's cause?

Hunter explained that "people always asked, 'Do you have someone in your family who is affected by it [this neurological condition]?' I said, 'No, I have a colleague [whose son has] it.' 'Why are you involved?' my friends would ask. I would respond, 'What do you mean?' They said, 'It's because the people who have the kids are the ones that are dealing day and night with crises with their kids [who are usually involved].' 'But,' I continued, 'my philosophy is the people who don't have that burden can at least raise the money, facilitate their research, and so on.' I feel the same way when I talk about programs for kids with learning disabilities in schools. Most parents are dealing with the kids. They shouldn't have to pay the double and triple push [for] what's needed [to advance their] cause."[10] His advice to younger colleagues, whom he still mentors, is to begin volunteering now for some community cause that they care about. His advice flows from his own experience and from the calls that he sometimes receives from colleagues who retire from their careers when they're older and ask for ideas about community volunteer work. Hunter told me that "sometimes, someone will call me saying, 'I'd like to get involved in charities,' but they haven't really done that before. [While] it's not impossible to do it at a later age, you have more value if you've grown up in that environment."[11]

Some of the reasons that Millennials offered for contributing back to the community blow apart the stereotypes of Millennials as being self-absorbed. Linda Archer served in the Peace Corps as a Youth Development Volunteer and continues to use her talents to develop youth leaders in her local community. In asking her about her passion for community, she exclaimed, "Being connected is such a big part of living, whether that's to the community that you live in, whether it's a community of artists, a community at work—everyone needs a community that they have, and that they feel like they can go to."[12] In a similar vein, another Millennial, Angela Krintz, began volunteering for a community group because she felt that it's "important for anyone especially now [to become involved with some community] because so many people do feel more isolated with all the technology. It gets you to be face-to-face with someone—no matter what kind of community. Community is something that keeps you going."[13]

One Millennial in my study had spent a year abroad in the Peace Corps as a Youth Development Volunteer, another was involved in the Special Olympics, and a third had been in Teach for America. These Millennials were determined to find ways to contribute back to their communities and they certainly made me feel proud and hopeful about the future. Understandably, their motivations were not identical to those of Baby Boomers. For example, some of the Millennials whom I interviewed understood that they would gain insights into themselves by connecting with a community. When I was speaking with Allan Sherman, a Millennial, about the value of community involvement and meeting people from diverse backgrounds, he remembered a piece of wisdom that one of his supervisors shared. "Look at the person in this room who you admire the most. And then I want you to look at the person who you may dislike or not get along with the most. Those are the two people you will learn the most about yourself from," and Allan added, "And that is so true [for participating in a volunteer community, too]."[14]

Rachel Nunez, a Millennial, summarized the value of regularly volunteering with others in person in an ongoing community. "I think [being part of a voluntary community] is a critical part of feeling like you belong. It's important for everybody to feel like they belong to a group and we don't have a lot of social capital today. There's a decline of those places where you can feel like you're part of something and really [be] responsible for . . . so coming together around something that's much more personal, much more significant, much more meaningful, it just develops a different kind of bond."[15] Her words echoed the sentiments of Baby Boomers and Millennials who shared this value of community service.

Can We Have Faith in
Intergenerational Faith Communities?

I specifically asked Boomers and Millennials about their views on faith-based communities and congregations, an area of personal expertise. Dr. Terri Elton and I wrote about the challenges that established and start-up Jewish and Protestant congregations face in our recent book, *Leading Congregations and Nonprofits in a Connected World: Platforms, People, and Purpose.*[16] But even after mulling over their challenges, I'm still unable to think of another kind of community or organization dedicated to bringing people together across the generations in what urban sociologists describe as a "third place" ("first place" is home and "second place" is work). According to the sociologist, Ray Oldenberg, third places "host the regular, voluntary, informal, and happily anticipated gatherings of individuals beyond the realms of home and work."[17] Oldenburg suggests that "main streets, pubs, cafes, coffeehouses, post offices, and other third places are the heart of a community's social vitality. . . . [They] promote social equity by leveling the status of guests, providing a setting for grassroots politics, creating habits of public association, and offering psychological support to individuals and communities."[18]

Unlike some other Western countries, there simply aren't many "third places" that organically promote intergenerational relationships in the United States. While religious congregations aren't "third places" in the way that town squares or pubs are, many seek to attract generationally diverse communities. Yet, in the Jewish community in the United States which I know well, I'm unable to think of one congregation or spiritual community that has an intergenerational council or committee that seek solutions to issues through diverse generational perspectives. Instead, congregations have atomized families and individuals into generational cohorts,[19] with programs and services for preschoolers, teens, seniors, etc. You can see that same generation-specific thinking at work when viewing a congregational budget, too, with line items that show a picture of a generationally segmented congregation.

The Boomers and Millennials whom I interviewed were almost evenly split in their current participation in a faith-based community. Some of those who didn't belong to a congregation now could envision themselves becoming more active at a later stage, while others had no future interest. But even those who were completely uninterested in a faith-based community were supportive of those who found community in a congregation. The concept of belonging to any kind of community was so valuable that it didn't matter whether that was a community of believers or a community of artists. Linda Archer, quoted earlier on her thoughts about community, also added, "I think if church is something that is important to them [individuals seeking a community], and if that's a faith-based community that is awesome, but it may not be so . . . I think that ultimately people should belong to a community that gives you happiness and fulfillment."[20] Gary Harper, a Boomer who is not a church-goer, made a similar comment. "Church can be a very important social event for many [and] can be very beneficial."[21]

We've already seen overwhelming statistics on social isolation and loneliness. As the Jungian analyst, James Hollis, notes,

> What most characterizes the modern era, going back four centuries, is that the responsibility for meaning and for the conduct of one's life has progressively shifted from tribal mythology and sacred institutions to the shoulders of the individual. No one whether pope or potentate, whether from the seat of mace or miter, today has the authority to define what you experience as real for you. . . . The claims of divine sanction by various religious and political leaders are still made today, but we know these leaders to be flawed human beings like the rest of us, just as capable of erring judgment and self-interested interpretations.[22]

While Hollis correctly observes that individuals don't need an external authority interpreting their subjective experiences, he fails to note that loneliness can be eased in trying to puzzle through new and complex situations with others in an open spiritual community; not the kind of community in which leaders feed answers to those who are seeking guidance, but one in which they facilitate conversations that enable wisdom to emerge from a contemporary group and transparently bring it into dialogue with ancient spiritual wisdom.

What caught my attention in my interviews was that Millennials and Boomers thought that ongoing involvement in some community was better than no community involvement. This suggests to me that a congregation's "religious" brand may not be an obstacle to those who are neutral about religion but feel positively about intergenerational community. In fact, if congregations can be more open within the boundaries of their mission, their inherited wisdom could be an asset. Why? Because the most effective religious leaders know how to apply "spiritual brakes" to accelerated change so that people can discuss broad questions like, "Just because we can do something new, should we? If we pursue the new, what do we gain and what do we lose?" Acknowledging my bias, I believe that congregations have an incredible opportunity to fill a void and help lift people out of their loneliness by finding an intergenerational community. Spiritual communities will first need their own help in learning how to differentiate between "multigenerational" and "intergenerational" and recognize that placing people of different generations in proximity with one another does not make a congregation intergenerational. But with intentionality and skilled people who can create a space for mutually enriching interactions, they have some advantage over other organizations because relationships really are at the heart of a spiritual community's mission.

Building on Existing Policies and Finding Free-Market Solutions

In today's political climate, the experts with whom I spoke were skeptical about the federal government's willingness to find common policy and program ground on intergenerational issues. While partisan politics was not new, they hadn't witnessed such unyielding unwillingness to even engage in conversations about finding common ground around issues that cut across party lines. However, some were more optimistic about the ability to work with local government officials.

Donna Butts, executive director of Generations United, explained that mayors are on the front line of governance. They keenly felt the impact of changes in eligibility and availability of federal and state funding on pressing issues that directly affected their citizens, like transportation, housing, and health care. She has seen how more cities are looking at building projects through an intergenerational lens and cited as an example intergenerational community centers that are designed to house a preschool, a senior center, and a homework hang out space for teens.[23]

Marc Freedman, chief executive officer of Encore, is also dubious about relying upon new policies at the federal level to promote intergenerational communities. But he is encouraged by the emergence of a greater number of market-based solutions, especially in housing: "I think that housing did more than anything else to separate the generations and so it's heartening to see this ferment in housing. A number of big home builders who have been players in the age-segregated part of the housing arena, in the active aging community, are starting to develop multigenerational housing units."[24]

Some city planners are also thinking openly about how to make intergenerational contact more organic by partnering with social entrepreneurs. For example, two recent graduates of MIT's master's program in urban planning, Noelle Marcus and Rachel Goor, designed a Web-based platform, Nesterly, that matches younger people who need affordable housing with older adults

who have room to spare. These older homeowners are willing to charge relatively more affordable rent to individuals who need a place to stay for longer
than one month. The goal of these graduates was to tackle housing problems
through an intergenerational lens: enabling older people to remain in their
homes that had become increasingly challenging for them to maintain, and
opening up affordable housing space for younger people who couldn't afford
to pay exorbitant rent. Nesterly's founders developed this concept in partnership with the city of Boston, and their goal is to expand to other cities. As
described on Nesterly's website, "In a twist that's unique to Nesterly, Guests
can also exchange help around the house for lower rent. Nesterly helps to
make intergenerational homesharing safe, transparent, and easy by providing
multi-tiered screening, customizable homesharing agreements, and a 24-hour
service team."[25]

Freedman also directed me to another small, market-based intergenerational experiment, Judson Manor, located in Cleveland's University Circle,[26]
which includes prestigious medical, educational, and cultural facilities like
the Cleveland Clinic, Case Western Reserve University, the Cleveland
Institute of Music, the Cleveland Institute of Art, and the Cleveland Public
Library. He viewed the Judson Manor experiment as both a promising and a
cautionary tale in trying to forge an intergenerational community.[27]

As you can imagine, Judson Manor attracted a highly educated and cul-
turally sophisticated group of senior residents, many of whom had taught at
these institutions. Despite their proximity to these institutions, age segregation persisted. Freedman explained that intergenerational connections
only began to change when a Judson Manor board member approached its
director with the idea of offering a limited number of free apartments to
music students at the Cleveland Institute of Music in exchange for their
performing concerts for residents. You can imagine how initially skeptical
the director was. To paraphrase his response, it was: "Do I really want to be
a college dorm resident advisor and a director of a residence for seniors?!"[28]
Understandably, he was concerned about the different challenges that each
population presented, what the dynamic would be in common spaces like
the dining rooms and kitchens, and in ensuring that younger residents had
more altruistic motives for wanting to reside with seniors than just looking
for free luxury space.[29]

Freedman recently visited Judson Manor and told me, "They now have
seven students doing it [living and performing there], and it's just turned out
to be spectacular, so far beyond the actual performances. All of these really
deep friendships have come out of it [this living arrangement]. One of the

most moving stories is of a woman living next door to a graduate violist who got engaged during her time living at Judson, who asked her eighty-six-year-old neighbor to be her flower girl, and the stories are all true. I mean, they make sense. It's all of these people who love the arts and all of these students who are so good at them, so it's like a little utopia."[30]

In one video interview about Judson Manor, the reporter lyrically states, "Music here is a bridge where the past and the future often pause to meet,"[31] as some of the senior residents had taught or been students at the Cleveland Institute of Music. In the same video, the reporter asked several elderly residents and several younger residents about their feelings in sharing space with people who are separated by decades. I watched Margaret Mitchell, one elderly resident, hesitate and respond, "That's where life is [being with young people]."[32] But I almost had the feeling that she really wanted to say, "You dimwit, how much better does it get?"—or I might have been projecting my response on to her. Daniel Parvin, a younger resident, answered the reporter by saying, "I have people to look up to and learn from. It's crazy to think as I talk with the centenarians here . . . they've lived four of my lifetimes, and they have all of that experience that I can ask them about."[33] Statements like these are like the sound of music to those who believe in the mutual benefits of intergenerational living.[34]

Intergenerational Communities: Beyond "Age-Friendly"

As I've written previously, "multigenerational" only indicates the number of generations of people alive at one time, but is silent on the question of relationships across the generations. "Intergenerational" is a value, expressing the many benefits that members of all generations experience when their daily interactions naturally involve people of all ages. Intergenerational efforts should not be confused with efforts to create "age-friendly" communities, meaning those communities that are changing their infrastructure and services to enable a growing aging population to remain "healthy, independent and autonomous long into their old age."[35] Intergenerational work encompasses "age-friendly" but also transcends the goal of enabling elderly people to remain living independently. "Intergenerational" means normalizing the experience of young, old, and everyone in-between being together, and replacing negative stereotypes of all generations with an empathetic understanding that each generation has something to offer to the other.

National Service?

Of the approximately thirty people whom I interviewed, all agreed that a year of national service in a structured program with diverse individuals, either after high school, college, or in later life, would be extremely valuable. In their opinions, it could help to restore a sense of being a part of a greater collective and erase the fear of "the other." Some people believed that incentivized service was preferable to mandatory service. Those who preferred incentivized service felt that it was unrealistic for our country to be able to successfully scale existing programs and create new ones so that this year of service would be valuable and transformative. Others believed that mandatory service wouldn't even stand a chance at an open discussion in our individualistic society. But what they lamented was that longstanding, existing government programs like the Peace Corps, Americorps, Senior Corps, and more recent programs like Teach for America, were still inadequately resourced, although they have been repeatedly evaluated and proven effective.

Several Boomers whom I interviewed had served in the military. They didn't enjoy all aspects of their service, but they grew to appreciate living with people in close quarters from different backgrounds. Mickey Hull, who had served during the Vietnam War said, "I had never met an African American until I had served in Vietnam."[36] His commanding officers also came from different regions of the country, and what also made his military service valuable was having the supervision of experienced personnel who knew how to create a cohesive unit. Military service may not be for everyone, and absent a major war, the United States military is likely to remain a voluntary army. But life in the military teaches enlisted men and women to live with diversity and interact with older generations.

Talk the Walk: Messaging Counts

Another insight that experts shared was the need to be thoughtful about the language that organizations use in trying to foster intergenerational communities. Mark L. Meridy, executive director of Dorot, described what happened when Dorot changed the language of "providing services to the elderly" to "engaging generations." He explained that sometimes when a staff member asked an elderly client if he or she needed a service, the answer might be "no." "However, when they [a staff member] asked the same person if they would like to provide a service to someone else, the answer is [more likely] to be 'Yes.'"[37] Meridy's point was similar to one made by Vandana Pant, senior director, Design and Innovation at Sutter Health, a lead team member who piloted an intergenerational program, linkAges. Initially, link-Ages was designed to provide one-to-one exchanges of services between members. But in a second iteration, "we actually introduced this idea of the members themselves being able to create groups on a platform, or members themselves being able to post the class they were offering."[38] The significant point in thinking about intergenerational communities is to remember that a person can be both in need of a service and capable of providing a service to someone else. Or, as Eugene Roehlkepartain of Search Institute said, before thinking in a top-down way about what program is needed, involve "innovative stakeholders," those who have a vested personal interest in an issue, as active partners in designing it.[39]

We don't have to count on grand policy designs to cultivate more intergenerational communities. Even if you've never thought about this issue before, there are enough examples in this chapter to stimulate your imagination about the possibilities for change that you can initiate through local government officials, business leaders, clergy, and other concerned citizens. In fact, one of the themes that I heard repeatedly from experts in the field is an over-reliance on policies to fix person-centered issues. As Roehlkepartain (cited above) said, "sometimes we over-rely on policy solutions, and that can sometimes set a different table, but we have to come to the table and [first] work together at that table to figure things out."[40] In other words, let the policies emerge from the people who do the work. Freedman, whom I quoted earlier, had similar views about programs: "You know I think programs can play an important positive role but, how do we bring people together in the central institutions of daily life in a way where proximity is even more important than programs."[41]

What You Can Do

1. If you're a Boomer, become a mentor to someone whose background is vastly different from your own. You might be that person who changes the trajectory of a young person's life. Don't worry—if you haven't been a mentor before, or seek to sharpen your effectiveness as a mentor, many organizations that work with volunteers offer some training that can help you grow. As you connect with someone younger through your mentoring relationship, try keeping a journal of what you're learning from this experience.

2. If you're a Millennial or Gen Xer and considering contributing time to a cause or organization, don't wait. As Hunter Weiss suggested, find a way to give a little something of yourself to another person. There are

720 hours in a thirty-day month and organizations in your community that would happily have you contribute only five hours per month of your time. You can search national platforms like Volunteer Match (https://www.volunteermatch.org) or Volunteers of America (https://www.voa.org) to locate available opportunities in your community, or you can contact your local United Way. Or find a friend who is already involved in an organization and double your investment in improving your community by deepening your relationship with your friend and working on a shared community cause.

3. If you work in an organization that seeks to meaningfully connect multiple generations, read *Matterness: Fearless Leadership for a Social World*, by Allison Fine.[42] With wit and wisdom, she lays out principles for a socially connected world to help organizational leaders hear customers, clients, donors, volunteers, and other constituents and make them matter. Fine has been a leader in the field of the impact of social media and networks on nonprofits, and this book is an important resource to help professional and volunteer leaders of organizations deeply engage with existing constituents and potentially re-engage others who had written off their value.

CHAPTER FIVE

~

Education

Anything, Anyone, Anytime, Anywhere

The current thinking among anthropologists, historians, and evolutionary biologists is that between seventy thousand and thirty thousand years ago, "the appearance of new ways of thinking and communicating" first occurred.[1] Yuval Harari, a prominent historian, refers to this as the beginning of the Cognitive Revolution.[2] That's when Homo sapiens developed "the ability to transmit information about things that do not really exist, such as tribal spirits, nations, limited liability companies and human rights."[3] Perhaps our predecessors, Neanderthals, and our earliest direct ancestors, Homo Sapiens, began to use language and symbolic thinking.[4] I can almost imagine the very first conversation between an early Homo Sapien parent dramatically explaining to his child about the dangers that he encountered while traveling to a friend's cave a half-mile away to learn a new skill or behavior. Acquiring an education was hard.

Fast forward to 2018, and if you live in a cold, snowy climate, you can still hear elderly people describe their terrifying treks through frequent blizzards to attend a school a mile or more away. We don't have written records to verify the veracity of this imagined first Homo Sapiens' dialogue between parent and child over the difficulties of acquiring an education, but my elderly Minnesota friends are not exaggerating because we have records of snowfall amounts when they were school-age children. As a native Boomer Philadelphian, I had it relatively easy because winters weren't as merciless. I either carpooled or used public transportation to reach my public high school, which meant a maximum, one-way commute of about one hour.

During my high school years, technology advances made learning some subject matter easier than in the past. For example, while students still had to master a mechanical slide rule for more complex mathematical calculations, we were also allowed to use handheld electronic calculators.

When I entered college in 1976, typewriters were recommended educational gear. Some of the more fortunate college students owned an IBM Selectric typewriter that replaced typing bars with golf-ball-shaped type heads with different kinds of fonts and a built-in correction key that covered errors with a white tape. (For those who are Gen X and younger, try to find an old standard typewriter if you want to appreciate the revolutionary progress that the correction key was. You could now backspace over a mistaken word or letter and correct it without having to retype an entire page, and no longer need to apply "white out" correction fluid to an error. Now that was progress!) As a college undergraduate from 1976 to 1980, some of my mysterious college friends disappeared at odd hours to use the computer lab at my college, where they learned exotic languages such as Fortran, SQL, and Cobol.

I've provided this very condensed, broad snapshot of education, as education required a significant amount of sacrifice until recently. You had to travel somewhere, often battling harsh weather and heavy traffic, and be physically present in a building. Educational technologies that we take for granted today (like the fact that I'm able to dictate drafts of entire books on a smartphone) were either nonexistent, limited in their functions if they did exist, costly, and financially unaffordable for many. But a paradox has emerged with the ease of access to abundant educational choices, one that our Neanderthal ancestors couldn't imagine and that some of us who are Boomers may forget. The explosion of educational options has made questions about how much education, what kind of education, and the best way to acquire an education confusing and uncertain. This paradox of having more options that generate greater uncertainty about the best educational choices means that post–high school education has become a source of misunderstanding between Baby Boomers and Millennials, and this divide will only deepen with younger generations.

These misunderstandings reflect 1) the dynamically evolving purpose of education, 2) the role of ongoing learning regardless of whether a person is mandated by a profession or employer to regularly take continuing education credits, and 3) the advantages and disadvantages of attending a traditional brick-and-mortar college with a campus, enrolling in a purely online bytes-and-clicks university, or a hybrid bricks-and-clicks college that requires learners to be physically present on a campus for limited amounts of time but enables them to take the majority of their courses online. Education is more closely tied today with employment, raising the stakes of identifying the right educational options the first time and lowering the value of a humanities education when the sciences currently open more doors to employment and help to future-proof job options. Additionally, older retired adult learners are a factor in considering education as they often have the discretionary time, personal curiosity, and funds to continue their education. Therefore, in this chapter, we'll be exploring attitudes and values about education along the lifespan and not limiting our discussion only to the issue of post–high school options.

The New Educational Landscape

To provide context for the views on education of those who participated in the research for this book, it's helpful to understand how radically the educational landscape has changed in only a generation. Here are two reputable sources of information about generational attitudes toward college education that together provide us with a broad and deep understanding of the changed profiles of college graduates. Beginning with Baby Boomers, when higher educational options became open more equally to women and men, and with the next two subsequent generations, Gen Xers and Millennials, the percentage of individuals who earned a college degree increased.[5] Moreover, the slight increase of Gen X women who received a college education compared with Gen X men grew significantly among Millennials. To summarize: the trajectory of those completing at least a bachelor's degree has been upward over the past five generations: the Greatest and Silent Generations, Baby Boomers, Gen Xers, and Millennials. The gap between men and women who were college-educated not only narrowed but was reversed. Many more Millennial women than men earned a bachelor's degree. Of course, minorities did not have the same access and are still too often disadvantaged at an early age, with negative implications for their likelihood of becoming college-educated. However, we now have a study that provides a more granular look at which Millennials have opted for college, with some surprising findings.

Cathy J. Cohen is the David and Mary Winton Green Professor of Political Science and chair of the Department of Political Science at the University of Chicago. She is also the founder and principal investigator of a project called GenForward, which conducts the GenForward Survey, described as "the first of its kind—a nationally representative survey of over 1,750 young adults ages eighteen to thirty-four conducted bi-monthly that pays special attention to how race and ethnicity shape how respondents experience and think about the world."[6] Her team focused on Millennial attitudes about education and included a series of questions about the importance that they attach to a college degree. She found that "62 percent of Asian Americans and 57 percent of Latinx believe a college education is necessary to be successful, while 55 percent of whites and 51 percent of African Americans say there are ways to succeed today without a college degree."[7] In interpreting how race and ethnicity may factor into attitudes about college education, Cohen suggests that "young African-American men and women often live in communities where access to a college education isn't guaranteed, and can be difficult to attain based on cost and how well their education prepared them. They have seen individuals in their communities find other ways to succeed. In fact, it's been a necessity."[8] She explains that white privilege may give access to successful career opportunities that are not open to minorities, and that some white Millennials whose parents did not attend college but were still able to provide for their families may have decided that it was unnecessary for them to earn a college degree.

For the purposes of this book, the caution that Cohen offered about not misinterpreting the data is especially relevant. She said that "it's important not to come away thinking African-American and white Millennials don't value education. I think instead what we're seeing here is that they understand that there *have to be multiple pathways to success*."[9] Speaking broadly, Millennials as a generational cohort are the most educated to date, but that blunt statistical observation obscures the many factors that have influenced Millennials' educational decision-making, including race, gender, and ethnicity. Cohen's observation that "there have to be multiple pathways to success" is consistent with the way that I described in chapter 2 how many Millennials approach decisions, exploring different pathways to identify and achieve their goals, in contrast to their Boomer predecessors who more typically set goals and plotted a linear progression to achieving them.

Millennials and younger generations had already become accustomed to using online educational resources like Kahn Academy and Wikipedia in their primary and high school years. By the time they were ready for college, they had many accredited post-secondary online options available to them. Unfortunately, some of these for-profit vocational programs and online colleges were just incredibly costly marketing scams. Graduates of these scandalous programs found that instead of improving their chances for better employment, they only accrued educational debt. Many of these bad online educational actors have gone out of business, and traditional brick-and-mortar universities typically offer some courses or complete degree programs online to remain competitive with their newer digital entrants. In fact, the most recent report that tracks trends in online learning found that "30 percent of all students in higher education are now taking at least one distance course."[10] However, while Millennials are the most educated generation to date, many are having "buyer's remorse" over the cost of their education and its economic consequences.[11]

That is one of several reason why Gen Z will think even more pragmatically about college than Millennials. There are now sophisticated app-based games that enable families to understand the costs of college more comprehensively, beyond tuition, room, and board. One such game, Payback, is the brainchild of Tim Ranzetta, who turned to Jenny Nicholson, an experienced web-based game designer on financial issues. In an interview with Ron Leiber, who writes the *New York Times* column, "Your Money," she explained why her firm took on Ranzetta's project: "Ms. Nicholson said . . . that the firm recognized that paying for college is not just about debt but also about investment. Every decision—from where you attend to what jobs and activities and classes and majors you choose while you are there—is about trade-offs. How much paid work is enough? How much socializing and spending on fun?"[12]

Players must also account for cash graduation gifts, the purchases of supplies like laptops, and participation in the Greek system. Leiber notes that "one of the cleverest things about the game is the constant, cumulative tabulation of focus (which paid work can reduce), connections (is an unpaid internship worth it?) and happiness. That last one comes from Ms. Nicholson's personal experience, for she eventually realized that focus and happiness were sometimes counterpoints and she might have received a better return on her investment in college if she'd had more fun and more friends."[13]

Additionally, Gen Z learners may more readily embrace world-class learning platforms like Coursera or edX that offer certificates, specializations, and degrees.[14] Platforms like Coursera and edX partner with outstanding universities from around the globe. They're able to provide students with the opportunity to learn from internationally recognized expert faculty members. Their flexible learning paths that empower students to customize their education with a global faculty is already challenging purely online universities, which themselves only became accredited in the early to mid-1990s.

Adding to the complexity of post–high school educational choices, some employers are relying less upon college degrees as proxies for competence and looking more closely at skills and performance.[15] And there are serious skills-based learning platforms for those of any age who want to continue to grow their knowledge and skills without having to pay exorbitant costs, including Udacity, LinkedIn Learning, and Mind Tools, to name a few.[16]

The marketplace will be the ultimate arbiter of how future generations approach higher education. Some post-Millennials will find alternative routes for education. But it's too soon to write off the value of a college degree, as Thomas L. Friedman observes when profiling AT&T, a global communications, media and entertainment, and technology giant. He describes how AT&T had to prepare a workforce that didn't exist so that it could exploit its unique position of being the exclusive carrier of the iPhone for several years when it was first launched in 2007. A significant part of that transformation was both skills-based and degree-based education for its workforce. AT&T developed educational partnerships on an unprecedented scale with Udacity and Georgia Tech, which designed an online master's degree in computer science specially designed for AT&T employees and offered them generous tuition assistance.[17]

As Friedman notes, AT&T has redefined the "new contract" between employer and employee, which offers job advancement and growth for employees who are willing to keep learning and adding value to the company. He quotes AT&T's Senior Executive Vice President for Human Resources, Bill Blase, who elaborates on the shared understanding of this "new contract":

> It is a contract between the company and employees. It's a new bargain. If you want to get an A in your performance review, now you have to do the "What" and the "How." The "How" is that you get along with people, you achieve results by effectively partnering and teaming and leading change through [and with] others and don't just sit in your cubicle. The "What" is that you are not only proficient in your job but that you are reskilling to improve your capacity, continuing to learn, and that you are aspiring to go beyond where you are. Maybe you're a salesperson and you're making yourself more valuable to the company by getting [to know] the technical side as well. You're not just selling products but understanding how our network works. Our best employees have it down and they know it is the What and the How.[18]

John Donovan, CEO, Communications at AT&T, adds, "you can be a lifelong employee if you are ready to be a lifelong learner. We will give you the platform but you have to opt in."[19] To remain competitive in the workforce today requires more individuals to embrace a mindset of lifelong learning, even if it is not a company requirement. And if you think that I'm exaggerating, here's my "oops" moment story that makes the point.

My Accidental LinkedIn
Connection with a Post-Millennial

LinkedIn recommended that I connect with someone named Josh Miller, a CEO of an organization called Deciding Edge, who lived in my area.[20] I hastily read his profile which read: "I am an entrepreneur and thought-leader. . . . I have . . . been mentored by topic experts such as Warren Buffett, discussed marketing strategy with Fortune 500 companies, and been featured in national publications. . . . I founded Deciding Edge in order to create a platform for organizations to better understand how to recruit, retain, and sell to the next generation about to take the economy by storm."[21] I invited Josh to connect and only after re-reading his bio, I realized that I had missed one important detail: it began with the words, "I am a 16-year-old student . . . "[22]

It's not unusual today for post-Millennials to have dabbled in business already while they are in high school. In fact, the Minnesota Vikings made news in September 2017 not because of a player, but because they were the first to hire a "Gen Z (that is, post-Millennial) advisor," Jonah Stillman, who had only graduated from high school a few months earlier. His responsibilities were to "consult with the Vikings on a variety of club business initiatives, including team marketing and fan activation efforts, Vikings Entertainment Network (VEN) and digital media content and strategy, U.S. Bank Stadium fan experience, STEM opportunities with the future Twin Cities Orthopedics Performance Center and workplace culture."[23] Was it a savvy move on the part of the Vikings? Time will tell, but they certainly selected a talented expert, who had co-authored *Gen Z @ Work: How the Next Generation Is Transforming the Workplace* with his father, David Stillman, a Gen Xer who is an expert on generations in the workplace.[24] The press release announcing this unusual hire explained that, "born between 1995 and 2012, Generation Z is considered to be independent and competitive workers who want to write their own job description and work for organizations with similar social values. They also have an incredible understanding of and passion for digital media."[25]

Almost all of my Boomer friends who worked during our junior high school and high school years had more modest expectations. I was a "stock boy" at a neighborhood shoe store when I was twelve years old, hustled to my neighbors' homes to shovel snow after a big storm before my competition arrived, and by high school was tutoring several middle school students for bar and bat mitzvah preparation. Sure, there were always one or two of our peers whom our friends could identify as likely to be a millionaire before age thirty, but many of us worked at the bottom of a ladder in the service and retail industries or did manual labor.[26] But Gen Z kids may have started their own businesses or raised funds on sites like Indiegogo to develop an app like Emma Yang did starting at age thirteen. Emma was inspired to improve the quality of life for people with Alzheimer's disease based on her experience with her grandmother who was affected by it.[27] Brains and not brawn can accelerate an adolescent's education in ways that were unthinkable not that long ago. Although our culture celebrates college dropouts like the late Steve Jobs, Bill Gates, Mark Zuckerberg, Lady Gaga, and Oprah Winfrey, the clear majority of accomplished people in industry, government, and the nonprofit sector have completed college.[28]

Are traditional colleges ready for this newest generation or will post-Millennials find that college education is too stifling? I asked David Stillman that question from both a professional and personal viewpoint. David readily admitted that he was ambivalent. Of course, he was proud of his son breaking new ground and acquiring the kind of education that college can't provide. But David, who has a humanities background, seemed a little unsettled with the reality of high school graduates moving so immediately into the workplace without at least some college education.

I also asked Boomer and Millennial interview subjects who were involved in my research for this book the following questions about post–high school education: 1) How important was it for you to graduate from college or vocational school? Was it your decision, or did anyone make it clear that you were going to college or a certain vocational school? 2) In addition to any continuing education requirements that you might have to fulfill, or had to fulfill, did you go back to school, earn a certificate, or other kinds of credential? Was that a choice that you made voluntarily or one that you felt you had to make because your employer had that expectation of you? 3) In hindsight, considering debt versus potential earnings, would your educational path be different today and what would you advise a high school junior or senior who is thinking about his or her next educational step?

It was difficult to identify any clear pattern about their views on these issues based on generational cohort age. For example, Rachel Nunez, a Millennial who had completed a bachelor's degree and was working in government believed that a four-year degree was an absolute necessity today. At the same time, she questioned why certain jobs required a master's degree and believed that some employers were too focused on credentials instead of performance and ability. Later in the same interview, she acknowledged that a college degree was not for everyone, even if finances were not an obstacle, and may not be the best or only way to receive an education given other options available.[29]

Another Millennial in my study, Allan Sherman, had earned a bachelor's and a master's degree in counseling in traditional classroom settings on campus. He could not envision doing his education any differently, even though it entailed a significant amount of sacrifice, as he continued to work during the day and on weekends to keep the cost of his education affordable. He explained that without a master's degree in counseling you had zero opportunity for developing a clinical practice. In addition, he valued the socialization and maturation that emerge from a traditional university experience and was concerned that those dimensions of education were being neglected in discussions about cost and value. He understood very well the need for efficiency but was unconvinced that doing a program completely online would have given him the more rounded experience of college life that contributed to his growth as a person.[30]

I heard from Baby Boomers who said that they would not do anything differently about their education if they were starting out today, and I heard others express regret that they had not earned a degree in the sciences or engineering, which they believed would be a better return on investment (ROI) and would have resulted in less college debt. Their logic was that they would have been employable immediately after college at a decent paying job and continue to advance in one of these fields. But during my interview with Gary Harper, a Baby Boomer, who expressed mild regret at not having majored in engineering as an undergraduate, he also shared the advice that he gave to his own Millennial children about education: "Don't worry about the money you're going to make. Find something that you enjoy doing and if you enjoy it enough and do it well enough, you'll make money."[31]

There were too few people and too many variables in my study to draw any definitive conclusions about their views toward additional certificates or ongoing education. Some of those whom I interviewed were in professions which required continuing education to maintain certification, while others were not but felt that it was imperative for them to find ways to keep learning to remain competitive. For example, someone who worked in the tech world had found that more experiential learning with a group of peers with whom he had developed a network to help scout trends and test ideas was critical to maintaining his state-of-the-art knowledge. Other Millennials were autodidacts and had learned much on their own and continued to do so in fields that required the use of technology. They didn't believe that it was necessary to have a degree or a credential and were confident that their track record and performance would enable them to progress if they kept on learning new skills.

There were several Baby Boomers who were no longer in the workforce but decided to enroll in formal academic programs that provided them with the structure to embrace new challenges, while other Boomers matriculated into demanding academic programs because they desired to change career directions. For example, one Baby Boomer who had not completed her bachelor's degree did so, and then a few years later, at age fifty-seven, decided to enter law school. A retired naval officer, who also had a Master of Business Administration degree, was currently completing a Master of Fine Arts, not because he expected to become a great artist, but because he wanted a structured program and faculty mentors. Still another Baby Boomer who had always had an appetite for learning about the multifaceted dimensions of his faith was gratified that he now had more time to pursue them vigorously through his faith community. And as we'll see later, some colleges and universities are capitalizing on Boomers' desires to continue learning by building housing for seniors on or near college campuses or through partnerships with housing developers. According to George Mason University adjunct professor and Senior Housing Administration Founding Director, Andrew Carle, "There are about four dozen senior housing and university partnership communities in the U.S.,"[32] or University-Based Retirement Communities, a term that Carle coined.

In summary, the shared points of view between Boomers and Millennials about the value of education were: 1) it's important to balance affordability and efficiency with the broader social experience of being on a college campus, and understand that education and maturation occur both within and outside of a classroom; 2) even if you believe that college is not for you now, try to earn an associate's degree, with the equivalent of what would be the generally accepted core requirements for a bachelor's degree, making possible completion of a degree easier; and 3) seek creative options for minimizing the cost of a college education, including living at home with a parent, splitting a four-year degree program between an accredited but less expensive community college for the first two years that seamlessly feeds students into a state university for the remaining two years. Aside from these several shared points of agreement, participants' views about college and graduate school education reflected the transitional state of higher education. Many of the people whom I interviewed still appreciated the value of a college degree, were also concerned about its "cost-benefit" ratio when weighing employment opportunities against college debt, and were considering newer, nontraditional avenues to gaining knowledge and skills outside of a physical or digital campus.

I'm not convinced that if I had a much larger sample of Boomers and Millennials that a clearer picture of the similarities and differences with regard to post–high school education would have emerged. And trends about how the newest and future generations will think about "higher education" are very fluid. We have reliable data clearly indicating that as a generation, Millennials are better educated than prior generations. But data are a snapshot in time of what currently is, and not a full-length movie of what will be. As big data, artificial intelligence, and machine learning converge and enable exponential work productivity with fewer human workers, there will be greater competition for a shrinking number of jobs at all levels. Based on my experience, I'm not sure that Baby Boomers fully appreciate how intertwined education and employment have become. For those Baby Boomers and for people of any generation involved in professions like medicine, law, teaching, counseling, and accounting, their continuing education requirements may be sufficient to enable them to remain securely in their professions, although as more routine tasks become automated, even in "white-collar" professions, their job security will also become more tenuous.

I titled this chapter, "Education: Anything, Anyone, Anytime, Anywhere." This title reflects the demands of the workplace and the opportunities and challenges facing today's employees, especially those who are younger. Boomers had the luxury of thinking about a lifelong career, and although some of those hopes were dashed by the great economic recession of 2007 and prior recessions, many Boomers could complete a bachelor's or master's degree, or have a vocational education that provided them with financial stability. But today, how can you possibly know what your educational path should be when the job that you have three years from now doesn't currently exist? One answer is to adopt the posture of becoming a lifelong learner, expect to acquire skills and knowledge through multiple learning channels, continue to network within and outside of your field, and recognize that continuous education is key to making yourself more valuable.

Is this concerning? Personally, I find it both exciting and problematic. The exciting dimension of this reality is that when you learn, you grow, and there are many psychosocial and cognitive benefits to learning. Additionally, classrooms are places where young and old can share space together, and coach one another both in content areas and life experiences. My concern is that given the current pragmatic push for STEM (Science, Technology, Education, and Math) education, we may wind up with a generation of young people who can precisely measure the impact of processes and purchases, but not understand the value that they add or detract from our individual humanity and collective well-being. Algorithms and machine learning will become increasingly better at predictive behavior, but authors, playwrights, poets, artists, and musicians also provide deep insights into the human personality.[33]

While many people are focused on wearable technologies, the next big trend that's on the foreseeable horizon is implantable technologies. Soon, more and more people will have a chip in their shoulder, or implanted in their hand, behind their ear, or inside of their brain, enabling all sorts of cognitive and physical enhancements that used to be the stuff of science fiction.[34] Like every other field, education will continue to experience tremendous marketplace-driven disruption, and even newer universities that offer only online degrees are just as at risk for disruption as traditional brick-and-mortar universities that blend real-time and online learning. Conversations across generations will be very helpful to individuals and communities in trying to gain a better grasp on the value and cost of the burgeoning options on the educational landscape.

What You Can Do

1. Increase your skills or knowledge in one educational area that you already know reasonably well, and one in which you know little about by enrolling in a course on Udacity, Coursera, or edX. In addition to acquiring new applied skills and academic knowledge, you'll gain a personal understanding of how rapidly education is being transformed and how accessible it has become. By starting with an area that you're already familiar with, you'll decrease any initial frustration that you may encounter with a new educational platform, although educational platforms are generally intuitive. And once you've tried learning in a content or skills area that you're familiar with, you'll be able to more confidently explore new areas of knowledge and expertise. By doing so, you'll continue to sharpen your brain and begin to develop yourself more as a person or professional in ways that may have unforeseen benefits. Also, try to participate in an online forum for learners and hear the perspectives of others from around the world.

2. If you have the knowledge, skills, and inclination, explore becoming an instructor on one of these or other platforms, or at your local community college or community center. The best teachers that I've had always embrace opportunities for learning, and there's nothing like presenting a class or workshop to others that pushes you to deepen your existing knowledge or skills.

3. If your learning style is more experiential, become involved in a structured network that meets on a regular basis to expand your educational horizons. Be counterintuitive and become a part of a group that is not directly related to your area of work. One of the most overlooked strategies for growing educationally is to expand your networks outside of your profession and learn how others look at issues from their perspectives. For example, everyone has issues with existing, new, and emerging technologies. Consider joining a networking group with a technological focus to learn what those with more expertise are focused on. As another example, museums and orchestras have had to reinvent themselves to engage younger audiences. If you're in the customer service business, try to learn from those involved in cultural institutions about strategies that they have used to maintain existing members, and to cultivate new audiences. While it's counterintuitive, you're likely to acquire novel and innovative ways of approaching your work by becoming a part of a professional network in a field of work that is different from your own. If you're unsure about how to find a network, ask some friends or colleagues, or visit a networking site like Meetup (www.meetup.com).

4. If you're a Boomer, and you have a Millennial family member, speak with her or him about the decision-making factors that went into a post–high school educational choice. Also, ask if your Millennial relative plans to continue his or her education either because it is a company or professional requirement, or because your younger family member believes that ongoing learning and experience are the keys to remaining competitive. You'll gain greater insight into the challenges that those who are Millennials and younger face about educational choices.

5. If you're a Millennial and experiencing some educational difficulties, ask a Boomer for ideas or help. Even if that Boomer doesn't know the specific skills or content area that you need, she or he may introduce you to others who do, or offer strategies for you to solve them by yourself. Remember that Boomers have life experience that you may be able to apply to your own situation.

6. If you have the financial means, or can pool funds with a group of people, create a giving circle to support a college scholarship fund through your local high school. A giving circle is a philanthropic structure that enables a group of people who care about a cause to define their mission and achieve it by scaling their impact by working with others. Many local community foundations or community philanthropies, like the United Way, provide the support and fiscal sponsorship to create a giving circle.

CHAPTER SIX

~

Are You Your Work?

Careers, Meaning, and Identity

Boomers And Millennials:
Work and Play Can/Not Coexist?

In chapter 2, we explored the generally negative stereotypes of career goals and work ethic that Boomers and Millennials had of one another. Boomers often remarked about the perceived lack of drive in Millennials and their indifference about their career goals. Millennials felt that Boomers were overly obsessed with their careers and couldn't understand why work, fun, and personal meaning were incompatible. Nor did they believe that peoples' identity should be so entangled with work that it limited their ability to cultivate other aspects of themselves through travel or other hobbies during their working years. Why defer an opportunity to travel to an exotic location later if you could scrape together an inexpensive way to do so now? Baby Boomers were the ones who created a "bucket list" of things to do upon retirement but Millennials wanted to kick the bucket out of sight, find meaning in work, have fun while they were healthy, and not gamble on some distant future time for greater enjoyment.

I wanted to find a way to verify this difference in their overall attitudes about work, and asked Millennials the following question: "Would you be willing to accept a completely lawful job for five years that had no personal meaning but paid you significantly more than what you are currently earning? You would not be able to retire from work after that five-year period, but you would earn a sufficient amount of money so that you could work at any job you wished for the rest of your life?" Without exception, the answer was, "No!" I wanted to make sure that I was being clear, so I asked the same question differently. "This job that provided you with no personal meaning would have a clear beginning, middle, and end, and after five years you would have no further commitment to it. Are you saying that you would be unwilling to trade off earning a significant amount of money for a limited time in exchange for the flexibility in your choice of work for the balance of your working years?" Again, without exception, their answer was a polite "thank you anyway" (and if I read some of their thought bubbles accurately, some answers were closer to, "Are you serious?").

Remember, I asked this question of Millennials who might have another four decades of working years ahead of them. Using forty years as an average number, that meant that they would be committing only five years, or 12.5 percent, of their time to unfulfilling lucrative work in return for lifelong career flexibility. Still, it was unthinkable to them that personal meaning was for sale.

I didn't ask Baby Boomers to imagine how they would answer that question if they were just beginning their careers. At some point during our working lives, we spent at least an equivalent of five years doing work that was lacking in meaning. In fact, we knew that our initial years of employment would likely be devoid of personal fulfillment, and if we had the audacity to challenge a supervisor who gave us an arbitrary deadline or task, we would hear some variation of "the speech": "I had to work long hours when I started doing grunt work and now it's your turn." Our goal was to successfully land a decent-paying first job, put the long hours in that were necessary for a next move up or out, continue to work hard, settle into a career until retirement, and use paid vacation time and the weekend for some relaxation and enjoyment. "Required hours" could be 9:00 a.m. to 5:00 p.m. for office or factory workers who "punched a clock,"[1] or if you were in senior management or practiced a profession like law, medicine, or accounting, you knew that you would be working anywhere between fifty and seventy hours per week pursuing a more lucrative career.

Millennials Learned from Boomers

How do we explain such vastly different attitudes about work between these two generations? Millennial children didn't randomly come into being; they are the offspring of Baby Boomer parents. Boomer parents (and I include myself) may want to reflect on the reigning values of raising young children in our day and ask if we need to take some ownership of those Millennial attitudes instead of rushing to find fault with them. Was there something in our parenting style that created and then fed a sense of "entitlement" that Boomers often complain about when it comes to Millennials? Was it too much "helicopter parenting" that contributed to Millennial children feeling like someone would always be there to bail them out literally and figuratively when they encountered trouble? Did we do the right thing in teaching them that "everyone is a winner" and collaboration is superior to competition, depriving them of the real-world experiences that they would face in which there are clear winners and losers?

At least one expert on generations in the workplace, David Stillman, believes so. Stillman, coauthor of the books *When Generations Collide*[2] and the *M-Factor: How Millennials are Rocking the Workplace*,[3] energetically stated that "Boomers raised their Millennial kids during the self-esteem movement—it was really about [parents saying to their children]: 'It doesn't matter what you're bad at, focus on what you're good at, find others that are good at what you're not, come together, two heads are better than one and collaborate, you bring a lot to the workplace, you're brilliant, you're great. You know, no one folds laundry like you, no one has a math test like you.' I mean, we really built them up so that when they entered the workforce, they were feeling really good about themselves. They were told they could be anything from an astronaut to a president. The economy was better, so they just were more confident, and they came in (to the workplace)—and what did we do? We called them 'entitled,' we told them they were 'spoiled,' and yet—the same people who complain to me about them, are the ones who raised them. So, while I think it's not fair for Millennials, they come across as, 'My way or no way—you're lucky to have me in this job, etc.'"[4]

Stillman recently coauthored another book on generations in the workplace with his son, Jonah Stillman, who belongs to the Gen Z or the post-Millennial generation.[5] I didn't want to miss an opportune moment with an expert to discuss differences in how Millennials and members of Gen Z relate to Boomers, and how Boomers feel about this newest generation that is entering the workforce. What did Stillman think? "[With Gen Z], it's not my way or no way. An easier way to say this—is while Millennials came across as 'this job is lucky to have me,' Gen Z feels lucky to have the job. So Boomers are going to love it. I think Boomers got sick of the, 'I have to talk to you about meaning in your job all the time. I've got to tell you how you're making a difference.' You know, Boomers, I think, are really sick of [the attitude that], 'Everyone has to feel good.' Now, Gen Z comes in and says, 'Tell me what I need. You know, I'm going to get a good grade. If not, fire me.'"[6]

Stillman is correct in noting how different economic times can influence attitudes toward work, although it's also true that many Millennials graduated from college during the recovery from the Great Recession, and painfully realized that self-esteem doesn't carry you very far when the job market bottoms out. But because Gen Xers and their Gen Z children grew up fully expecting to compete in a global business environment, these two generations sandwiching Millennials, one older (Gen X) and one younger (Gen Z), have expressed some difficulties in working with Millennials, whom they feel expect too much, too soon, and with too little effort.

Yet, let's give Millennials a little more credit. Perhaps Millennials saw the trade-offs between work and any other kind of life outside of work and concluded that the disadvantages outweighed the advantages. Their behavior may be a corrective critique of having watched Baby Boomers downsized, outsourced, retrenched and, in some cases, abandoned by their "corporate families." "Work-life balance" was a felicitous phrase that sounded nice, but one that was elusive. And especially for women, the mantra of "you can have it all" turned out to be the first half of an elliptical sentence. The second, unspoken half that turned out to be truer to reality was, "You can have it all . . . if you work crazy hours and feel regularly torn between family and work." And it was rare for fathers to receive "paid time off" to help at home when a new baby arrived, and Millennials know that it was generally their moms who spent more time with them from the moment that they were born.

But there are more complex factors that make discussions between Baby Boomers and their Millennial children a "third rail" that sparks heated discussion. To simplify some of these differences, I'd like to introduce two contrasting pairs of work-related concepts that speak to how significantly the time in which Boomers entered the workforce has changed in comparison with their Millennial children. These two contrasting pairs of terms are the "organization man" and "the corporation," versus the "portable leader" and "flash organization."

The Organization Man versus the Portable Leader

The term "organization man" derives from a book of the same title written by William H. Whyte Jr. in 1956. In this book, Whyte describes with some dismay the willingness of individuals to conform to an organizations' norms and expectations to advance professionally, but at the cost of sacrificing their individual creativity. By fitting into the corporate culture and turning themselves into organization men they could expect certain substantial benefits in return (and the book appeared at a time when men almost exclusively ruled corporate culture).

Over time, the phrase "the organization man" became shorthand for the trust and commitment that existed between the company and the employee starting in the post-Eisenhower years through close to the end of the last century. An employee who worked hard could reasonably expect stable employment. There were peaks and valleys in the economy, and employees who worked in high-end manufacturing sectors (like the automotive and household appliance industries) were especially vulnerable to economic fluctuations and might find themselves temporarily out of a job. But they typically were able to find equivalent and gainful employment within a relatively short time. In return for hard work, organizations provided a regular paycheck with annual salary increases, health care benefits, various kinds of retirement savings plans and a certain amount of paid vacation time and sick leave. In return, employees would demonstrate loyalty and commitment to "the organization." Boomers, who might have had revolutionary ideals in their younger years, came to value job security and conformity, extending the shelf life of the "organization man," a conceptual phrase that had staying power even when women had entered the corporate and professional worlds.

While the pace of innovation at work began to increase with the widespread introduction of personal computers, and then networked personal computers in the mid-1990s, employees could absorb the rate of change and had middle management to support them. At least through the 1990s and often until the beginning of the Great Recession of 2007,[7] many Baby Boomers could count on a job for life, moving vertically up the company ladder a couple of times during a career, or relocating to another company or industry with similar compensation and benefits. Older Boomers were not "job hoppers" as there was still a remnant of a social contract between the organization and the individual that provided employees with greater job security that has by now vanished. For many older Boomers, those born between 1945 and 1955, their rite of passage into mandatory retirement at age sixty-five was a party thrown by coworkers and paid for by the company, and a gift of a gold watch, symbolizing the hoped-for golden dreams of retirement years ahead.

Without romanticizing the recent past, job stability was much more predictable because the United States economy was less integrated into a global economy and not nearly as subject to forces beyond its control. Remember, the North American Free Trade Agreement, or NAFTA, which eventually eliminated tariffs for manufactured goods among three strong trading partners—the United States, Canada, and Mexico—only went into effect on January 1, 1994.[8] NAFTA was an important milestone in accelerating the globalization of the United States economy, along with the entry of the United States into the World Trade Organization, or WTO, in 1995, "the only global international organization dealing with the rules of trade between nations."[9]

Around the same time, the state of personal computing and the Internet began to change the workplace. According to a Pew Research Center report commissioned for the twenty-fifth anniversary of the World Wide Web in 2014, only 14 percent of American households had Internet access in 1995 and of those, only 2 percent had a relatively fast modem for that time, 28.8 kilobits per second (Kbps). By 2014, only twenty-five years later, over 81 percent of Americans said that they accessed the computer either at home, work, or school. Smartphone penetration into American society, which allows for mobile work, has been even more dramatic. Apple's iPhone, which accelerated interest in these devices, was introduced in 2007. By the beginning of 2018, 94 percent of individuals between the ages of 18 and 29 owned a smartphone, 89 percent of individuals between the ages of 39 and 50 owned a smartphone, and 73 percent of individuals between the ages of 51 and 64 owned a smartphone.[10]

These trade agreements, data on computer usage and statistics on Internet access (which is increasingly mobile), and China's rise as a global economic power are relevant to understanding differing attitudes around work between Baby Boomers and Millennials. While globalization and stiff economic competition increased right before the eyes of Baby Boomers during their working years, we can remember a time when there were no cell phones and blazing down the Internet highway meant owning a "56K" modem (or more technically accurate, a 56 Kbps modem). However, as direct witnesses to such rapid change, Boomers may have difficulty in gauging its dramatic impact on the next generations. For Boomers, these were changes to which they had to adapt while having a job, but they were the harsher realities into which Gen Xers and Millennials were born. These two younger generations have had to contend with a workplace that is much more competitive because of globalization and technology from the beginning of their first search for work, often without adequate emotional and educational preparation.

If "the corporation" and the "organization man" still have some nostalgic pull for Boomers, for Gen Xers and those younger, those concepts needed to be substituted with "the portable leader" and the "flash organization." These exact phrases may not attain the same venerable vernacular status as the "organization man" did, but they certainly reflect the realities of today's workplace. The phrase "portable leader" appeared in a recent article titled, "The Portable Leader is the New 'Organization Man.'"[11] The author, Gianpiero Petriglieri, is one of three distinguished researchers of organizational leaders who studied how today's individuals seek to control their professional destinies in a fluid, global economy. A portable leader is a person who, according to the researchers, is one who feels "confident enough to *leave* one [a job]," in contrast to the "organization man" whose goal was to remain in a job! The researchers further explain that the allure of some prominent companies to talented employees is their corporate training programs, that offer an implicit promise that "working here today will make you a leader elsewhere tomorrow."[12]

In a related vein, individuals who acquired certification through reputable executive educational programs chose them because, "rather than striving to find, and ease the transition to, a single future dream job, the people we studied engaged in a broader yet more immediate project: crafting a 'portable self' that would be valued at Blue [the fictional name that the authors gave to one executive training program] and beyond—a self as a leader. 'Being a leader' was shorthand for being in charge of one's destiny, connected and useful to others, even in the absence of the mooring and direction of a traditional career ladder in a single company."[13]

The "portable leader" does not expect long tenure at one organization but seeks to future-proof his or her options to remain competitive by being able to move into different corporate settings multiple times, given today's fluid, global, and hypercompetitive workplace.

All large corporations are not going to disappear, but today's workers also recognize that both legacy institutions and startups that became huge disruptors of an industry may themselves be disrupted. And because it's difficult to compete with the 3Ms and Facebooks of the world, a new organizational model that two Stanford professors, Melissa Valentine and Michael Bernstein have studied is emerging on a broader scale: "the flash organization."[14] These are organizations that come together to complete a complex project and then disband. Think Hollywood and movies in trying to understand this organizational model. "Temporary organizations capable of taking on complicated projects have existed for decades, of course, perhaps nowhere more prominently than in Hollywood, where producers assemble teams of directors, writers, actors, costume and set designers, and a variety of other craftsmen and technicians to execute projects with budgets in the tens if not hundreds of millions."[15]

The flash organization is now viable outside of Hollywood for several reasons: big data that generate algorithms and online platforms are the new matchmakers of the work world. They can connect superior talent from any-where in the world with employers' needs, and the people behind the plat-forms are learning how to better assure quality control and become specialists in facilitating project management and execution. The pharmaceutical and software industries are already experimenting with this organizational model, and even a quick online search at sites like Gigster, Business Talent Group, and 99designs suggest that "the company," in some cases, may have a rival in ephemeral pop-up organizations built through networks of talented individu-als and facilitators for a limited duration.[16] Many Boomers had some experi-ence with "the corporation" that provided stability and security and lived as or remembered the "organization man." But Millennials need to be "portable leaders" because of technology and globalization which have increasingly enabled the emergence of here-today, gone-tomorrow "flash organizations."

Also, if you're a Boomer, try and put yourself in the place of a younger Millennial. When you were beginning your career, if someone asked you about your career aspirations, you had a relatively limited number of profes-sions, industries, or trades available in which you could work. But how can a Millennial project a career trajectory when the job that he or she has three years from now may not exist today? Isn't it more productive for Millen-nials to think about the kinds of skills, experiences, and mentorships that are likely to help them with the emergence of new and yet-to-be imagined employment opportunities? Uber, Airbnb, 3D and early-stage 4D printing,[17] data scientists, holographic producers of experiences—these are companies, concepts, and technologies that didn't even exist long ago. Anticipating the future and preparing for it by continuing to acquire new skills, building net-works, and developing talents not related to your job are more important for Millennials than attempting to map a rough career trajectory given the rapid acceleration of change and innovation.[18] If Millennials can't shake the label of "job hoppers," that is, individuals who feel no attachment to workplaces or professions, they have good reasons.[19]

And Stillman, whom I quoted earlier, anticipates the potential for even greater clashes across four generations of working adults now in the workplace unless there is more conversation "up front" around team-based projects that involve members of different generations. Boomers who are still employed are used to working in structured, hierarchical organizations and may assume that their experience endows them with automatic project leadership and control. Some Boomers also make clear that they believe they have little to learn from younger generations. While they have be-come more accustomed to working with Gen Xers, they also are working with two additional younger generations in the workforce, Millennials and post-Millennials, and these two generations have different work styles. Millennials, as Stillman notes, have

> A really collaborative mentality. We all come together, innately we play to our skills, two heads are better than one, we're only as strong as our weakest link, and then together, we'll all knock this out of the park. There are no winners or losers, it's a participation-award mentality. But, Gen Z is way more competitive and independent. They're more like, "Keep your nose out of my stuff because we're both probably competing for the same job, and I really don't want a team grade. I don't want to be held accountable for your work, I want my own individual grade, and I'm going to be really competitive and independent. I don't like all these team meetings and rah-rah." So I think some of our biggest collisions are on the horizon—between this collaborative, Millennial team generation and a competitive-driven, Gen Z, independent generation.

That's why Stillman believes that initial discussion around two areas needs to be clarified to avoid confusion in the workplace. "Roles need to be really clear. Who's taking notes, who's doing follow up, we're all playing a role," to preempt misunderstanding and annoyance by having clear agreements, and that applies to people who work in the same building, or in distributed teams across different time zones and cultures.[20] The other issue that team members need to agree upon, regardless of age, is, "Who's making decisions here, and then who are we reporting to? We've got to be held accountable, so our reporting structure needs to be determined up front."[21] Stillman also added that those decisions should be based on skill set and performance and not on tenure and age. The "chain of command" for each project may differ, and during a project, work flow will be more fluid than in the past, but the most important criteria for judging the success of intergenerational organizations are their performance outcomes.[22]

Another business expert, organizational futurist Daniel Burrus, offers some optimism of a different kind in having multiple generations in the workplace. He writes, "It will be increasingly difficult to attract and keep talent."[23] But this is a "Soft Trend," defined by Burrus as one that individuals can influence because any company or organization can create an environment where both young and old come together to focus on actively reinventing their industry and creating transformational change.[24] Burrus has seen this happen when a leader or group of influencers in an organization believe that "we're all [inherently] connected unless we chose to be disconnected, and it's the disconnection that causes disharmony, and the assumptions that we make about one another are often wrong."[25]

In my interviews with Baby Boomers and Millennials, they generally felt that they were treated respectfully by one another. As in any new job, a Millennial had to earn the trust of colleagues through consistently reliable and high-quality performance. At the same time, those Boomers who had been supervised by individuals who were younger by a generation generally did not care, with a few exceptions. For example, one Boomer, Jack Jones, categorically said that he learned nothing from a younger colleague who supervised him because his value set and metrics about what mattered were so vastly different.[26] But, in the words of another Boomer, Keith Wilbert, "Age doesn't matter to me much if they [younger supervisors] are competent. But I can't take incompetence at any age."[27]

To conclude this section on the sharp contrasts between the ways that Boomers' and Millennials' work environments have changed, I've created a simple table. The table is simple, but their contrasts are powerful and can help each generation take a step back to appreciate why their values about work are so different.[28]

If Boomers and Millennials display different attitudes toward work, it's for good reason. The relative job stability and benefits that Boomers could rely upon are relics for many Millennials.

Table 6.1.

Baby Boomers	Millennials
More than 40 percent of older Boomers stayed with one employer for greater than 20 years	Significantly more "job hopping" and projected shorter stays at companies or organizations
Greater job security	Job insecurity; try to earn extra income through participation in "gig" economy
Promotions often tied to seniority	Keep your resume warm and LinkedIn profile up-to-date
Continuing education if mandated by profession	Self-mandated necessity to keep learning and add value to employer
Typical benefits: 2–3 weeks paid vacation, national holidays; health insurance and defined benefit pension (employee and employer contributed, but employer contribution was greater or equal to employee contribution)	Typical benefits: 2–3 weeks paid vacation, national holidays; health insurance and 401K retirement plans (with higher employee contribution)
Keep your head down and do your work	Speak up because performance carries more weight than seniority
Retire between ages 65 and 67	Yet-to-be-determined

In fact, some Millennials are encountering their own unique version of generational dislocation. Boomers had to become digital immigrants to keep pace with their Millennial digital-native coworkers. Now, some Millennials are having to contend with a new reality of becoming "digital nomads." They may literally have to travel the globe for long stretches of time based on their willingness and desire to maintain employment. Currently, there are two global companies that have expanded the idea of co–working spaces into co–living spaces: Roam (launched in 2015) and WeLive (launched in 2016, and grew from WeWork, a co–working space launched in 2010).[29] These two companies might more accurately be described as nascent movements that are poised to meet the need of a global, permanent class of people who want a place that feels like home without owning a home, and a ready-made human community to mitigate against the damaging effects of social isolation.

Boomer Life Post–Full-Time Work: Please Don't Call It Retirement

Any discussion about work would be incomplete without also talking about how Boomers are redefining life after employment. Notice that I didn't use the word "retirement." Why? Because the word "retirement" no longer defines or signifies what it used to for those who completed their employment years. In my interviews with Baby Boomers who had already retired, only one of them was nominally comfortable with the word "retirement" to describe this stage of life, while the others had mild to strong negative reactions to it. In the words of another Boomer, Hunter Weiss, who retired voluntarily at age fifty-five and has been devoting much of his time to charitable causes, "Retirement conjures up images of someone sitting in a rocking chair. . . . There are some people who say to me, 'You're retired, I'll never retire . . .' but [I understand that] the word conjures up biases, like you're out to pasture, not making money."[30]

Another Baby Boomer, Jack Jones, who stopped working full-time eight years ago but is consulting one day a week in the medical field, said that he spent about three years planning for what his life would be like when he was no longer working full-time. This individual had entered medicine because he wanted to help the quality of life of his patients and make a broader contribution to the well-being of his community. He realized that if he wanted to continue to live a purposeful, post-work life, then he needed to plan for it intentionally. And that's what he did for three years. He described the financial, emotional, and intellectual work that went into preparing for a fulfilling next stage of life, and he provided great insight for those who are contemplating "retirement." He explained how he envisioned life as consisting of three chapters: growing up, developing career and family life, and beginning a third chapter of "doing something else meaningful." This stage of life is not retirement but turning a page to a new chapter and finding other forms of being productive. "You can't retire *from* something, you have to retire *to* something, so you better have a good definition of what you should do with your life when you leave your current career."[31] To paraphrase his words, a life of meaning won't magically appear on your doorstep after your last day of work; you must lay down your own pathways to meaning. (Ironic—isn't that what Millennials are trying to do in the workplace!?)

I heard similar comments about life after employment from other Baby Boomers whom I interviewed for this book. They all stressed the importance of financial security, although their wealth varied significantly. But their shared point was that you need to establish some baseline of financial security that you can live with, understanding that the feeling of no longer earning money while watching dollars flow out of your retirement savings was an emotional adjustment. Another younger Boomer, Gary Harper, whose guiding values were "live, love, learn," offered a simple definition of financial security: "I never wanted to be rich, but just wanted to be able to eat steak when I wanted to."[32] The across-the-board sentiment of participants was that they wanted to be "comfortable," although each one had a different standard of what constituted "comfort."

Another common theme without exception was a desire on the part of those who were Baby Boomers to remain connected with younger generations. That was true whether they were still in the workforce or no longer employed. One Baby Boomer couple that had just retired decided to spend a winter in Mexico, where they are considering permanent relocation. They registered for a volunteer program where they interact with middle school students for an hour each week. For the first thirty minutes, they speak only English and help students improve their English language skills, and for the second half-hour, these students speak to them only in Spanish, helping them acquire Spanish language proficiency. Two other different Baby Boomers in this study returned to school, one to complete a degree in fine arts, the other to earn a law degree. Despite the disparate nature of their respective academic programs, they each mentioned how they enjoyed their contact with younger students. From their interactions with younger students, it sounded like they were informally available as calming presences, and their lived experience of resilience in the face of difficult situations were sources of inspiration for younger students.

There is a significant industry of "encore" opportunities for Baby Boomers, both those who are still employed and those who are in their post-employment years, which you can read about in appendix C. The presence of organizations including Generations United, Encore, Dorot, and linkAges (a pilot program that was acquired by Help-Full, Inc., in January 2018), whose senior leaders were interviewed for this volume, testifies to the revolutionary transformation of the stage of life that we used to call retirement. These organizational websites offer valuable advice for ways to continue to be productive and to grow in what one Boomer called this "third chapter of life." But there is one article written in 2006 by a prominent attorney, James Freund, that is especially saturated with wisdom for Boomers, and I believe for Gen Xers as well.

Freund titled his article, "A Retirement Scorecard," playing off of the balanced scorecard in business, a tool that uses metrics in key internal business functions to improve performance and outcomes.[33] In his article, Freund analyzes the pros and cons of retirement. For the purposes of this chapter, what interests me most is not his recommended decision-making guide for when it's time to retire, but what he refers to as the "package deal," that is, the inherently contradictory benefits and liabilities of retirement. He tries to balance fairly the pretty parts of retirement with its challenges.[34]

Paraphrasing his wisdom, he explains that the relief of not being on call for clients is counterbalanced with the realization that you are not as indispensable as you thought. The drudgingly predictable routine of a workday, which can feel stifling toward the end of one's career, must be weighed against the challenge of owning your own schedule. He notes that while that sounds enticing, it can be overwhelming at first to realize that you're now responsible for using your time purposefully.[35] If your work is your identity, and you give up something for which you were known, what does that do to your self-esteem? Those are some of the questions that he addresses, and he also recommends having some "fun," which is, after all, one of the reasons for leaving a career.[36] But the most interesting observation that he makes relates to solitude.

While Freund directs his comments toward lawyers and those in other professions, I think that they are more universal and applicable to any person who leaves the workforce. He writes, "I think you need to become immersed in at least one activity with the following characteristics:

1. It should be something you can do primarily by yourself, without the need of someone in a supporting cast.
2. It involves a skill that will require effort on your part to become proficient at and that holds out the prospect of continued improvement.
3. It produces something you can view with pride, and perhaps show off to others."

These three points are an elaboration of his earlier observation in his article that "you have to learn how to be good company for yourself."[37]

The images that Boomers unconsciously hold of retirement naturally relate to experiences with their own aging family members a generation ago. But of course, those images are outdated, as many people can expect to lead active and productive lives well beyond eighty years old. In 1950, the average life expectancy at birth was sixty-eight years and continued to rise steadily to seventy-six years in 1991.[38] However, Baby Boomers "have the longest life expectancy in history. The average 65-year-old today can expect to live to 84.3—nearly three years longer than a 65-year-old in 1980."[39] Advertisements often portray the face of aging with glitzy shots of elderly people doing impossible skateboarding routines or running marathons. I admit that I'm jaded about those kinds of advertisements, perhaps because I could never perform these athletic feats in my younger days, but mainly because they present a lopsided view of aging. Maintaining good health and physical activity are essential at all stages of life, and if you have the physical ability to compete in age-appropriate athletic sports, I think that's fantastic! But there are other ways of climbing mountains, and they include embracing activities that challenge us, require us to develop new skills, and engage with new people across the generational spectrum. The post-work years can be exceptionally fulfilling, and as much as we give attention to Gen Xers, Millennials, and post-Millennials, and their different entryways and byways into and around work, it's an exciting time to be a Baby Boomer and have so many opportunities to embrace a different kind of growth. It seems to me like that's another conversation that members of all generations could enjoy together.

What You Can Do

1. If you're a Baby Boomer, and you're a few years away from retirement, begin preparing for it now. If you don't already have a financial plan-

ner, ask for a recommendation from a peer who has recently retired. You may be an excellent manager of your own finances, but when entering a new stage of life, draw upon the expertise of a trusted professional who has helped hundreds of people create a financial plan. Have conversations with your peers who have been retired for several years and hear directly from them how they have navigated this transition, and especially what life was like for them during the first year. You can also visit Boomer-focused organizations like Age Wave, that describes itself as "the world's leader in understanding the effects of an aging population on the marketplace, the workplace and our lives" and AARP, another organization that is designed for individuals who are approaching or in retirement.[40] Even if you haven't been a planner for much of your life, this stage especially requires planning because of the potential for being more vulnerable to health, emotional, and financial wellness issues. Include other family members in thinking about your plans. They may have some additional insights, and while you don't need their permission to pursue your dreams, by speaking with them you can set their expectations for how you envision life and relationships, and also model for them the value of intergenerational conversation.

2. If you're an employer, learn more from trusted sources about engagement and retention of younger employees. There is a tremendous amount of literature and hype on this topic, so carefully vet what you read. Personally, I prefer independent think tanks like the Pew Research Center and Gallup as starting points for keeping abreast of generational trends and practical ideas for boosting engagement and retention; local business or association trade groups are also often good sources of ideas.[41] With several generations in the workplace and complex business regulations, it's important to understand how different generations define and prioritize a benefit. For example, companies like Gradifi work with employers to help younger workers pay down their college debt, a benefit that the Baby Boomer employer might not think of but that can help Millennials who are very concerned about it.[42]

Here's another example of how one Gen X business founder and owner, Lili Hall, decided to take her values and embed them into the culture of her company from the very beginning. She explained that "culture is everything to our company, and people work hard and [I began to think about] what we can be doing to make their lives a little bit better."[43] Her company has grown, and she now has a business partner, but even in her company's early days, she thought creatively about how to support her employees in simple ways, like assuming the financial costs of having a chiropractor visit her office once per week and arranging membership for her employees in a workout studio near her office.

Most uniquely, Lili Hall partnered with a law firm that offers workshops on preparing legal documents like advance medical directives, wills, estate planning and various kinds of powers of attorney that employees are unlikely to think about until that catastrophic trigger event happens to a family member. As she said, "You have to stop and think about what people are going through and creatively think about what they need that you may be able to provide."[44] Because the context of work has changed, and employers must make difficult decisions about benefits, they can improve retention and engagement of employees when they understand the value that different generations attach to a benefit. While these benefits might make a company more competitive, as Lili explained, "no one really knows what's going on in someone else's life, and when you hear a person [employee] and see his or face and they say, 'Thank you so much,' you realize that what companies traditionally offered is different than what they might need today."[45] As Hall shows, there may be some relatively small costs to offering these kinds of "benefits," but I left our conversation inspired by how a small business can make a huge difference in employees' lives if business owners take the time to see them as people.

3. Finally, regardless of age and stage, learn a new skill, find a hobby if you don't have one or invest more in one that you enjoy, join a local networking group that speaks to your personal or professional interests, or enjoy a vast, open world of learning on platforms like Coursera or edX, Kahn Academy, Udacity, TED Talks, or podcasts on public radio or television. Explore these sites, set your learning goals, and then enjoy! There is an abundance of learning options and, depending upon your budget, you can take advantage of many free opportunities or relatively inexpensive ones.

~

CHAPTER SEVEN

We're All Perennials, So Let's Act Together!

And to you youngsters out there, remember that you have to wake up every day with a purpose in life.

—Advice given by a one-hundred-year-old man to guests at his centennial birthday celebration on June 10, 2018

It's Personal and Professional

I want to answer a question that many people asked me when they learned that I was writing a book on intergenerational relationships and communities: why are you interested in this topic? "Fair question," I answered, and realized that "because I think that it's important" was a lazy response—to them and to me. What was driving me toward this issue of intergenerational connections?! My answer is both professional and personal.

In retrospect, my professional interest began when I was a freshly minted congregational rabbi in 1985. I learned that, in a typical day in a congregation, I might be telling stories to preschool children in the morning, participating in an intergenerational book review discussion with my congregation's Sisterhood Group during lunch, helping teenagers prepare for a bar or bat mitzvah in the afternoon, and meeting with three generations of a grieving family that had lost a loved one later in the evening in preparation for a funeral the next day. And on each Sabbath, I encountered all ages, from the very young to the very old.

While I was unfamiliar with the meaning of "intergenerational," I quickly realized that I was going to need a repertoire of approaches to connect with so many diverse generations. I entered the rabbinate because I cared about "community," but when I graduated from rabbinical school I naively equated community with institutions and sometimes prioritized "correct" principles over relationships with people. I had an outstanding academic education, it just didn't have much to do with my daily work as a congregational rabbi. That's why I decided to apply for a first position as "assistant rabbi" in a large congregation, where I could be mentored by an exceptional senior rabbi. I also enrolled in two graduate-level courses on human development and family systems over the next several years, connected with several experts for advice on issues that were generation-specific, and also reached out to others who helped me learn to speak and work intergenerationally.

Then, beginning about ten years ago, conversations about aging parents, the delayed development of adolescent children entering adulthood, employment struggles of middle-aged people (often men), and the status of personal relationships became frequent topics of discussion when I was with my Baby Boomer peers. Whether I was having coffee with a friend or socializing at a holiday celebration, the first part of every conversation was often about one of these issues. What was odd was that I didn't initiate these discussions—they found me, and on some mysterious level, I believe that my earlier years in a congregation and the discussions that started about a decade ago were inviting me to explore them for some larger purpose. Also, I'm a younger Baby Boomer with parents and in-laws in their mid-to-upper eighties, Millennial children, and post-Gen Z grandchildren, so I am experiencing parts of the story about which I have written.

During this decade of personal experience and formal study, I've come to believe that every Boomer has the same story to tell, but with different variations. Whether it's the single, seventy-year-old parent who is still working but also taking care of elderly parents, the fifty-five-year-old married couple that is providing much more emotional and financial support to a child than they had expected, or professionals who have been highly successful but are now struggling to keep pace with the velocity of change at work, I sensed that these were not random conversations, but somehow interrelated. Professionally and personally, my experiences reinforced my intuitive feeling that we had arrived at some inflection point that I couldn't quite name. But now, I can "connect the dots" across these earlier and more recent experiences and answer the "why" of undertaking this research and writing endeavor: we live more joyfully, purposefully, and wisely when we are a part of an intergenerational community and we infuse greater empathy into the universe for generations to come.

I've also come to understand that the labels that we've given to the six generations alive today had hindered my ability to weave the connective strands of these conversations sooner.[1] These labels have some utility. They help us clarify generational distinctions in behaviors and attitudes toward relationships, work, family, and community that are the result of our being born into historical contexts with different events that influenced our values. But these labels obscure what every generation has in common with the other and they drive wedges across the generations that pull us further apart.

Why? Because discussions of difference can be conversation stoppers. Generational differences often encourage individuals in a conversation to assert that their way of thinking or acting is superior to that of the "other." You've probably experienced the aftermath of emotions of one of those conversations with someone who is older or younger, where you leave feeling further misunderstood and without any incentive to try and see the world through that other person's point of view. Marketers of goods, services, and products have a vested financial interest in highlighting generational differences, but as individuals, we have a greater societal interest in identifying frameworks that unite people of every age. So, here you have it: this volume is another effort to unite more people around the value of intergenerational living.

Neither Boomer nor Millennial, But Perennial

Until age twenty-seven, I had lived in two large cities: Philadelphia and New York. I grew up with some green space but was mostly surrounded by brick, cement, and asphalt. When my wife and I lived in our first apartment in New York, I used to joke that I was going "urban hunting," which meant strategically placing "roach motels" throughout our apartment at bedtime and setting an occasional mousetrap. While I left my East Coast city roots decades ago, I never developed an appreciation for gardening, and to this day, the only time that I've picked up a shovel of earth has been at a Jewish funeral, where it's customary to place some earth upon the casket. But when I met with Dr. David Alter, one of the experts whom I interviewed for this book, he began speaking about his perennial plants and how the prior year's seeds carried the flowers of the future. I was captivated by what he said as I thought that perennials might serve as one metaphor to help us reclaim organic intergenerational relationships.

After the interview, I searched the Web for a very basic explanation of perennials. I learned that "Perennial plants . . . have a very different survival and reproduction strategy [from annual plants]. They are long-lived plants, and can live from many years to many centuries, depending on the species. . . . In Nature, *most of the plants on the planet are perennials*! The majority of all terrestrial (land based) and freshwater aquatic plants are perennial plants."[2] I also read that with perennials, "Generally, the top portion of the plant dies back each winter and regrows the following spring from the same root system."[3] Maybe I should have taken up gardening as a hobby after all! "Perennial" was such an apt metaphor for unearthing the enduring tasks of discarding, retaining, and renewing that characterizes the broad work of every generation, tasks that generational labels have pushed underground.

If most plants are perennials, I also wondered if a promising strategy for thriving into the future will be through intergenerational collaboration. After all, perennials require not only the dimension of space but also time, because each season's variety has roots from the past and seeds for the future within it. And if you've guessed that my question about collaboration as a survival strategy led me to refresh my memory of evolutionary biology and Charles Darwin's theories on "the survival of the fittest," you're correct. The only problem was that after dedicating over a full year almost exclusively to research for writing this book, I wasn't in the mood to read Darwin's *The Origin of Species* (over five hundred pages) and *The Descent of Man* (over eight hundred and fifty pages). But fortunately, Dr. Christopher L. Kukk recently was interested in delving into Darwin's works, which he needed to do in writing his recent book, *The Compassionate Achiever: How Helping Others Fuels Success.*[4]

Kukk knew that he would have to defend his idea that our survival has always been more dependent upon collaboration than competition. In reviewing many of Darwin's works, and those of more contemporary biologists like Edward O. Wilson, best known for his studies of the social life of ants and bees and the light that they shed on human interactions, Kukk concluded that "Darwin's research shows that 'survival of the kindest' is more correct for explaining which species climb the evolutionary ladder efficiently and effectively."[5] In fact, building upon the theories and research of Darwin, Herbert Spencer,[6] and Wilson, Kukk explains why groups of compassionate people have a clear advantage over groups of self-interested individuals:

> The members of the selfish group are looking out only for themselves, and if others in their group fall, they see it as strengthening their own survival within it: One less competitor to worry about. Over time, as Darwin noted,

their membership dwindles relative to the compassionate group. As E. O. Wilson writes in "The Meaning of Human Existence": "Within groups selfish individuals beat altruistic individuals, but groups of altruists beat groups of selfish individuals."[7]

I know that I'm reiterating what much ancient and contemporary wisdom, and many philosophical, psychological, and faith traditions have said in stating that to be human is to have a deep relationship with another person, someone who accepts us unconditionally and who we accept unconditionally in return. But as I've watched statistics of social isolation increase, I want to add an intergenerational twist to this insight. In addition to having several close friends who are approximately our own age, I want to advocate that we have at least one close friend who is a generation older and one close friend who is a generation younger. Call it the "Perennial Challenge," one that will help us discard negative, age-based stereotypes that harden generational silos, maintain our empathy through reciprocal learning about the events that shaped us, and invest in a future that views members of different generations as having a stake in one another's success. What I'm calling the "Perennial Challenge" is a manifestation of Kukk's hopeful phrase, "the survival of the kindest."

When I interviewed Baby Boomers and Millennials, I asked them two questions about friendships. I wanted to know how many close friends they had who were approximately their age, and if they had at least one close friend who was a generation older or a generation younger, excluding family members. You might be thinking, "Why would I want or need to have a close relationship with someone who is at a different stage of life? Isn't having a close friend who is my contemporary enough?"

It's a reasonable question, but if we remain within our own generational orbit, we're likely to miss the timeless tasks that we share with those who came before us and with those who will follow. Broadly, these tasks are to look critically at the assumptions of the prior generation and determine which we need to reject because they restrain greater human potential that resides within us, maintain those that are still positive today, and try to prepare ways for the next generation to make their future better than our own. The context in which we do this work changes, and today's disruptive times and differentiated generational labeling may cause us to feel less connected with the past and despairing of the future. But this is our shared perennial task.

I realize that this is the kind of sweeping generalization that can make a discerning reader skeptical. But when you take a step back and look at the arc of human history, individuals in each generation have shown that they have the freedom to act in a way that says, "We are not bound by the path of our parents or more distant ancestors. We can distinguish between what they have left as an inheritance that is worth continuing and also reject their mistakes. We do not have to make a binary choice of accepting or discarding everything." What's even more remarkable is that whether in antiquity, when kings were considered as deities and people were their property, or in modernity, when oppressive governments still brutalize their citizens, you don't have to look far for examples of courageous individuals who have harvested parts of the past to plant a brighter future that they know they will not live to see.

That process is still alive now. If you're a United States citizen and a Baby Boomer, you may have been a part of the protest movement that helped to end the Vietnam War, and if you're a Millennial, you may have helped to change history by electing the first African American president. If you're a Millennial, you may be creating a better future through work that you're doing in the life sciences. If you're a Baby Boomer, perhaps you're changing a disadvantaged young person's life trajectory by volunteering in a school, because you're teaching more than discrete educational skills—you've become an inspirational presence. Everyone has the power to engage in this perennial process of retaining parts from our past that are usable, relinquishing pieces that have constrained us, and renewing the capacity for a better future for the next generation. A handful of people in every generation do so in large ways, but an even larger number of people have anonymously taken up this perennial process and developed relationships that have changed the world for the better. So rather than limit ourselves to one generational label that sociologists ascribe to us ("I'm a Boomer;" "I'm a Millennial"), why not call ourselves Perennials, people who possess the potential to repeat the process of questioning assumptions and aspiring for positive change regardless of age?[8]

During my interviews, and in additional less-structured conversations with members of different generations, I heard a common theme about wanting to be "respected" and "heard." Young adults want to be heard and respected by those who are older. "Being heard" doesn't just mean people politely listening and agreeing during a conversation. Rather, it means that the listener is curious and open to learning about another point of view. "Being respected" doesn't mean that someone else will automatically agree with your opinion on a given issue. In fact, they may challenge you. But it does mean that someone views you as capable of making thoughtful choices—even if that means making a mistake or two along the way. That's the "unconditional" piece of

Perennial relationships, giving people the freedom to choose their own path in the way that someone hopefully gave to us as an unconditional gift.

And the same holds true for those who are older. An elderly person may be treated deferentially but not feel respected or heard. Older people may feel like those around them no longer take them seriously, either because they're perceived as not being "productive," "tech savvy," or "aware of today's new realities." It's as if they've been stamped with a product expiration date that has passed. Many younger people see older people, exchange a quick friendly greeting, but communicate that they would prefer to put them back on the shelf because of their perceived irrelevance. But while yogurt and milk sour, fine art appreciates with age. And a long life often has an asymmetrical beauty that bears the scars of experience and strengths of healing.

What rang so clearly throughout my interviews with people of different ages, whether they were eighteen or eighty, is how they expressed the same sentiment of feeling less valuable than those in other generations. For older adolescents, sometimes it's because people are dismissive of their lack of experience. For the elderly, the cause may be tied to a perception that they are living in the past. But while the causes may be different, the feelings of social isolation and irrelevance are painfully similar. Where are the spaces for conversations that can enable members of different generations to talk about what it feels like to be lacking in value in comparison with others? And following those conversations, what kind of changes can be enacted to restore feelings of equal dignity and self-worth, regardless of age?

One of my friends and colleagues in the field of intergenerational relationships, Stuart Himmelfarb, spoke with me about the concept of "reciprocal mentoring."[9] That phrase really resonated with me, as it provided an imaginative way of expressing how people from different generations can enliven one another through reciprocal relationships. Stuart was part of a diverse, self-organized group of volunteers who decided to dedicate time to rebuilding New Orleans after Hurricane Katrina in 2011, a group that continues to volunteer time and service. (In 2017, they shifted their location to Houston, which had suffered devastating floods). In reflecting on his years of volunteering, he wrote, "I noticed something when I'd arrive at a job site: it made no difference if the site manager or other worker was 22 or 42 or 62. We were there to learn what to do and all that mattered was clear instructions from someone who knew their way around a construction site. The fact that I was joined by my twenty-something son made no difference—he, too, benefited from the same guidance. Age didn't matter; guidance, experience, and knowledge did."[10] Based on those ongoing experiences, and his additional efforts to try and help faith communities value sustainable intergenerational volunteer opportunities, Himmelfarb coined the phrase "reciprocal mentoring." By that, he means that "we should no longer rely on old stereotypes when pairing people up to learn from each other. If there is true communication and an openness to learning from someone whether he or she is younger or older, then the outcome of the mentoring relationship has a higher likelihood of success. Knowledge gets conveyed to the person who needs it."[11]

Himmelfarb speaks to the reciprocal joy of learning and sharing between Boomers and Millennials around work that directly improves people's lives. That same enriching mutual reciprocity can also occur between Boomers and those a generation above. John Leland, a Boomer-age reporter for the *New York Times*, wrote a series of articles in 2015 profiling six individuals who were at least eighty-five years old. His goal was to tell the stories of what it was like to experience life as an elderly individual. However, he did not anticipate the impact that those stories would have on shaping his own life. In a follow-up article several years later he wrote, "The six became models for the challenges in my own life, living examples of resilience, gratitude and the wisdom that comes from living through ups and downs in history."[12] Leland was so profoundly affected by his experience that he wrote a book titled, *Happiness Is a Choice You Make: Lessons from a Year among the Oldest Old.*[13]

Search Institute[14] is conducting pioneering research in refining and applying its five dimensions of "developmental relationships" to enable young people to overcome the high percentages of social isolation that they are reporting. These five elements are:

- Express CARE
- CHALLENGE growth
- Provide SUPPORT
- Share POWER
- Expand POSSIBILITIES.[15]

By asking, "what happens in relationships that contribute to learning, growing, and thriving?"[16] the researchers were able to move beyond obvious clichés like, "relationships are important," to identifying and then offering specific ideas that help adolescents thrive into adulthood. They offer fifty-five recommendations and examples of how to bring this framework of developmental relationships to adults, parents, teachers, and youth workers. Anyone who works with youth can apply these elements to their work.

While Search Institute conducts research on youth and adolescents, I asked one of the lead researchers on this project, Dr. Eugene Roehlkepartain, if he believed that these five elements of developmental relationships might have broader generational application. He responded, "We haven't researched that yet, but I'm not sure why they couldn't."[17] Later, when interviewing Dr. David Alter for this book,[18] I asked him if he was familiar with Search Institute's developmental relationships framework. Although Search Institute and the clinic that Alter founded are both located in the Minneapolis metropolitan area, there was no reason for him to be aware of this framework, so I brought a copy of the report that described it. Before I was able to ask him if he thought that these developmental rubrics might be applied across other generations, he preempted me by commenting, "I don't see why this framework is limited to adolescents. In fact, this is the kind of work that I do with my clients of all ages [that is, 'challenging growth,' 'expanding possibilities,' etc.]."[19]

Daniel Burrus, an internationally renowned futurist and innovation expert argues that "we are standing at the base of a mountain of disruption and change, that's filled with problems and transformational opportunities as well as the ability to innovate at levels mankind has never before experienced. The speed at which we are all approaching the mountain is increasing at an exponential rate, and the mountain is steep. That means good navigation is a must."[20] One navigational "tool" that we can use to shape disruptive forces into productive outcomes is intergenerational collaboration. Working across generations enables us to use our collective intelligence and perspectives to see together what we are unable to perceive alone.

Shimon Peres, the late prime minister and president of the State of Israel, and Nobel Peace Prize recipient in 1994, died on September 28, 2016. Among his many distinguished accomplishments, this global elder statesman founded the Peres Center for Peace and Innovation. Shortly before his death, he observed,

> Technological progress has created bridges across borders and languages and cultures. We have yet to fully comprehend the opportunities that will continue to grow from this transformational interconnectivity. Yet transformations, however worthy, do not follow a clear path. One cannot forge connections without the prior existence of gaps, but one also cannot forge connections if those gaps are too wide. In today's world, the separation between generations is wider than the separation between nations, and it is the young who now hold the power to create greater global impact than statesmen and generals ever could.[21]

Peres wrote these words when he was ninety-three years old! He maintained remarkable insight into humanity's most pressing issues and he pegged generational divides as one of them. But he also lived and died an optimist, filled with remarkable vision and hope for the ability of ordinary individuals to do extraordinary things, especially when leaders who are entrenched in thinking about issues in only one way make ample space for fresh generational perspectives.

Connecting Generations: A Time to Act

One of my clergy colleagues once told me that he called the time that he and his volunteer leaders used to plan for the future an "advance" instead of a "retreat." I understand why he wanted to project forward movement to his leaders, but in concluding this book, I'd like to retreat in order to advance. I'll return to the assumptions that motivated me to explore how uplifting intergenerational relationships can be and raise some questions that will hopefully advance the desires of even more people to develop or deepen their own intergenerational relationships.

The following is a reminder that the three assumptions that informed my thinking about this book were:

1. We need fulfilling relationships with people our own age and across the generations to lead lives that are rich in meaning and purpose.
2. Social and technological revolutions create powerful waves of isolation that disconnect us from one another.
3. Regardless of age, we're all experiencing a feeling of ongoing disequilibrium, as if we can never adapt quickly enough to the changes swirling around us. Whether you're eighty or twenty-eight years old, if you compare how you're living many aspects of your life today, they are probably different than only a few years ago and are likely to be different a few years from now.

Before I wrote this book, I had a hunch that these assumptions were interrelated, but I wasn't certain that I was correct, nor could I clearly see how they fit into a coherent pattern. I was just left with men's intuition (I'm egalitarian so I can use this phrase). I've learned to accept that I have the kind of curiosity (or obsession) that sometimes leads me down empty rabbit holes, and at other times to unanticipated treasures.[22] Fortunately, in researching this book, my journey was filled with winnings—new people, new ideas, new sources of inspiration, and expanded purpose. As so many people generously shared their perspectives and wisdom, I now understand just how integrally connected these three assumptions are, and I hope that by listening to their stories and ideas you also feel the great potential of intergenerational connections as an uplifting response to the many forces that drive us apart.

We've seen that while the work of creating intergenerational community is difficult, it's possible. To be fully transparent, I'm advocating that this work is more than possible or preferable—it's imperative. Why? Because with six generations of people alive at one time as the new norm, we'll need to reset our thinking about the most precious assets in our communities: our young and our old. Building bridges between young and old is an endeavor that involves all generations because to get across the bridge, you must go through the generations in-between.

So, we're left with two alternatives. The first alternative is to build two incomplete halves of a bridge that aren't far-reaching enough to connect and complete a whole. Alternative 1 will guarantee generational isolation and hostilities because the bridge is useless in this condition and will stand as a reminder of a missed opportunity to create a vital connection, with one generation blaming the other. Alternative 2 is to complete the bridge's sections and make a unique structure that is open for all generational traffic. That's a task that would call forth our deepest capacity for empathy because we would have to make this bridge accessible to people with vastly differing driving abilities and usable for a variety of vehicles. In return, we would not feel as cut off and isolated from one another and we could experience the beauty of intergenerational connections more frequently.

Like the late Nobel Peace Prize winner, Shimon Peres, I'm optimistic about this second alternative based on the stories and insights of those who participated in this research project. I know that we can find new language, metaphors, and frameworks for re-engaging together in the perennial task of harvesting usable wisdom from the past, and challenging assumptions that restrain our ability to create a better world. We don't need anyone's permission to begin that process because we're already empowered to initiate changes in our local communities if we choose. I'm committing to strengthening intergenerational communities as one of my personal top priorities. Will you join me in doing so?

What You Can Do

1. Think big at the local level. Learn about issues and people in your own neighborhood by opening a free account on a platform like Nextdoor. com, whose mission is "to provide a trusted platform where neighbors work together to build stronger, safer, happier communities, all over

the world,"[23] and then decide, preferably with one person from a different generation, upon one intergenerational change that you can make in your neighborhood.

2. Judith Turner, Senior Program Officer for Volunteer Services and Intergenerational Programs at Dorot,[24] noted that "whether we teach children attitudes about aging, they learn them anyway. Children absorb whatever they hear or see about anything, including aging. Through culture, humor, and [relationships with] peers, they form attitudes and adopt values."[25] One of her goals is to create a community that thinks differently about what aging looks like. What negative stereotypes about individuals from other generations do you hold that you are now ready to discard? How will you hold yourself accountable? Will you remain silent when you hear another person stereotype someone by age, or will you try to educate that person about the benefits of working intergenerationally, which begins by discarding age-based stereotypes?

3. For your reflection, I leave you with some wise words from several experts on their vision of an intergenerational community:

- "I think my one learning [in working on intergenerational issues] has been that loneliness is a very real issue that people don't like to acknowledge—reaching out through available networks is a first step in connections. Simplicity of engagement, and easy, clear messaging on safety and enjoyable opportunities, are perhaps critical to network adoption."[26] —Vandana Pant, Senior Director, Design and Innovation at Sutter Health and lead team member of linkAges

- "Throughout our history, our coming together as one America across race, age, and other differences has made our nation stronger. The changes we face today push this narrative like never before."[27] —Donna Butts, Executive Director, Generations United

- "My vision, and our vision for the organization [Dorot], is really being able to improve the health and well-being of not only the older adults that we serve, but the volunteers that we engage, and being able to serve and engage exponentially more people, because it [engagement] provides a certain human touch that you don't get from technology . . . a connection that you don't get from simply speaking over the telephone. [Engagement] provides something which I think is void from so many of our personal existences these days that

it really fills a very, very important niche within the community."[28]
—Mark L. Meridy, Executive Director, Dorot

- "[In an intergenerational community] all people are valued, and not only have something to contribute but are expected to contribute to the common good, and [an intergenerational community is one in] that we change the normative expectation from "retired to play golf" to "retired to move in a different role in the community and still play golf"; and also [intergenerational community] is about the idea that we're not just doing parallel play in communities, where the seniors do good stuff over here, college kids do something over here, but that there are spaces, intentional times, places, and opportunities where seniors, high school kids, and middle-aged people like me, all get a chance to learn from each other, contribute to each other, and work on shared goals and priorities."[29] —Eugene Roehlkepartain, Vice President of Research and Development, Search Institute

4. Finally, I invite you to write your own vision of an intergenerational community and place it in a prominent location as a reminder of your role in helping to create an intergenerational future!

~

Family Technology Action Plan

Prepared by Rhonda K. Hauser, MA, Parenting Coach and Educational Consultant

Overview

The primary purpose for creating a family technology action plan is to establish clear, implementable, and sustainable goals and boundaries for using technological devices with your children. This includes the use of iPhones, iPads, computers, video games, virtual reality, television screens and in-home theaters.

Foundational Principle

Technological devices can serve different purposes: a) passive consumption (i.e., watching a video/movie), b) interactive experiences (i.e., playing a game, taking pictures, reading a book), c) communication (i.e., texting, social media, email), or d) research/work (e.g., homework, Internet search).

A technological device is a *tool*. The use of technological devices in your family should be used to *enhance* an experience or *solve* a problem.

Technological devices should *never* be used as a bribe, punishment, or a quick response to tantrums or boredom.

Action Plan

1. PURPOSE: Begin by considering the purpose for the technological device. Will it enhance an experience or solve a problem? Is it being

used to avoid or prevent something (e.g., prevent a tantrum, prevent boredom)?

2. EXPECTATIONS: Develop and communicate clear expectations (what the device can be used for), guidelines (how and when can the device be used) and boundaries/consequences (how long can a device be used and what happens if there is failure to comply with the expectations and guidelines). Keep the expectations, guidelines, and boundaries consistent and predictable over time.

3. AVOID:
   • Using devices as company or as background noise;
   • Using devices at meals—meals are an important time to establish direct communication skills and build family relationships;
   • Using devices at bedtime—all use of devices should end at least thirty to sixty minutes prior to bedtime;
   • Using devices as a solution to boredom—boredom is an opportunity for children to discover, invent, and create and should be reframed as a time to explore possibilities rather than turning to a device as an easy solution.

4. TECHNOLOGY-FREE: Create a media-free zone in your home where neither children nor adults have access to technological devices.

5. TIME: Limit the time your children engage in technology/media activities on a daily basis (no screen time for children under age 2; 30–60 min/day for children 2–5 yrs; 60–75 min/day for children 6–8 yrs). Be consistent and use resources, if necessary, to assist you in staying consistent (e.g., Kidslox, Screen Time Parental Control, Our Pact).

6. MONITOR: Always accompany your child when they are browsing the Internet and monitor the sites they visit.

7. INTERACTION: Your child learns best from direct human interactions, so whenever possible, interact directly with your child during screen usage.

8. ADDICTION: Watch for signs of technology addiction (e.g., desire for constant tech/media companionship, inability to disengage from device when required to do so, change in sleep patterns or overall behavioral expression).

9. MULTIDIMENSIONAL: Suggest how a child might use a technological device to enhance an experience rather than as just a unidimensional or simple-purpose activity (e.g., go on a nature walk and use an iPhone/iPad to take pictures or record sounds; read a book

together and then on a computer look up other books by same author; help your child research an answer to a question he/she may have).

10. MODEL: Always model appropriate usage of technological devices in front of your children (e.g., put away devices at meals, respect media-free zones in house, refrain from checking your own devices when interacting with your children).

APPENDIX B

~

Health Care Transition Discussion Guide

Prepared by Sherrill Zehr, PhD, RN, Health Care Industry Management Consultant

The following questions are offered as a conversation framework to help uncover some of your own hidden stereotypes, disappointments, and stories that can be present when a loved one's health is declining. Having proactive conversations before a crisis occurs with family members of different generations can increase your self-understanding and preparedness for change, and enable you to identify issues that only an intergenerational perspective can bring to light. It is assumed that the person in declining health as well as the involved family and any support individuals would participate in these conversations as they are able during the ongoing cycles of care.[1]

Declining Health and Mobility

- When I see ____ in declining health, it makes me want to ____.
- During this time, I am afraid for him/her *and* me because ____.
- Because of ____ declining health and not being able to be in her/his usual role in our family, I feel ____.
- How can we help each other deal with the losses that are taking place for each of us (loss of my time, loss of the ability to talk with this person, loss of emotional support once given, loss of my "comfort zone," loss of my day-to-day functioning, loss of my living arrangement)?
- During times of change, I feel respected when ____.
- There are written documents (living will, health care directive, power of attorney, POLST or Physician Orders for Life Sustaining Treatment) that can help define how our loved one wants to be cared for during

declining health. How would having this information early in our discussion help our ability to plan?

Expectations of the Health Care System

- My beliefs and past experiences about the capability of (hospital, assisted living, nursing home, home health, hospice) to do a good job taking care of ____ include ____.
- Because of these beliefs, I see my role in helping ____ transition to multiple levels of care throughout his/her illness as needing to be *minimal, a lot, or overwhelming.*
- Three things the health care system can help us with are ____.
- Will the primary care physician and his/her team be willing to coordinate the care through multiple transitions and specialty appointments? Have we asked him/her to describe this care coordination role to us and how we fit in?
- Do we have a contact person at each transition—the discharging entity and the receiving entity—that we can call any time with questions?
- How can we advocate for ____ during this time of transition? What does that look like?
- What technologies and additional services are available to support care giving? Which ones am I comfortable using?

Expectations of the Family

- What changes are taking place in the way we interact as a family?
- As we go through these changes, what does the "new" reality look like? Feel like?
- The top three priorities in this "new" reality, at least today, are ____.
- Is it OK not to participate in meeting these priorities? How do we come to this decision?
- How do I balance my needs with the needs of others (for example, location of care facility based on family convenience or needs of the individual)?
- What is it like being the one receiving the care rather than the one giving it (for example, a person in declining health now being taken care of by daughter/son)?
- If I need to step up to the plate and take on a new role (for example, a grandson or daughter-in-law becomes caregiver), this makes me feel ____.

- Three areas we as a family/support system handle well include ____.

Evolving Reality

- What have I lost in this new reality (a partner, family member, living situation, control of daily activities, role in family)?
- What have I gained (deeper relationships, greater understanding of declining health challenges, increased insight into my own feelings)?
- Three things that are staying the same are ____.
- Do I have any regrets in this new reality? What are they?
- What has helped or hindered us during this time of constant change?
- What must I continue to do or have to maintain my equilibrium in this evolving reality?

© July 2018 Sherrill Zehr, PhD, RN (sherrill@zbreakthrough.com)

APPENDIX C

~

Individual Experts and Organizational Resources

Prepared by Hayim Herring, PhD

I interviewed thirteen experts on intergenerational issues. Some of them lead organizations whose mission is focused exclusively on fostering intergenerational communities. Others have deep expertise in one specific generational cohort, but their mission is to make connections between members of that generation and other generations. I've also included several private practitioners whose work involves meeting with family members from multiple generations, or with clients who span several generations. I'd like you to learn more about them and their work because I found them to be inspirational and motivational and you may, too.

Prior to writing this book, I only personally knew a few of these experts, some well and others casually. Regardless of any existing relationship, they were equally generous in sharing their expertise and experience. Many of them even asked if we could extend our allotted meeting time, and all of them responded to my additional follow-up questions! If you ever need reassurance that there are many good people in the world who care deeply about individuals of all ages, intergenerational relationships, and the quality of our communities, you'll find them on this list, and in the organizations in which they work.

I encourage you to become familiar with their websites and the abundant resources that they offer, both those that are available for purchase and as complimentary downloads. I have used many resources from these websites in researching this book, but to help you begin, I've highlighted one free downloadable resource, link to a free subscription, or web page with organizational resources. I'm sure that you'll find them valuable, and I encourage you to also share them with friends and family members.

Organizational Experts

Encore.org "is [an] innovation hub tapping the talent of people ages 50+ as a force for good."[1] Expert interviewed: "Marc Freedman, the president and CEO of Encore.org, is a renowned social entrepreneur, thought leader, and writer . . . [and] has pioneered innovative programs and sparked a growing movement in the United States and beyond to tap the talent and experience of people past midlife as a human resource for solving our most vexing social problems."[2] Recommended resource: Gen2Gen, a site filled with ideas on how to mobilize "1 million adults 50+ to help young people thrive,"[3] that has a Top 10 list of intergenerational movies to inspire adults 50+ to mentor in real life.[4]

Generations United "improve[s] the lives of children, youth, and older people through intergenerational collaboration, public policies, and programs for the enduring benefit of all."[5] Expert interviewed: Donna Butts, executive director, is "an internationally sought-after speaker, author and advocate [who] frequently speaks on intergenerational connections, grandparents raising grandchildren and policies effective across the lifespan."[6] Recommended resource: *Creating an Age-Advantaged Community: A Toolkit for Building Intergenerational Communities that Recognize, Engage, and Support All Ages.*[7]

DOROT, Inc. "alleviate[s] social isolation among the elderly and provides services to help them live independently as valued members of the community. DOROT, Inc. serves the Jewish and wider community, bringing the generations together in a mutually beneficial partnership of elders, volunteers and professionals."[8] Experts interviewed: Mark L. Meridy, executive director; Judith Turner, senior program officer for volunteer services and intergenerational programs. Mark has over twenty-five years' experience in non-profit management and administration with expertise in gerontology. In prior nonprofit leadership roles in the field of aging, he has focused on senior housing, case management, and transportation.[9] Judith provides leadership and direction to DOROT's approximately seven thousand volunteers each year. She served a five-year term with Mayor Bloomberg's commission of the Age-Friendly NYC project.[10] Recommended resource: To view a comprehensive list of services and organizations that support elderly individuals, their caregivers, and organizations that work with elderly individuals, please visit http://www.dorotusa.org/site/PageServer?pagename=seniors_resources_D#.W1uCCtVKjIV.[11]

linkAges "is a community that helps members form meaningful connections with people of all ages through rewarding exchanges of abilities and interests. Communities are strengthened as members connect with one another to share and learn skills or to give and receive help. Members earn hours by providing services to other members, and then use those hours to receive services in return. linkAges was created in 2015 by Sutter Health with a goal of creating healthy communities beyond the doctor's office. In 2018, Sutter Health transitioned ownership of linkAges to Help-Full (Help-Full. com). Help-Full's vision is a global community where we help each other age with more joy and vitality."[12] Expert interviewed: Vandana Pant, senior director, design and innovation at Sutter Health. Recommended resource: *Highlights from the linkAges Community Evaluation* (2016).[13]

Search Institute "bridges *research* and *practice* to help young people be and become *their best selves*."[14] Expert interviewed: Eugene Roehlkepartain, PhD, vice president of research and development, "is widely recognized for his expertise in child, youth, and family development in community contexts. He has particular expertise in family strengths and engagement, positive youth development, international youth development, and spiritual development."[15] Recommended resource: *The Developmental Relationships Framework*, where "Search Institute has identified five elements—expressed in 20 specific actions—that make relationships powerful in young people's lives."[16]

Individual Experts

Rabbi Kassel Abelson is rabbi emeritus of Beth El Synagogue in Minnesota. Except for his service as a chaplain in the United States Army Air Corps during World War II and several years serving a congregation in Columbus, Georgia, his association with Beth El began in 1948 as assistant rabbi, and concluded in 1992, when he transitioned from senior rabbi to rabbi emeritus.[17] While in the active rabbinate, he was an innovator in programming from tots to teens, for adults through developing home-based study groups, a prolific writer of Jewish legal opinions on contemporary issues, and an international leader of one of the major Jewish denominations (Conservative Judaism). Among his enduring contributions to the Jewish community, he helped to pave the way for the ordination of female rabbis in the 1980s and, more recently, for gay and lesbian Jews in the 1990s. In the broader community, he was at the forefront of efforts in the United States in improving relations between Christians and Jews, and on the local level with people of color.

Dr. David Alter has "worked in the field of clinical psychology for nearly 30 years. [His] areas of interest and expertise involve brain-behavior relationships (Neuropsychology), mind-body relationships (Health Psychology) and how to treat the various conditions that affect brain, mind, body and soul."[18] Alter "is a founder and Clinical Director of Partners in Healing of Minneapolis [and] . . . has a longstanding interest in a wide range of healing approaches that he utilizes in his therapy work with adult clients. His work emphasizes ways that clients can learn to access and activate inner healing resources. He draws on both western and eastern healing traditions."[19] He is a coauthor of *Staying Sharp: 9 Keys for a Youthful Brain through Modern Science and Ageless Wisdom*.[20] Recommended resource: For more information, visit David's blog at https://www.drdavidalter.com/blog.[21]

Daniel Burrus (www.burrus.com) is "one of the world's leading futurist speakers on global trends and innovation. The *New York Times* has referred to him as one of the top three business gurus in the highest demand as a speaker. He is a strategic advisor to executives from Fortune 500 companies helping them to develop game-changing strategies based on his proven methodologies for capitalizing on technology innovations and their future impact. He is the author of seven books, including best-sellers *Flash Foresight* and *The Anticipatory Organization: Turn Disruption and Change into Opportunity and Advantage*."[22] Recommended resource: For more information, subscribe to Daniel Burrus's newsletter, "Strategic Insights Newsletter: Game Changing Strategies for Shaping the Future."[23]

"Stuart Himmelfarb is a Senior Fellow at NYU's Wagner School of Public Service. He has held professional and volunteer leadership positions in the Jewish community. His encore career at UJA Federation followed twenty-five years in marketing, advertising, media, research and consulting. He co-founded and was president of CollegeTrack, Inc., which became the leading college market research and consulting company, and which he sold to Roper Starch Worldwide."[24] Himmelfarb is also "CEO of B3/The Jewish Boomer Platform, an independent, non-profit initiative dedicated to engaging—or re-engaging—Baby Boomers in Jewish life and to changing the conversation in the Jewish community about aging."[25] Recommended resource: "Service-Learning and Jewish Baby Boomers: An Emerging Opportunity or a Best-Missed Chance."[26]

Susan Link "practices in the areas of estate planning, probate, and trust administration" at Maslon LLP, located in Minneapolis, Minnesota. "She works closely with families to plan the disposition of their assets, both during lifetime and at death, and to accomplish the optimal estate, gift tax, and philanthropic planning for clients through wills, trusts, and other instruments."[27] She was selected for inclusion in the *Best Lawyers in America* 2018; was recognized on the 2017 Top 100 Minnesota Super Lawyers list and the 2017 Top 50 Women Minnesota Super Lawyers list; and was selected as a recipient of a 2018 Hennepin County Bar Association (HCBA) Excellence Award in recognition of her work as a founder and program director of Minnesota Wills for Heroes (WFH) for more than a decade. WFH provides free legal services to the families of the state's First Responders—EMTs, police, firefighters, and more—who daily risk their lives to help others.[28] To learn more about Wills for Heroes, visit http://www.willsforheroes.org.

David Stillman has been researching, writing, consulting, and speaking about the generations in the workplace for organizations and world-renowned Fortune 100 companies, ranging from the IRS to MTV for nearly twenty years. He cofounded Bridgeworks, an organization dedicated to researching, writing, and speaking on generational gaps in the workplace and marketplace, which he later sold. David is an international game-changing entrepreneur, bestselling author, and inspiring presenter. He coauthored the bestsellers *When Generations Collide* and *The M-Factor: How the Millennials Are Rocking the Workplace* and has received distinguished awards including several gold medals at the New York Film Festival and the CLIO Award. David continues to pioneer work in generational trends and translate them into innovative strategies, now with his Gen Z son, Jonah Stillman. As founders of GenZGuru (http://genzguru.com/home), father and son are fostering new generational dialogues, and their ground-breaking book, *Gen Z @ Work*, is the first to introduce Gen Z in the workplace. Recommended resource: Check out their GenZGuru blog at http://genzguru.com/blog.[29]

Sherrill Zehr, PhD, RN (sherrill@zbreakthrough.com) consults with the health care industry to integrate the acute and post-acute systems. As a former psychiatric nurse, college dean, and health system operations director, she brings an academic and practical approach to design and implement initiatives that define the gray areas for patients and families as they navigate the health care continuum. This combined approach supports an accelerated learning process and provides increased insight into process management, communication practices, and behavior.[30]

Notes

Introduction

1. My friends are real but the names that I've used are fictitious.

2. Matthew Clifford and Eva Chiang, "The Great American Principal Turn-over—And How Districts Can Stop the Churn," *RealClear Education* (August 25, 2016), https://www.realcleareducation.com/articles/2016/08/25/the_great_ameri can_principal_turnover_1303.html. The average tenure for high school principals is approximately three years.

3. Jean M. Twenge, "Have Smartphones Destroyed a Generation?" *The Atlantic* (September 2017), https://www.theatlantic.com/magazine/archive/2017/09/has-the -smartphone-destroyed-a-generation/534198/.

4. I interviewed nine Baby Boomers, eight Millennials, and thirteen experts from eleven different organizations (two experts were from the same organization). Experts included one member of the Greatest Generation, Baby Boomers, and Gen Xers.

5. "The Whys and Hows of Generations Research," Pew Research Center (September 3, 2015), http://www.people-press.org/2015/09/03/the-whys-and-hows-of -generations-research/. For the purposes of this book, I use the generational cohort years from the Pew Research Center, although there are some social scientists who demarcate the generations with slight variations. Also, for the purposes of this book, I treat individuals from the Greatest and Silent Generations together, as they have more generational continuity with one another than do other generations, and because this is a small study of relatively active, well, elderly individuals. The names and years of the generations are Millennials (born after 1980–2000); Generation Xers (born 1965–1980); Baby Boomers (born 1946–1964); and the Greatest Generation/Silent Generation (respectively, those born before 1928, and those born from

1928 to 1945). The generally accepted cohort name for individuals born after 2000 is still in flux. Current candidates include "Gen Z," "post-Millennials" and the "i-Gen."

6. Richard Fry, "Millennials Projected to Overtake Baby Boomers as America's Largest Generation," Pew Research Center (March 1, 2018), http://www.pewre search.org/fact-tank/2016/04/25/millennials-overtake-baby-boomers/.

7. "Political Polarization in the American Public: How Increasing Ideological Uniformity and Partisan Antipathy Affect Politics, Compromise and Everyday Life," Pew Research Center (June 12, 2014), http://www.people-press.org/2014/06/12/political-polarization-in-the-american-public/.

8. Richard Fry, Ruth Igielnik, and Eileen Patten, "How Millennials Today Compare with Their Grandparents 50 Years Ago," Pew Research Center (March 16, 2018), http://www.pewresearch.org/fact-tank/2018/03/16/how-millennials-compare-with-their-grandparents/.

9. Ibid. The story of educational progress for Native Americans and racial and ethnic minorities of color was not nearly as rosy, but that subject matter is complex and that is why researchers who focus on economic and educational achievements and disparities of these groups carefully distinguish among them. That kind of research is beyond the scope of this general overview of educational options, but many of the topics and recommendations of this volume are still applicable to all people.

Chapter One

1. Johann Hari, "Everything You Think You Know about Addiction Is Wrong," TEDGlobalLondon video, 14:43, June 2015, https://www.ted.com/talks/johann_hari_everything_you_think_you_know_about_addiction_is_wrong.

2. MedicineNet, "Medical Definition of Epidemic," last modified May 13, 2016, https://www.medicinenet.com/script/main/art.asp?articlekey=3273.

3. Richard C. Dicker et al., *Principles of Epidemiology in Public Health Practice*, 3rd ed. (Atlanta, GA: US Department of Health and Human Services, 2012), https://www.cdc.gov/ophss/csels/dsepd/ss1978/ss1978.pdf.

4. Donna Butts (executive director, Generations United), in discussion with author on November 21, 2017.

5. Vivek H. Murthy, "Work and the Loneliness Epidemic," *Harvard Business Review* (September 2017), https://hbr.org/cover-story/2017/09/work-and-the-loneliness-epidemic. Not included in this series is another article on the loneliness of the CEO: Thomas J. Saporito, "It's Time to Acknowledge CEO Loneliness," *Harvard Business Review* (February 15, 2012), https://hbr.org/2012/02/its-time-to-acknowledge-ceo-lo.

6. Twenge, "Have Smartphones Destroyed a Generation?" (see introduction, n. 3).

7. Generations United and The Eisner Foundation, *I Need You, You Need Me: The Young, the Old, and What We Can Achieve Together*, Executive Summary (May 2017), 2. https://dl2.pushbulletusercontent.com/meKWf8Kr67yddSbALqs18KWN-

NIqQci4I/GU-Exec-Summary-WEB.pdf. This report commissioned an online Harris Poll from February 15 to 17 among 2,171 US adults, ages 18 and above.

8. Eugene Roehlkepartain et al., *Relationships First: Creating Connections That Help Young People Thrive* (Minneapolis, MN: Search Institute, 2017), 2, http://page. search-institute.org/relationships-first-020217a.

9. Leland Kim, "Loneliness Linked to Serious Health Problems and Death among Elderly: UCSF Researchers Find Social Factors Play Major Role in Older Adults' Health," University of California, San Francisco (June 18, 2012), https://www.ucsf.edu/ news/2012/06/12184/loneliness-linked-serious-health-problems-and-death-among -elderly.

10. Sutter Health: Palo Alto Medical Foundation, *Highlights from the link-Ages Community Evaluation* (2016), http://www.mitimebanks.org/wp-content/up-loads/2011/12/linkAges-Community-Evaluation-Highlights.pdf.

11. Dhruv Khullar, "How Social Isolation Is Killing Us," *The New York Times* (December 22, 2016), https://www.nytimes.com/2016/12/22/upshot/how-social-iso-lation-is-killing-us.html?mcubz=0.

12. Laura Entis, "Chronic Loneliness Is a Modern-Day Epidemic," *Fortune* (June 22, 2016), http://fortune.com/2016/06/22/loneliness-is-a-modern-day-epidemic/; Jane E. Brody, "Social Interaction Is Critical for Mental and Physical Health," *The New York Times* (June 12, 2017), https://www.nytimes.com/2017/06/12/well/live/ having-friends-is-good-for-you.html?mcubz=0&_r=3.

13. Emma Seppala and Peter Sims, "The Average American Has Only One Close Friend—Here's How We Got to This Point," *Business Insider* (July 16, 2017), http:// www.businessinsider.com/emma-seppala-the-average-american-has-only-one-close -friend-2017-7.

14. Miller McPherson, Lynn Smith-Lovin, and Matthew E. Brashears, "Social Isolation in America: Changes in Core Discussion Networks over Two Decades," Abstract, *American Sociological Review* (June 1, 2006), http://journals.sagepub.com/ doi/abs/10.1177/000312240607100301?ssource=mfc&rss=1&.

15. Sabrina Tavernise, "U.S. Suicide Rate Surges to a 30-Year High," *New York Times* (April 22, 2016), https://www.nytimes.com/2016/04/22/health/us-suicide-rate-surges-to-a-30-year-high.html.

16. Mitch Prinstein, "Popular People Live Longer," *New York Times* (June 1, 2017), https://www.nytimes.com/2017/06/01/opinion/sunday/popular-people-live-longer .html?mcubz=0&_r=0.

17. Ibid.

18. David DiSalvo, "Loneliness Is a Mind Killer—Study Shows Link to Rapid Cognitive Decline in Older Adults," *Forbes* (July 24, 2015), https://www.forbes. com/sites/daviddisalvo/2015/07/24/loneliness-is-a-mind-killer-study-shows-link-with -rapid-cognitive-decline-in-older-adults/#435600cb7aec.

19. Julianne Holt-Lunstad, Timothy B. Smith, and J. Bradley Layton, "Social Relationships and Mortality Risk: A Meta-Analytic Review," *PLOS Medicine*

(July 27, 2010), http://journals.plos.org/plosmedicine/article?id=10.1371/journal.pmed.1000316.

20. Avshalom Caspi et al., "Socially Isolated Children 20 Years Later: Risk of Cardiovascular Disease," *Archives of Pediatrics & Adolescent Medicine* 160, no. 8 (2006): 805–811, doi: 10.1001/archpedi.160.8.805.

21. Khullar, "Social Isolation."

22. Brody, "Social Interaction."

23. Rakesh Kochhar and Anthony Cillufo, "How Wealth Inequality Has Changed in the U.S. Since the Great Recession, by Race, Ethnicity and Income," Pew Research Center (November 1, 2017), http://www.pewresearch.org/fact-tank/2017/11/01/how-wealth-inequality-has-changed-in-the-u-s-since-the-great-recession-by-race-ethnicity-and-income/.

24. Thomas L. Friedman, *Thank You for Being Late: An Optimist's Guide to Thriving in the Age of Accelerations* (New York: Farrar, Straus and Giroux, 2016), 27–35.

25. WP Master, "99Designs x WP Master," 2018, https://wpmaster.com/99designs-x-wp-master/.

26. Richard Fry, "It's Becoming More Common for Young Adults to Live at Home—and for Longer Stretches," Pew Research Center (May 5, 2017), http://www.pewresearch.org/fact-tank/2017/05/05/its-becoming-more-common-for-young-adults-to-live-at-home-and-for-longer-stretches/. Only very recently, it appears that more Millennials are beginning to purchase homes. See, for example, Barry Ritholtz, "Millennials Are Out of the Basement and Into Buying Homes," *Bloomberg Opinion* (February 2, 2018), https://www.bloomberg.com/view/articles/2018-02-02/millennials-are-out-of-the-basement-and-into-buying-homes.

27. Alzheimer's Association, "2017 Alzheimer's Disease Facts and Figures," *Alzheimer's & Dementia* 13 (2017): 325–373, https://www.alz.org/documents_custom/2017-facts-and-figures.pdf. Current estimates in the United States are that approximately 10 percent of adults who are sixty-five and older have Alzheimer's dementia, a figure that rises to close to 40 percent of adults who are eighty-five and older; "Quick Facts," Alzheimer's Association, 2018, https://www.alz.org/facts/. In other words, given the size of the Baby Boomer population, approximately every 66 seconds someone in the United States develops Alzheimer's dementia.

28. National PACE Association, "Is PACE for You?" 2018, http://www.npaonline.org/pace-you#History.

29. United Hospital Fund, "NORC Blueprint: A Guide to Community Action," 2015, http://www.norcblueprint.org/faq/.

30. Ibid.

31. Katherine A. Ornstein et al., "Epidemiology of the Homebound Population in the United States," *JAMA Internal Medicine* 175, no. 7 (2015): 1,180–1,186, https://jamanetwork.com/journals/jamainternalmedicine/fullarticle/2296016?resultClick=3.

32. Marc Freedman, personal interview with author, January 19, 2018.

33. Ibid.

34. While I use the terms "digital media" and "social media" interchangeably throughout this book, digital media encompasses the full range of capabilities that we have to be our own creators of content (film, music, podcasts; not only blogs) and experiences through augmented and virtual reality technologies, and our own manufacturers of products through technologies like 3-D printing. Baby Boomers may be more familiar with the term "social media" and identify it with social media sites like Facebook and LinkedIn. While "digital media" may be a less familiar term to them, it more accurately conveys a fuller landscape of possibilities that younger generations already experience.

35. Jana Riess, "The Bible in Emojis? Terrific Idea, Sloppy Execution," *Religion News Service* (June 1, 2016), https://religionnews.com/2016/06/01/the-bible-in-emojis-terrific-idea-sloppy-execution/.

36. "Number of Apps Available in Leading App Stores as of 1st Quarter 2018," Statistica (2018), https://www.statista.com/statistics/276623/number-of-apps-available-in-leading-app-stores/.

37. Sherry Turkle, *Reclaiming Conversation: The Power of Talk in a Digital Age* (New York: Penguin Press, 2015), 21.

38. Ibid., 21–22.

39. "Mobile Fact Sheet," Pew Research Center (February 5, 2018), http://www.pewinternet.org/fact-sheet/mobile/.

40. Victoria Rideout, *The Common Sense Census: Media Use by Kids Age Zero to Eight* (San Francisco: Common Sense Media, 2017), https://www.commonsensemedia.org/sites/default/files/uploads/research/0-8_executivesummary_release_final_1.pdf.

41. "Your Eyes Really Are the Window to Your Soul," *Psychology Today* (December 31, 2015), https://www.psychologytoday.com/blog/talking-apes/201512/your-eyes-really-are-the-window-your-soul.

42. Twenge, "Have Smartphones Destroyed a Generation?"

43. Ibid.

44. Ibid.

45. Ibid.

46. "Mobile Fact Sheet," Pew Research Center (February 5, 2018), http://www.pewinternet.org/fact-sheet/mobile/.

47. Twenge, "Have Smartphones Destroyed a Generation?"

48. Keith Wilbert, personal interview with author, January 31, 2018.

49. Turkle, *Reclaiming Conversation*.

50. Linda Archer, personal interview with author, December 1, 2017.

51. Ibid.

52. Ibid.

53. David Alter, personal interviews with author, November 8 and December 6, 2017.

54. Better Angels, 2017, https://www.better-angels.org; Civil Conversations Project, 2018, http://www.civilconversationsproject.org. While this is not a personal endorsement, see these websites for examples.

Chapter Two

1. English Oxford Living Dictionaries, s. v. "entitled," accessed June 10, 2018, https://en.oxforddictionaries.com/definition/entitled.

2. I also had approximately five additional less structured conversations with Millennials, and seven less structured conversations with Baby Boomers.

3. Sutter Health, "linkAges Community Evaluation"; and Roehlkepartain et al., *Relationships First.*

4. Shabbat 89b.

5. Actually, it was my colleague's mother who relayed this suggestion and as I'd like to continue my friendship with both of them, I'm exercising discretion in not revealing their names.

6. Fry, Igielnik, and Patten, "Millennials Today."

7. Lydia R. Anderson, "Generational Differences during Young Adulthood: Families and Households of Baby Boomers and Millennials," *Family Profiles* (Bowling Green, OH: National Center for Family and Marriage Research, 2017), https://www.bgsu.edu/ncfmr/resources/data/family-profiles/anderson-families-households-boomers-millennials-fp-17-07.html.

8. Ibid.

9. Joseph Campbell with Bill Moyers, *The Power of Myth* (New York: Anchor Books, 1991), 120.

10. Jack Weinberg, interview with *San Francisco Chronicle* reporter, November 1964, at University of California–Berkeley. This quote is often incorrectly attributed to social activist, Jerry Rubin, but it was most like first said by Jack Weinberg, another social activist and organizer of the "Free Speech Movement."

11. Linda Archer, personal interview with author, December 1, 2017.

12. For a more erudite explanation than I have provided, just search the Internet for the term, "adulting," and many online book retailers will be happy to sell you several volumes on this topic.

13. Rachel Nunez, personal interview with author, October 29, 2017.

14. Sharri Bear, personal interview with author, October 25, 2017.

15. This refrain is from the song "I Won't Grow Up"—one of the more famous songs of the Broadway musical, *Peter Pan*, first produced on Broadway in 1954.

16. Sandra Petrowski, personal interview with author, November 10, 2017.

17. Ellen Roos, personal interview with author, November 8, 2017.

18. Sam Baglioni, personal interview with author, October 25, 2017.

19. Allan Sherman, personal interview with author, November 11, 2017.

20. Gary Harper, personal interview with author, October 25, 2017.

21. Angela Krintz, personal interview with author, November 22, 2017. Angela's suggestion about how problematic an overabundance of choice can be was already well-documented by social psychologist Barry Schwartz in the first edition of his book, *The Paradox of Choice: Why More is Less* (New York: HarperCollins Publishers Inc., 2003).

22. For more information about the concept of emerging adulthood, check out Jeffrey Jensen Arnett's book *Emerging Adulthood: The Winding Road from the Late Teens through the Twenties* (New York: Oxford University Press, 2015).

23. Meg Jay, "Why 30 Is Not the New 20," TED2013, video, 14:46, February 2013, https://www.ted.com/talks/meg_jay_why_30_is_not_the_new_20.

24. Sam Baglioni, personal interview with author, October 25, 2017.

25. Rachel Nunez, personal interview with author, October 29, 2017.

26. Keith Wilbert, personal interview with author, January 31, 2018.

27. Jack Jones, personal interview with author, December 22, 2017.

28. Keith Wilbert, personal interview with author, January 31, 2018.

29. Ibid.

30. Gary Harper, personal interview with author, October 25, 2017.

31. Sam Baglioni, personal interview with author, October 25, 2017.

32. Ellen Roos, personal interview with author, November 8, 2017.

33. Rachel Nunez, personal interview with author, October 29, 2017.

34. Linda Archer, personal interview with author, December 1, 2017.

35. Billy Thane, personal interview with author, November 3, 2017.

36. Rachel Nunez, personal interview with author, October 29, 2017.

37. Jingjing Jiang, "Millennials Stand Out for Their Technology Use, But Older Generations Also Embrace Digital Life," Pew Research Center (May 2, 2018), http://www.pewresearch.org/fact-tank/2018/05/02/millennials-stand-out-for-their-technology-use-but-older-generations-also-embrace-digital-life/.

38. Jerry Seinfeld, "The Old Man," *Seinfeld*, season 4, episode 17, directed by Tom Cherones, aired February 18, 1993 (Los Angeles, CA: Castle Rock Entertainment, 1993).

39. Gary Harper, personal interview with author, October 25, 2017.

40. Keith Wilbert, personal interview with author, January 31, 2018.

41. John Jolet, personal interview with author, November 3, 2017.

42. Angela Krintz, personal interview with author, November 22, 2017.

43. Billy Thane, personal interview with author, November 3, 2017.

44. Rachel Nunez, personal interview with author, October 29, 2017.

Chapter Three

1. Quoted in David Remnick, "Leonard Cohen Makes It Darker," *New Yorker* (October 17, 2016), https://www.newyorker.com/magazine/2016/10/17/leonard-cohen-makes-it-darker.

2. Michael Dimock, "Defining Generations: Where Millennials End and Post-Millennials Begin," Pew Research Center (March 1, 2018), http://www.pewresearch.org/fact-tank/2018/03/01/defining-generations-where-millennials-end-and-post-millennials-begin/.

3. Skylar Werde, "Early Boomers + Generation Jones: Meet the Two Boomer Subgroups," *Bridgeworks* (blog), November 9, 2015, http://www.generations.com/2015/11/09/early-boomers-generation-jones-meet-the-two-boomer-subgroups/.

4. Harry Chapin, vocal performance of "Cat's in the Cradle," by Sandy Chapin and Harry Chapin, released on January 1, 1974, on *Verities & Balderdash*, Warner/Chappell Music, Inc., 1974, compact disc.

5. The following is the author's recommendation made in consultation with the author's daughter, Tamar Krivosha: To maintain a healthy relationship when your child is ready to learn how to drive, strongly consider asking a trusted friend to teach your child or invest in a few private driving lessons as an alternative to being your child's driving instructor. It's a much better option than debriefing with your child after a practice run on a major highway with a fifty-five-mile-per-hour speed limit—this is not a good time to doubt your ability to merge lanes, and then to illustrate the point by removing both hands from the steering wheel, thrusting them in the air for dramatic effect, and screaming, "I can't do it."

6. Erik Sherman, "Why Millennials Boomerang Home: It's Not Student Loans. It's Worse," *Forbes* (January 11, 2017), https://www.forbes.com/sites/er iksherman/2017/01/11/why-millennials-boomerang-home-its-not-student-loans-its -worse/#5677e5a45d86.

7. "Grandfamilies Statistics," Generations United, accessed June 21, 2018, http:// www2.gu.org/OURWORK/Grandfamilies/GrandfamiliesStatistics.aspx. Grandfami- lies are families headed by grandparents and other relatives who are sharing their homes with their grandchildren, nieces, nephews, and/or other related children. Some grandfamilies are multigenerational households where a parent works long hours and wants the child close to family while he or she is at work. However, no parents are present in more than a third of grandfamily households. Grandparents stepped in to provide care when their parents could not care for the children.

8. "Older Drivers Set Record for Second Year: Licensed Drivers over 65 Con- tinue to Increase, Teen Drivers Remain at Near-Record Lows," US Department of Transportation, last modified November 27, 2017, https://www.transportation.gov/ briefing-room/fhwa2017.

9. I'm seriously considering codifying that in my will that "the family cell phone plan" does not extend to grandchildren. But I'm counting on cell phones being replaced by implantable chips that will enable us to be our own mobile communica- tions devices.

10. Fry, "Live at Home."

11. Gary Harper, personal interview with author, October 25, 2017.

12. Ibid.

13. Robin Marantz Henig, "The Age of Grandparents Is Made of Many Trag- edies," *Atlantic* (June 1, 2018), https://www.theatlantic.com/family/archive/2018/06/ this-is-the-age-of-grandparents/561527/.

14. Wright, "8 Modern In-Law Units," *Dwell* (May 13, 2017), https://www.dwell .com/article/8-modern-in-law-units-12c75f54. An Accessible Dwelling Unit (ADU) is defined as having a second small dwelling that sits on the same property as a regular single-family house, or is attached to it. Typically, these take on the form of an apart- ment over the garage, a tiny house on a foundation in the backyard, or a basement apartment. For a comprehensive overview of ADUs, you can visit the website of the American Association of Retired Persons (AARP) at www.aarp.org, or consult the following article on AARP.org: Rodney Harrell, "Creating Room for Accessory

Dwelling Units," AARP (November, 2017), www.aarp.org/livable-communities/housing/info-2015/accessory-dwelling-units-model-ordinance.html.

15. Jack Jones, personal interview with author, December 22, 2017.

16. "Wills For Heroes," Minnesota State Bar Association, accessed June 21, 2018, https://www.mnbar.org/about-msba/related-organizations/wills-for-heroes#.WyJzSad Kg2w. Wills for Heroes currently operates in twenty-seven states.

17. Susan Link, personal interview with author, December 26, 2017. Susan is an attorney at Maslon LLP in Minneapolis, MN.

18. "Grandfamilies," Generations United, accessed June 21, 2018, https://www.gu.org/explore-our-topics/grandfamilies/.

19. Ibid.

20. Generations United, *Raising the Children of the Opioid Epidemic: Solutions and Support for Grandfamilies*, accessed June 21, 2018, https://dl2.pushbulletusercontent.com/qdCNUO2JMMZKzKRjyIlwbgjMtf39xkKa/16-Report-SOGF-Final.pdf.

21. "Grandfamilies," Generations United.

22. Rachel Botsman, "Co-Parenting with Alexa," *New York Times* (October 7, 2017), https://www.nytimes.com/2017/10/07/opinion/sunday/children-alexa-echo-robots.html?action=click&pgtype=Homepage&clickSource=story-heading&module=region&region=region&WT.nav=region&_r=0.

23. Ibid.

24. Anya Kamenetz, "Our Screenless Future Calls for Augmented Parenting," Fast Company (January 29, 2018), https://www.fastcompany.com/40478880/our-screenless-future-calls-for-augmented-parenting.

25. Rhonda Hauser, personal interview with author, June 14, 2018. Hauser owns a private parenting and educational consulting practice. You can learn more about her work at http://aleapofaction.com.

26. Ibid.

27. Ibid.

28. Ibid.

29. Dorothy A. Miller, "The 'Sandwich' Generation: Adult Children of the Aging," *Social Work* 26, no. 5 (1981), 419–23, https://www.jstor.org/stable/23712207?seq=1#page_scan_tab_contents.

30. Priscilla Quentin, personal interview with author, December 6, 2017.

31. Ibid.

32. Ibid.

33. Ibid.

34. Sam Baglioni, personal interview with author, October 25, 2017.

35. Linda Archer, personal interview with author, December 1, 2017; "Living Wills and Advance Directives for Medical Decisions," Mayo Clinic, last modified November 11, 2014, https://www.mayoclinic.org/healthy-lifestyle/consumer-health/in-depth/living-wills/art-20046303. Living wills and other advance directives are written, legal instructions regarding your preferences for medical care if you are unable to make decisions for yourself. Advance directives guide choices for doctors and

caregivers if you're terminally ill, seriously injured, in a coma, in the late stages of dementia, or near the end of life.

36. Kass Abelson, personal interview with author, January 23, 2018.

37. "Just-in-Time," Toyota, accessed June 21, 2018, http://www.toyota-global .com/company/vision_philosophy/toyota_production_system/just-in-time.html.

38. For more resources on limiting your kids' interaction with technology, check out the following websites: https://www.zerotothree.org/, https://www.commonsense media.org, and https://www.naeyc.org.

39. Susan Link, personal interview with author, December 26, 2017.

40. For more information on grandfamilies, visit http://www.gu.org.

41. If you'd like to volunteer, check out these organizations: https://www.search -institute.org/, https://encore.org/, http://www.help-full.com/about-us/index.html, and www.dorotusa.org.

Chapter Four

1. Donna Butts, personal interview with author, November 21, 2017.

2. Note: communities can also perpetrate base acts and are not inherently good or evil. In using the word "community" in this chapter, I'm referring to altruistic communities.

3. Norman V. Peale, "Confident Living," *Greensboro Daily News*, February 15, 1959.

4. Hayim Herring and Terri Martinson Elton, *Leading Congregations and Nonprofits in a Connected World: Platforms, People, and Purpose* (Lanham, MD: Rowman & Littlefield, 2017), 9–14; 21–42.

5. Later, I'll share their views on whether they believe that this service should be mandatory or incentivized.

6. Robert D. Putnam, *Bowling Alone: The Collapse and Revival of American Community* (New York: Simon and Schuster, 2001), 402.

7. Thomas H. Sander and Robert D. Putnam, "Still Bowling Alone? The Post-9/11 Split," *Journal of Democracy* 21, no. 1 (2010): 9–16, doi: 10.1353/jod.0.0153.

8. John Jolet, personal interview with author, November 3, 2017.

9. Celia Dent, personal interview with author, November 29, 2017.

10. Hunter Weiss, personal interview with author, January 25, 2018.

11. Ibid.

12. Linda Archer, personal interview with author, December 1, 2017.

13. Angela Krintz, personal interview with author, November 22, 2017.

14. Allan Sherman, personal interview with author, November 11, 2017.

15. Rachel Nunez, personal interview with author, October 29, 2017.

16. Herring and Elton, *Leading Congregations*. In addition to our recent study and publication, I've worked with several hundred Jewish congregations or spiritual communities and rabbis for over thirty years.

17. "Ray Oldenburg," Project for Public Spaces, last modified December 31, 2008, accessed July 19, 2018, https://www.pps.org/article/roldenburg.

18. Ibid.

19. Many congregations have one-off programs in which multiple generations mingle, but that is not the same as sustained intergenerational programming, or having a standing intergenerational committee that can address issues that are of interest or concern to multiple generations, like education, community service, and spirituality.

20. Linda Archer, personal interview with author, December 1, 2017.

21. Gary Harper, personal interview with author, October 25, 2017.

22. James Hollis, *Finding Meaning in the Second Half of Life* (New York: Gotham Books, 2005), 188.

23. Donna Butts, personal interview with author, November 21, 2017.

24. Marc Freedman, personal interview with author, January 19, 2018.

25. "Frequently Asked Questions," Nesterly, accessed July 19, https://www.nest erly.io/faq.

26. Judson Manor is a facility of Judson Services, Inc., which "is a not-for-profit, interdenominational organization . . . [that offers] independent living, assisted living, memory support services, short-term rehabilitative and long-term skilled nursing care, community memberships, outreach initiatives, and home care options." "About Us," Judson, accessed July 19, 2018, https://www.judsonsmartliving.org/about.

27. Marc Freedman, personal interview with author, January 19, 2018.

28. Ibid.

29. You can watch the full video describing this experiment at https://www.jud sonsmartliving.org/about/intergenerational-programs/.

30. Marc Freedman, personal interview with author, January 19, 2018.

31. "Music Students Living at Cleveland Retirement Home," CBC News video, 10:37, posted on July 12, 2016, https://www.cbc.ca/news/thenational/music-students -living-at-cleveland-retirement-home-1.3311116.

32. Ibid.

33. Ibid.

34. Also, see chapter 5, where I describe a trend in the housing market to build housing for seniors on or near college campuses or through partnerships with housing developers.

35. "Age-Friendly Cities and Communities," World Health Organization, accessed July 19, 2018, http://www.who.int/ageing/projects/age-friendly-cities-commu nities/en/.

36. Mickey Hull, personal interview with author, October 4, 2017.

37. Mark L. Meridy, personal interview with author, October 17, 2017.

38. Vandana Pant, personal interview with author, September 29, 2017.

39. Eugene Roehlkepartain, personal interview with author, October 20, 2017.

40. Ibid.

41. Marc Freedman, personal interview with author, January 19, 2018.

42. Allison H. Fine, *Matterness: Fearless Leadership for a Social World* (Legacy Books, LLC: 2014).

Chapter Five

1. Yuval Noah Harari, *Sapiens: A Brief History of Humankind* (London: Vintage Books, 2014), 22–44.

2. Ibid., 23.

3. Ibid., 41.

4. Ibid., 41–44.

5. Nikki Graf, "Today's Young Workers are More Likely than Ever to Have a Bachelor's Degree," Pew Research Center (May 16, 2016), http://www.pewresearch .org/fact-tank/2017/05/16/todays-young-workers-are-more-likely-than-ever-to-have-a-bachelors-degree/.

6. "A Survey of the GenForward Project at the University of Chicago," Gen Forward, accessed June 28, 2018, https://genforwardsurvey.com/.

7. "GenForward: Millennials' Political Views," GenForward, September 12, 2017, https://genforwardsurvey.com/assets/uploads/2017/09/GenForward-Education -Survey-Fact-Sheet.pdf.

8. Janet Nguyen and David Brancaccio, "Do Millennials Think College Is Worth the Cost?" *Kera News* (October 3, 2017), http://keranews.org/post/do-Millennials -think-college-worth-cost.

9. Ibid. (emphasis mine)

10. Digital Learning Compass, "Distance Education Enrollment Report 2017," accessed July 1, 2018, http://onlinelearningsurvey.com/reports/digtiallearningcom passenrollment2017info.pdf.

11. "Rising Student Debt Weighs Heavily on Millennials: Student Debt Jumps 150 Percent," The Center for Generational Kinetics (September 18, 2017), http:// genhq.com/rising-student-debt-weighs-heavily-Millennials/.

12. Ron Lieber, "A Game to Help Students Pay the Right Price for College," *New York Times* (September 29, 2017), https://www.nytimes.com/2017/09/29/your -money/paying-for-college/payback-college-loans.html.

13. Ibid.

14. For more information, visit www.Coursera.org and www.edX.org.

15. Gwen Moran, "Employers like EY and IBM Are Now Hiring Workers with out College Degrees," Fast Company (May 15, 2018), https://www.fastcompany .com/40565547/why-some-companies-are-dropping-degree-requirements-in-hiring.

16. For more information, visit www.linkedin.com/learning, https://www.mind tools.com/community/index.php, or www.udacity.com.

17. Friedman, *Thank You for Being Late*, 213–219.

18. Ibid., 218.

19. Ibid.

20. Here is an excerpt of my private message exchange with Josh on LinkedIn, which he gave me permission to use: "Hi, Josh—I'm writing a book on the value of intergenerational relationships. I honestly thought you were much older from your profile. How would you feel about my using our exchange as an example of Gen Z/ post-Millennials being entrepreneurial?"

21. Josh Miller, LinkedIn, accessed July 1, 2018, https://www.linkedin.com/in/joshmillerceo/.

22. Ibid.

23. Rochelle Olson, "In Hiring of Teenage Consultant, Vikings Take Long-Term View of Fan Base," *StarTribune* (September 15, 2017), http://www.startribune.com/minnesota-vikings-hire-18-year-old-to-connect-with-gen-z/444200463/.

24. David Stillman and Jonah Stillman, *Gen Z @ Work: How the Next Generation Is Transforming the Workplace* (New York: Harper Business, 2017).

25. Patrick Redford, "Vikings Hire Teen Consultant to Teach Them How to Be Cool," *Deadspin* (September 13, 2017), https://deadspin.com/vikings-hire-teen-consultant-to-teach-them-how-to-be-co-1806527641.

26. One day, I might describe my brief stint working side-by-side with Nebraska Cornhusker football players doing road construction. They had a good sense of humor as they watched me struggle to remove a manhole cover from a street. "Impossible," I declared, after trying for about ten minutes, until I watched one of them walk calmly toward it and lift it without breaking a sweat.

27. "Entrepreneur of the Week: Emma Yang, Timeless," The Longevity Network (March 1, 2017), https://www.longevitynetwork.org/exclusive/entrepreneur-of-the-week-emma-yang-timeless/.

28. Jonathan Wai, "The Myth of the College Dropout," *CBS News* (April 21, 2017), https://www.cbsnews.com/news/the-myth-of-the-college-dropout/. One tech mogul, Peter Thiel, even started The Thiel Fellowship which is "a two-year, $100,000 grant for young people who want to build new things instead of sit in a classroom." To learn more, visit "FAQ," Thiel Fellowship, accessed July 1, 2018, http://thielfellowship.org/faq.

29. Rachel Nunez, personal interview with author, October 29, 2017.

30. Allan Sherman, personal interview with author, November 11, 2017.

31. Gary Harper, personal interview with author, October 25, 2017.

32. Joseph Pimentel, "College Students, Boomers Now Neighbors as Senior Housing Goes Up Near Universities," Bisnow (January 3, 2018), https://www.bisnow.com/national/news/senior-housing/is-building-senior-housing-next-to-universities-the-next-big-housing-trend-in-the-us-83208.

33. Machine learning and neural networks haven't produced the kind of music and poetry that are comparable to the most brilliant composers and poets yet. But work has been underway to give Mozart and Shakespeare a run for their money. For example, see Kyle McDonald, "Neural Nets for Generating Music," Artists and Machine Intelligence (August 25, 2017), https://medium.com/artists-and-machine-intelligence/neural-nets-for-generating-music-f46dffac21c0, and "Human or Machine: Can You Tell Who Wrote These Poems?" *NPR* (June 27, 2016), https://www.npr.org/sections/alltechconsidered/2016/06/27/480639265/human-or-machine-can-you-tell-who-wrote-these-poems.

34. "The Day I Got Microchipped," Fast Company (January 23, 2018), video, https://www.fastcompany.com/video/the-day-i-got-microchipped/CZ2x7ukV.

Chapter Six

1. Country Music Hall of Fame musician, Dolly Parton, composed and sang the hit song, "9 to 5" in 1980, that captured especially for female secretaries the grind of daily work and the failure of the men whom they supported to recognize their talent.

2. Lynne C. Lancaster and David Stillman, *When Generations Collide: Who They Are, Why They Crash, How to Solve the Generational Puzzle at Work* (New York: HarperCollins, 2002).

3. Lynne C. Lancaster and David Stillman, *The M-Factor: How the Millennial Generation is Rocking the Workplace* (New York: HarperBusiness, 2010).

4. David Stillman, personal interview with author, October 19, 2017.

5. Stillman and Stillman, *Gen Z @ Work: How the Next Generation is Transforming the Workplace* (New York: HarperBusiness, 2017).

6. David Stillman, personal interview with author, October 19, 2017.

7. Liz Spayd, "As Recession Forces Layoffs, Older Workers Feel Targeted; Area, Nation Have Rise in Bias Complaints," *Washington Post*, September 29, 1992, https://www.highbeam.com/doc/1P2-1027461.html. Spayd reported that "the jobless rate among the 55-and-over group has almost doubled since the recession began in the spring of 1990, from 2.8 percent to 5.4 percent."

8. See Office of the United States Trade Representative, "North American Free Trade Agreement (NAFTA)," accessed July 4, 2018, https://ustr.gov/trade-agreements/free-trade-agreements/north-american-free-trade-agreement-nafta, and Chad P. Bown, "What Is NAFTA, and What Would Happen to U.S. Trade without It?" *Washington Post*, May 18, 2017, https://www.washingtonpost.com/news/monkey-cage/wp/2017/02/15/what-is-nafta-and-what-would-happen-to-u-s-trade-without-it/?utm_term=.65b83e042cde for further explanation of NAFTA, the trade benefits it offered, and how unions and the United States government have viewed its advantages and disadvantages.

9. World Trade Organization, "The WTO," accessed February 11, 2018, https://www.wto.org/english/thewto_e/thewto_e.htm.

10. "Mobile Fact Sheet," Pew Research Center (February 5, 2018), http://www.pewinternet.org/fact-sheet/mobile.

11. Gianpiero Petriglieri, "The Portable Man is the New 'Organization Man,'" *Harvard Business Review* (August 10, 2017), https://hbr.org/2017/08/the-portable-leader-is-the-new-organization-man.

12. Gianpiero Petriglieri, Jennifer Louise Petriglieri, and Jack Denfeld Wood, "Fast Tracks and Inner Journeys: Crafting Portable Selves for Contemporary Careers," *Administrative Science Quarterly* (July 12, 2017), doi:10.1177/0001839217720930.

13. Ibid.

14. Noam Scheiber, "The Pop Up Employer: Build a Team, Do the Job, Say Goodbye," *New York Times* (July 12, 2017), https://www.nytimes.com/2017/07/12/business/economy/flash-organizations-labor.html?emc=eta1.

15. Ibid.

16. Companies such as these provide high-quality developers, designers, consultants, and more to individuals or companies. For more information, visit https://gigster.com, https://businesstalentgroup.com/, and https://99designs.com/.

17. "4D Printing: Revolutionizing Material Form and Control," Stratasys, accessed February 13, 2018, http://www.stratasys.com/industries/education/research/4d-printing-project. Stratasys, a leader in 3D printing, is collaborating with the Massachusetts Institute of Technology's Self-Assembly Lab on 4D printing to develop the next stage of rapid prototyping, using new materials that enable objects to change over time with built-in self-programmed functions.

18. Kevin Granville, "How to Manage Your Career," *New York Times* (January 28, 2018), https://www.nytimes.com/guides/business/manage-your-career.

19. Amy Adkins, "Millennials: The Job-Hopping Generation," Gallup Business Journal (May 12, 2016), https://news.gallup.com/businessjournal/191459/millennials-job-hopping-generation.aspx.

20. David Stillman, personal interview with author, November 1, 2017.

21. Ibid.

22. Ibid.

23. Daniel Burrus, *The Anticipatory Organization: Turn Disruption and Change into Opportunity and Advantage* (Austin, TX: Greenleaf Book Group Press, 2017), 23.

24. Ibid., 21.

25. Daniel Burrus, personal interview with author, June 27, 2018.

26. Jack Jones, personal interview with author, December 22, 2017.

27. Keith Wilbert, personal interview with author, January 31, 2018.

28. Information regarding these contrasting working environments are based on the following sources: "Here's Why Your Parents Stayed at the Same Job for 20 Years," Associated Press (May 10, 2016), http://fortune.com/2016/05/10/baby-boomers-millennials-jobs/; Andrew Dugan and Bailey Nelson, "3 Trends That Will Disrupt Your Workplace Forever," Gallup Business Journal (June 8, 2017), https://news.gallup.com/businessjournal/211799/trends-disrupt-workplace-forever.aspx; Brandon Rigoni and Bailey Nelson, "Few Millennials Are Engaged at Work," Gallup Business Journal (August 30, 2016), https://news.gallup.com/businessjournal/195209/few-millennials-engaged-work.aspx?utm_source=link_newsv9&utm_campaign=item_211799&utm_medium=copy; Kevin Granville, "How to Manage Your Career," https://www.nytimes.com/guides/business/manage-your-career.

29. For more information, visit https://www.roam.co/, https://www.welive.com/, and https://www.wework.com/.

30. Hunter Weiss, personal interview with author, January 25, 2018.

31. Jack Jones, personal interview with author, December 22, 2017 (emphasis mine).

32. Gary Harper, personal interview with author, October 25, 2017.

33. Robert S. Kaplan and David P. Norton, "The Balanced Scorecard—Measures that Drive Performance," *Harvard Business Review* (January-February 1992), accessed on July 5, 2018, https://hbr.org/1992/01/the-balanced-scorecard-measures-that-drive-performance-2.

34. James Freund, "A Retirement Scorecard," *Delaware Lawyer* 24, no. 2 (2006): 8–11, http://delawarebarfoundation.org/delawyer/Volume_24_Number_2_Summer _2006.pdf.

35. Ibid., 10.

36. Ibid.

37. Ibid.

38. U.S. Census Bureau, "Sixty-Five Plus in the United States," U.S. Department of Commerce, last modified October, 31, 2011, https://www.census.gov/population/ socdemo/statbriefs/agebrief.html.

39. Sally Abrahms, "Five Myths about Baby Boomers," *Washington Post* (November 6, 2015), https://www.washingtonpost.com/opinions/five-myths-about-baby -boomers/2015/11/06/44ca943c-83fb-11e5-8ba6-cec48b74b2a7_story.html?utm_term= .d64411cacf4e.

40. Visit http://agewave.com/. If you click on the "What We Do" tab, you'll find a list of reports and publications that speak to the financial, educational, recreational, and emotional aspects of retirement. Also check out https://www.aarp.org/.

41. For more information, visit http://www.pewresearch.org/ and https://www .gallup.com/home.aspx.

42. For more information, visit https://www.gradifi.com/. (This is not an endorsement of Gradifi or any other company but an illustration of the changing meaning of employee benefits.)

43. Lili Hall, personal interview with author, May 3, 2018. Hall is president and CEO of Knock, Inc., "an independent full-experience creative agency driven by design and powered with meaning" ("What We Do," Knock, Inc., accessed July 4, 2018, https://knockinc.com/about/).

44. Lili Hall, personal interview with author, May 3, 2018.

45. Ibid.

Chapter Seven

1. Again, Gen Z or post-Millennials, Millennials, Gen Xers, Baby Boomers, the Silent Generation, and the Greatest Generations.

2. Angelo Eliades, "Perennial Plants and Permaculture," Permaculture Research Institute (June 6, 2012), https://permaculturenews.org/2012/06/06/perennial-plants -and-permaculture/.

3. "Annual, Perennial, Biennial?" Wildflowers in Bloom, accessed January 24, 2018, https://aggie-horticulture.tamu.edu/wildseed/growing/annual.html.

4. Christopher L. Kukk, *The Compassionate Achiever: How Helping Others Fuels Success* (New York: HarperOne, 2017).

5. Christopher Kukk, "Survival of the Fittest Has Evolved: Try Survival of the Kindest," NBC News (March 7, 2017), https://www.nbcnews.com/better/relation-ships/survival-fittest-has-evolved-try-survival-kindest-n730196.

6. Herbert Spencer was a contemporary of Darwin and as Kukk notes, coined the phrase, "survival of the fittest" after reading Darwin's works.

7. Kukk, "Survival of the Kindest."

8. Gina Pell, "Meet the Perennials," The What (October 19, 2016), http://thewhatlist.com/meet-the-perennials/. Gina Pell, cofounder of a website called The What, suggested using this term in a blog post titled "Meet the Perennials" in a more generic critique against marketers who, in her opinion, often artificially segment individuals by age. While I want to credit her for her suggestion, and only became aware of it after I wrote an earlier draft of this manuscript, I want to deepen its evocative imagery by drawing upon psychological and theological thought.

9. Himmelfarb is the CEO of the nonprofit B3/The Jewish Boomer Platform. "B3 is dedicated to engaging—or re-engaging—Jewish Baby Boomers in Jewish life." (B3/The Jewish Boomer Platform, accessed October 8, 2018, http://www.b3platform.org/index.html.) For more information, visit the website http://www.b3platform.org/index.html.

10. Stuart Himmelfarb, personal correspondence with author, January 24, 2018.

11. Ibid.

12. John Leland, "When Old News Is Good News: The Effect of 6 Elderly New Yorkers on One Middle-Aged Reporter," New York Times (January 3, 2018), https://www.nytimes.com/2018/01/03/insider/when-old-news-is-good-news-the-effect-of-6-elderly-new-yorkers-on-one-middle-aged-reporter-85-and-up.html.

13. John Leland, Happiness Is a Choice You Make: Lessons from a Year among the Oldest Old (New York: Sarah Crichton Books/Farrar, Straus and Giroux, 2018).

14. You can learn more about Search Institute in appendix C.

15. Roehlkepartain et al., Relationships First.

16. Ibid.

17. Eugene C. Roehlkepartain, personal interview with author, October 17, 2017.

18. Alter is a neuropsychologist and founder and clinical director of Partners in Healing, a holistic center for health and wellness that strives to integrate the best of Western and Eastern healing systems.

19. David Alter, personal interview with author, November 8, 2017.

20. Burrus, The Anticipatory Organization, 45.

21. Shimon Peres, No Room for Small Dreams: Courage, Imagination, and the Making of Modern Israel (New York: Custom House, 2017), 223.

22. I'm very grateful that my wife has learned to accept this annoying character trait.

23. Nextdoor, "About Nextdoor," accessed July 18, 2018, https://nextdoor.com/about_us.

24. For information about Dorot, visit http://www.dorotusa.org/site/PageServer?pagename=homepage_DOROT.

25. Judith Turner, personal interview with author, October 2, 2017.

26. Vandana Pant, personal interview with author, September 29, 2017.

27. Donna Butts, personal interview with author, February 27, 2018.

28. Mark L. Meridy, personal interview with author, October 17, 2017.

29. Eugene Roehlkepartain, personal interview with author, October 20, 2017.

Appendix B

1. In framing this Health Care Transition Discussion Guide, I have drawn upon the work of William Bridges, *Managing Transitions: Making the Most of Change*, 3rd ed., with Susan Bridges (Boston: Da Capo Lifelong Books, 2016).

Appendix C

1. Encore.org, "Who We Are," accessed July 27, 2018, https://encore.org/.

2. Encore.org, "Marc Freedman," accessed July 27, 2018, https://encore.org/marc -freedman/.

3. Generation to Generation, "About Generation to Generation," accessed July 29, 2018, https://generationtogeneration.org.

4. Generation to Generation, "Top 10 Gen2Gen Mentoring Movies," Encore. org, accessed July 27, 2018, https://encore.org/the-top-10-gen2gen-mentoring-movies-of-all-time.

5. Generations United, "Our Mission," accessed July 27, 2018, https://www .gu.org/who-we-are/mission/.

6. Generations United, "Donna Butts," accessed July 27, 2018, https://www .gu.org/people/donna-butts/.

7. Generations United, *Creating an Age-Advantaged Community: A Toolkit for Building Intergenerational Communities that Recognize, Engage, and Support All Ages*, accessed July 27, 2018, https://www.gu.org/app/uploads/2018/06/Intergenerational -Toolkit-CreatingAgeAdvantagedCommunities.pdf.

8. DOROT, "Our Vision and Mission," accessed July 27, 2018, http://www.doro tusa.org/site/PageServer?pagename=about_mission_D#.W1t7yNVKjIV.

9. "DOROT Welcomes New Executive Director," *Generations* (Fall 2009): 1, http://www.dorotusa.org/site/DocServer/Generations_Fall_2009.pdf?docID=1541.

10. This bio was written in part by Mark L. Meridy and Judith Turner.

11. DOROT, "National Resources," accessed July 27, 2018, http://www.dorotusa. org/site/PageServer?pagename=seniors_resources_D#.W1uCCtVKjIV.

12. linkAges Community, "About Us," accessed July 27, 2018, https://commu nity.linkages.org/about-us/.

13. Sutter Health: Palo Alto Medical Foundation, *Highlights from the link-Ages Community Evaluation* (2016), http://www.mitimebanks.org/wp-content/up loads/2011/12/linkAges-Community-Evaluation-Highlights.pdf.

14. Search Institute, accessed July 27, 2018, https://www.search-institute.org/.

15. Search Institute, "Leadership Team," accessed July 27, 2018, https://www .search-institute.org/.

16. Search Institute, *The Developmental Relationships Framework*, accessed July 27, 2018, https://www.search-institute.org/wp-content/uploads/2018/05/Developmental-Relationships-Framework_English.pdf.

17. Beth El Synagogue, "Clergy," accessed July 29, 2018, https://www.besyn.org/about/leadership/clergy/; Kate Dietrick, "Rabbi Kassel Abelson Papers Available to Public," *Continuum* (February 28, 2018), https://www.continuum.umn.edu/2018/02/rabbi-kassel-abelson-papers-available-public/.

18. "David Alter, PhD, LP," LinkedIn, accessed July 30, 2018, https://www.linkedin.com/in/drdavidalter/.

19. Partners in Healing, "Dr. David Alter, PhD, LP," accessed July 30, 2018, http://www.pih-mpls.com/.

20. Henry Emmons and David Alter, *Staying Sharp: 9 Keys for a Youthful Brain through Modern Science and Ancient Wisdom* (New York: Touchstone, 2015).

21. David Alter, *Enlarging Your Life Year-by-Year* (blog), accessed July 27, 2018, https://www.drdavidalter.com/blog.

22. Burrus Research, "About Daniel Burrus," accessed July 30, 2018, https://www.burrus.com/about/about-daniel-burrus/.

23. Burrus Research, "Strategic Insights Newsletter: Game Changing Strategies for Shaping the Future," accessed July 27, 2018, https://www.burrus.com/resources/strategic-insights-enewsletter/.

24. B3/The Jewish Boomer Platform, "Welcome to B3," accessed July 29, 2018, http://www.b3platform.org/aboutbio.html.

25. New York University–Wagner, "Stuart Himmelfarb," accessed July 29, 2018, https://wagner.nyu.edu/community/faculty/stuart-himmelfarb.

26. David M. Elcott and Stuart Himmelfarb, "Service-Learning and Jewish Baby Boomers: An Emerging Opportunity or a Best-Missed Chance?" *Journal of Jewish Communal Service* 87, no. 1/2 (Winter/Spring 2012): 198–206, http://jcsana.hs-cluster-1.net/upimagesjcsa/198.pdf.

27. Maslon LLP, "Susan J. Link," accessed July 27, 2018, http://maslon.com/slink.

28. Ibid.

29. David Stillman and Jonah Stillman, *GenZGuru* (blog), accessed July 27, 2018, http://genzguru.com/blog.

30. This bio was written by Sherrill Zehr.

~

Works Cited

Abrahms, Sally. "Five Myths about Baby Boomers." *Washington Post* (November 6, 2015). https://www.washingtonpost.com/opinions/five-myths-about-baby -boomers/2015/11/06/44ca943c-83fb-11e5-8ba6-cec48b74b2a7_story.html?utm _term=.d64411cacf4e.

Adkins, Amy. "Millennials: The Job-Hopping Generation." Gallup Business Journal (May 12, 2016). https://news.gallup.com/businessjournal/191459/millennials-job -hopping-generation.aspx.

Agewave. "About Agewave." Accessed October 7, 2018. http://agewave.com/.

Alter, David. *Enlarging Your Life Year-by-Year* (blog). Accessed July 27, 2018. https:// www.drdavidalter.com/blog.

Alzheimer's Association. "2017 Alzheimer's Disease Facts and Figures." *Alzheimer's & Dementia* 13 (2017): 325–373. https://www.alz.org/documents_custom/2017 -facts-and-figures.pdf.

Alzheimer's Association. "Quick Facts." 2018. https://www.alz.org/facts/.

Anderson, Lydia R. "Generational Differences during Young Adulthood: Families and Households of Baby Boomers and Millennials." *Family Profiles*. Bowling Green, OH: National Center for Family and Marriage Research, 2017. https:// www.bgsu.edu/ncfmr/resources/data/family-profiles/anderson-families-households -boomers-millennials-fp-17-07.html.

"Annual, Perennial, Biennial?" Wildflowers in Bloom. Accessed January 24, 2018. https://aggie-horticulture.tamu.edu/wildseed/growing/annual.html.

Arnett, Jeffrey Jensen. *Emerging Adulthood: The Winding Road from the Late Teens through the Twenties*. New York: Oxford University Press, 2015.

B3/The Jewish Boomer Platform. Accessed October 8, 2018. http://www.b3platform .org/index.html.

Beth El Synagogue. "Clergy." Accessed July 29, 2018. https://www.besyn.org/about/leadership/clergy/.

Botsman, Rachel. "Co-Parenting with Alexa." *New York Times* (October 7, 2017). https://www.nytimes.com/2017/10/07/opinion/sunday/children-alexa-echo-robots.html?action=click&pgtype=Homepage&clickSource=story-heading&module=region&region=region&WT.nav=region&_r=0.

Bown, Chad P. "What Is NAFTA, and What Would Happen to U.S. Trade without It?" *Washington Post* (May 18, 2017). https://www.washingtonpost.com/news/monkey-cage/wp/2017/02/15/what-is-nafta-and-what-would-happen-to-u-s-trade-without-it/?utm_term=.65b83e042cde.

Bridges, William. *Managing Transitions: Making the Most of Change*. 3rd ed. With Susan Bridges. Boston: DeCapo Lifelong Books, 2016.

Brody, Jane E. "Social Interaction Is Critical for Mental and Physical Health." *The New York Times* (June 12, 2017). https://www.nytimes.com/2017/06/12/well/live/having-friends-is-good-for-you.html?mcubz=0&_r=3.

Burrus, Daniel. *The Anticipatory Organization: Turn Disruption and Change into Opportunity and Advantage*. Austin, TX: Greenleaf Book Group Press, 2017.

Burrus Research. "About Daniel Burrus." Accessed July 30, 2018. https://www.burrus.com/about/about-daniel-burrus/.

Burrus Research. "Strategic Insights Newsletter: Game Changing Strategies for Shaping the Future." Accessed July 27, 2018. https://www.burrus.com/resources/strategic-insights-enewsletter/.

Campbell, Joseph, Moyers, Bill. *The Power of Myth*. New York: Anchor Books, 1991.

Caspi, Avshalom, HonaLee Harrington, Terrie E. Moffitt, Barry J. Milne, and Richie Poulton. "Socially Isolated Children 20 Years Later: Risk of Cardiovascular Disease." *Archives of Pediatrics & Adolescent Medicine* 160, no. 8 (2006): 805–811. doi: 10.1001/archpedi.160.8.805.

Chapin, Harry, and Sandy Chapin. "Cat's in the Cradle." Warner/Chappell Music, Inc., 1974, compact disc. Released on January 1, 1974.

Clifford, Matthew, and Eva Chiang. "The Great American Principal Turnover—And How Districts Can Stop the Churn." *RealClear Education* (August 25, 2016). https://www.realcleareducation.com/articles/2016/08/25/the_great_american_principal_turnover_1303.html.

"The Day I Got Microchipped." Fast Company (January 23, 2018). Video. https://www.fastcompany.com/video/the-day-i-got-microchipped/CZ2x7ukV.

Dicker, Richard C., Fátima Coronado, Denise Koo, and Roy Gibson Parrish. *Principles of Epidemiology in Public Health Practice*. 3rd ed. Atlanta, GA: U.S. Department of Health and Human Services, 2012. https://www.cdc.gov/ophss/csels/dsepd/ss1978/ss1978.pdf.

Dietrick, Kate. "Rabbi Kassel Abelson Papers Available to Public." *Continuum* (February 28, 2018). https://www.continuum.umn.edu/2018/02/rabbi-kassel-abelson-papers-available-public/.

Digital Learning Compass. "Distance Education Enrollment Report 2017." Accessed July 1, 2018. http://onlinelearningsurvey.com/reports/digtiallearningcompassenrollment2017info.pdf.

Dimock, Michael. "Defining Generations: Where Millennials End and Post-Millennials Begin." Pew Research Center (March 1, 2018). http://www.pewresearch.org/fact-tank/2018/03/01/defining-generations-where-millennials-end-and-post-millennials-begin/.

DiSalvo, David. "Loneliness Is a Mind Killer—Study Shows Link to Rapid Cognitive Decline in Older Adults." *Forbes* (July 24, 2015). https://www.forbes.com/sites/daviddisalvo/2015/07/24/loneliness-is-a-mind-killer-study-shows-link-with-rapid-cognitive-decline-in-older-adults/#435600cb7aec.

DOROT. "National Resources." Accessed July 27, 2018. http://www.dorotusa.org/site/PageServer?pagename=seniors_resources_D#.W1uCCtVKjIV.

DOROT. "Our Vision and Mission." Accessed July 19, 2019. http://www.dorotusa.org/site/PageServer?pagename=homepage_DOROT.

"DOROT Welcomes New Executive Director." *Generations* (Fall 2009): 1. http://www.dorotusa.org/site/DocServer/Generations_Fall_2009.pdf?docID=1541.

Dugan, Andrew, and Bailey Nelson. "3 Trends That Will Disrupt Your Workplace Forever." Gallup Business Journal (June 8, 2017). https://news.gallup.com/businessjournal/211799/trends-disrupt-workplace-forever.aspx.

Elcott, David M., and Stuart Himmelfarb. "Service-Learning and Jewish Baby Boomers: An Emerging Opportunity or a Best-Missed Chance?" *Journal of Jewish Communal Service* 87, no. 1/2 (Winter/Spring 2012): 198–206. http://jcsana.hs-cluster-1.net/upimagesjcsa/198.pdf.

Eliades, Angelo. "Perennial Plants and Permaculture." Permaculture Research Institute (June 6, 2012). https://permaculturenews.org/2012/06/06/perennial-plants-and-permaculture/.

Emmons, Henry, and David Alter. *Staying Sharp: 9 Keys for a Youthful Brain through Modern Science and Ancient Wisdom*. New York: Touchstone, 2015.

Encore.org. "Marc Freedman: President and CEO." Accessed February 13, 2018. https://encore.org/who-we-are/team/marc-freedman/.

Encore.org. "Who We Are." Accessed July 27, 2018. https://encore.org/.

Entis, Laura. "Chronic Loneliness Is a Modern-Day Epidemic." *Fortune* (June 22, 2016). http://fortune.com/2016/06/22/loneliness-is-a-modern-day-epidemic/.

"Entrepreneur of the Week: Emma Yang, Timeless," The Longevity Network (March 1, 2017). https://www.longevitynetwork.org/exclusive/entrepreneur-of-the-week-emma-yang-timeless/.

"FAQ." Thiel Fellowship. Accessed July 1, 2018. http://thielfellowship.org/faq.

Fine, Allison H. *Matterness: Fearless Leadership for a Social World*. Legacy Books, LLC: 2014.

Freund, James. "A Retirement Scorecard." *Delaware Lawyer* 24, no. 2 (2006): 8–11. http://delawarebarfoundation.org/delawyer/Volume_24_Number_2_Summer_2006.pdf.

Friedman, Thomas L. *Thank You for Being Late: An Optimist's Guide to Thriving in the Age of Accelerations*. New York: Farrar, Straus and Giroux, 2016.

Fry, Richard. "It's Becoming More Common for Young Adults to Live at Home—and for Longer Stretches." Pew Research Center (May 5, 2017). http://www.pewre

search.org/fact-tank/2017/05/05/its-becoming-more-common-for-young-adults-to -live-at-home-and-for-longer-stretches/.

Fry, Richard. "Millennials Projected to Overtake Baby Boomers as America's Largest Generation." Pew Research Center (March 1, 2018). http://www.pewresearch.org/ fact-tank/2016/04/25/millennials-overtake-baby-boomers/.

Fry, Richard, Ruth Igielnik, and Eileen Patten. "How Millennials Today Compare with Their Grandparents 50 Years Ago." Pew Research Center (March 16, 2018). http://www.pewresearch.org/fact-tank/2018/03/16/how-millennials-compare -with-their-grandparents/.

Generation to Generation. "About Generation to Generation." Accessed July 29, 2018. https://generationtogeneration.org.

Generation to Generation. "Top 10 Gen2Gen Mentoring Movies." Encore.org. Accessed July 27, 2018. https://encore.org/the-top-10-gen2gen-mentoring-movies -of-all-time.

Generations United. "Creating an Age-Advantaged Community: A Toolkit for Building Intergenerational Communities that Recognize, Engage, and Support All Ages." Accessed July 27, 2018. https://www.gu.org/app/uploads/2018/06/ Intergenerational-Toolkit-CreatingAgeAdvantagedCommunities.pdf.

Generations United. "Donna Butts." Accessed July 27, 2018. https://www.gu.org/ people/donna-butts/.

Generations United. "Our Mission." Accessed July 27, 2018. https://www.gu.org/ who-we-are/mission/.

Generations United. *Raising the Children of the Opioid Epidemic: Solutions and Support for Grandfamilies*. Accessed June 21, 2018. https://dl2.pushbulletusercontent.com/ qdCNUO2JMMZKzKRjyIlwbgjMtf39xkKa/16-Report-SOGF-Final.pdf.

Generations United and the Eisner Foundation. *I Need You, You Need Me: The Young, the Old, and What We Can Achieve Together*. Executive Summary (May 2017). https://dl2.pushbulletusercontent.com/meKWf8Kr67yddSbALqs18KWN- NIqQci4I/GU-Exec-Summary-WEB.pdf.

GenForward. "A Survey of the GenForward Project at the University of Chicago." Accessed June 28, 2018. https://genforwardsurvey.com/.

GenForward. "GenForward: Millennials' Political Views." September 12, 2017. https://genforwardsurvey.com/assets/uploads/2017/09/GenForward-Education-Sur vey-Fact-Sheet.pdf.

Graf, Nikki. "Today's Young Workers are More Likely than Ever to Have a Bachelor's Degree." Pew Research Center (May 16, 2016). http://www.pewresearch.org/ fact-tank/2017/05/16/todays-young-workers-are-more-likely-than-ever-to-have-a -bachelors-degree/.

"Grandfamilies." Generations United. Accessed June 21, 2018. https://www.gu.org/ explore-our-topics/grandfamilies/.

"Grandfamilies Statistics." Generations United. Accessed June 21, 2018. https://www.gu.org/grandfamilies-statistics/.

Granville, Kevin. "How to Manage Your Career." *New York Times* (January 28, 2018). https://www.nytimes.com/guides/business/manage-your-career.

Harari, Yuval Noad. *Sapiens: A Brief History of Humankind*. London: Vintage Books, 2014.

Hari, Johann. "Everything You Think You Know about Addiction Is Wrong." TEDGlobalLondon. Video, 14:43. June 2015. https://www.ted.com/talks/johann _hari_everything_you_think_you_know_about_addiction_is_wrong.

Harrell, Rodney. "Creating Room for Accessory Dwelling Units." AARP (November, 2017). www.aarp.org/livable-communities/housing/info-2015/accessory -dwelling-units-model-ordinance.html.

Henig, Robin Marantz. "The Age of Grandparents Is Made of Many Tragedies." *Atlantic* (June 1, 2018). https://www.theatlantic.com/family/archive/2018/06/this -is-the-age-of-grandparents/561527/.

"Here's Why Your Parents Stayed at the Same Job for 20 Years" Associated Press (May 10, 2016). http://fortune.com/2016/05/10/baby-boomers-millennials-jobs/.

Herring, Hayim, and Terri Martinson Elton. *Leading Congregations and Nonprofits in a Connected World: Platforms, People, and Purpose*. Lanham, MD: Rowman & Littlefield, 2017.

Hollis, James. *Meaning in the Second Half of Life*. New York: Gotham Books, 2005.

Holt-Lunstad, Julianne, Timothy B. Smith, and J. Bradley Layton. "Social Relationships and Mortality Risk: A Meta-Analytic Review." *PLOS Medicine* (July 27, 2010). http://journals.plos.org/plosmedicine/article?id=10.1371/journal.pmed.1000316.

"Human or Machine: Can You Tell Who Wrote These Poems?" *NPR* (June 27, 2016). https://www.npr.org/sections/alltechconsidered/2016/06/27/480639265/ human-or-machine-can-you-tell-who-wrote-these-poems.

Jay, Meg. "Why 30 Is Not the New 20." TED2013. Video, 14:46. February 2013. https://www.ted.com/talks/meg_jay_why_30_is_not_the_new_20.

Jiang, Jingjing. "Millennials Stand Out for Their Technology Use, But Older Generations Also Embrace Digital Life." Pew Research Center (May 2, 2018). http://www.pewresearch.org/fact-tank/2018/05/02/millennials-stand-out-for-their -technology-use-but-older-generations-also-embrace-digital-life/.

Judson. "About Us." Accessed July 19, 2018. https://www.judsonsmartliving.org/about.

"Just-in-Time." Toyota. Accessed June 21, 2018. http://www.toyota-global.com/com pany/vision_philosophy/toyota_production_system/just-in-time.html.

Kamenetz, Anya. "Our Screenless Future Calls for Augmented Parenting." Fast Company (January 29, 2018). https://www.fastcompany.com/40478880/our-screenless -future-calls-for-augmented-parenting.

Kaplan, Robert S., and David P. Norton. "The Balanced Scorecard—Measures that Drive Performance." *Harvard Business Review* (January-February 1992). Accessed July 5, 2018. https://hbr.org/1992/01/the-balanced-scorecard-measures-that -drive-performance-2.

Khullar, Dhruv. "How Social Isolation Is Killing Us." *The New York Times* (December 22, 2016). https://www.nytimes.com/2016/12/22/upshot/how-social-isolation- is-killing-us.html?mcubz=0.

Kim, Leland. "Loneliness Linked to Serious Health Problems and Death among Elderly: UCSF Researchers Find Social Factors Play Major Role in Older Adults'

Health." University of California San Francisco (June 18, 2012). https://www.ucsf
.edu/news/2012/06/12184/loneliness-linked-serious-health-problems-and-death
-among-elderly.

Knock, Inc. "What We Do." Accessed July 4, 2018. https://knockinc.com/about/.

Kochhar, Rakesh, and Anthony Cillufo. "How Wealth Inequality Has Changed in
the U.S. Since the Great Recession, by Race, Ethnicity and Income," Pew Research
Center (November 1, 2017), http://www.pewresearch.org/fact-tank/2017/11/01/
how-wealth-inequality-has-changed-in-the-u-s-since-the-great-recession-by-race-
ethnicity-and-income/.

Kukk, Christopher L. *The Compassionate Achiever: How Helping Others Fuels Success.*
New York: HarperOne, 2017.

Kukk, Christopher. "Survival of the Fittest Has Evolved: Try Survival of the Kindest." NBC News (March 7, 2017). https://www.nbcnews.com/better/relationships/
survival-fittest-has-evolved-try-survival-kindest-n730196.

Lancaster, Lynne C., and David Stillman. *The M-Factor: How the Millennial Generation is Rocking the Workplace.* New York: HarperBusiness, 2010.

Lancaster, Lynne C., and David Stillman. *When Generations Collide: Who They Are,
Why They Crash, How to Solve the Generational Puzzle at Work.* New York: HarperCollins, 2002.

Leland, John. *Happiness Is a Choice You Make: Lessons from a Year among the Oldest
Old.* New York: Sarah Crichton Books/Farrar, Straus and Giroux, 2018.

Leland, John. "When Old News Is Good News: The Effect of 6 Elderly New Yorkers on One Middle-Aged Reporter." *New York Times* (January 3, 2018). https://
www.nytimes.com/2018/01/03/insider/when-old-news-is-good-news-the-effect-of
-6-elderly-new-yorkers-on-one-middle-aged-reporter-85-and-up.html.

Lieber, Ron. "A Game to Help Students Pay the Right Price for College." *New York
Times* (September 29, 2017). https://www.nytimes.com/2017/09/29/your-money/
paying-for-college/payback-college-loans.html.

linkAges Community. "About Us." Accessed July 27, 2018. https://community.link-
ages.org/about-us/.

LinkedIn. "David Alter, PhD, LP." Accessed July 30, 2018. https://www.linkedin.
com/in/drdavidalter/.

Maslon. "Susan J. Link." Accessed July 27, 2018. http://maslon.com/slink.

Mayo Clinic. "Living Wills and Advanced Directives for Medical Decisions."
Last modified November 11, 2014. https://www.mayoclinic.org/healthy-lifestyle/
consumer-health/in-depth/living-wills/art-20046303.

McDonald, Kyle. "Neural Nets for Generating Music." Artists and Machine Intelligence (August 25, 2017). https://medium.com/artists-and-machine-intelligence/
neural-nets-for-generating-music-f46dffac21c0.

McPherson, Miller, Lynn Smith-Lovin, and Matthew E. Brashears. "Social Isolation
in America: Changes in Core Discussion Networks over Two Decades." Abstract.
American Sociological Review (June 1, 2006). http://journals.sagepub.com/doi/abs/1
0.1177/000312240607100301?ssource=mfc&rss=1&.

MedicineNet. "Medical Definition of Epidemic." Last modified May 13, 2016. https://www.medicinenet.com/script/main/art.asp?articlekey=3273.

Miller, Dorothy A. "The 'Sandwich' Generation: Adult Children of the Aging." *Social Work* 26, no. 5 (1981): 419–23. https://www.jstor.org/stable/23712207?seq=1#page _scan_tab_contents.

Miller, Josh. LinkedIn. Accessed July 1, 2018. https://www.linkedin.com/in/josh-millerceo/.

"Mobile Fact Sheet." Pew Research Center (February 5, 2018). http://www.pewinter net.org/fact-sheet/mobile/.

Moran, Gwen. "Employers like EY and IBM Are Now Hiring Workers without College Degrees." Fast Company (May 15, 2018). https://www.fastcompany.com/40565547/ why-some-companies-are-dropping-degree-requirements-in-hiring.

Murthy, Vivek H. "Work and the Loneliness Epidemic." *Harvard Business Review* (September 2017). https://hbr.org/cover-story/2017/09/work-and-the-loneliness-epidemic.

"Music Students Living at Cleveland Retirement Home." CBC News video, 10:37. Posted on July 12, 2016. https://www.cbc.ca/news/thenational/music-students -living-at-cleveland-retirement-home-1.3311116.

National PACE Association. "Is PACE for You?" 2018. http://www.npaonline.org/ pace-you#History.

Nesterly. "Frequently Asked Questions." Accessed July 19. https://www.nesterly.io/faq.

New York University–Wagner. "Stuart Himmelfarb." Accessed July 29, 2018. https:// wagner.nyu.edu/community/faculty/stuart-himmelfarb.

Nextdoor. "About Nextdoor." Accessed July 18, 2018. https://nextdoor.com/ about_us.

Nguyen, Janet and David Brancaccio. "Do Millennials Think College Is Worth the Cost?" *Kera News* (October 3, 2017). http://keranews.org/post/do-millennials-think-college-worth-cost.

"Number of Apps Available in Leading App Stores as of 1st Quarter 2018." Statistica (2018). https://www.statista.com/statistics/276623/number-of-apps-available-in -leading-app-stores/.

Office of the United States Trade Representative. "North American Free Trade Agreement (NAFTA)" Accessed July 4, 2018. https://ustr.gov/trade-agreements/ free-trade-agreements/north-american-free-trade-agreement-nafta.

"Older Drivers Set Record for Second Year: Licensed Drivers over 65 Continue to Increase, Teen Drivers Remain at Near-Record Lows." U.S. Department of Transportation. Last modified November 27, 2017. https://www.transportation. gov/briefing-room/fhwa2017.

Olson, Rochelle. "In Hiring of Teenage Consultant, Vikings Take Long-Term View of Fan Base." *StarTribune* (September 15, 2017). http://www.startribune.com/ minnesota-vikings-hire-18-year-old-to-connect-with-gen-z/444200463/.

Ornstein, Katherine A., Bruce Leff, Kenneth E. Covinsky, Christine S. Ritchie, Alex D. Federman, Laken Roberts, Amy S. Kelley, Albert L. Siu, and Sarah L. Szanton.

"Epidemiology of the Homebound Population in the United States." *JAMA Internal Medicine* 175, no. 7 (2015): 1,180–1,186. https://jamanetwork.com/journals/jamainternalmedicine/fullarticle/2296016?resultClick=3.

Partners in Healing. "Dr. David Alter, PhD, LP." Accessed July 30, 2018. http://www.pih-mpls.com/.

Peale, Norman V. "Confident Living." *Greensboro Daily News* (February 15, 1959).

Pell, Gina. "Meet the Perennials." *The What* (October 19, 2016). http://thewhatlist.com/meet-the-perennials/.

Peres, Shimon. *No Room for Small Dreams: Courage, Imagination, and the Making of Modern Israel.* New York: Custom House, 2017.

Petriglieri, Gianpiero. "The Portable Man is the New 'Organization Man.'" *Harvard Business Review* (August 10, 2017). https://hbr.org/2017/08/the-portable-leader-is-the-new-organization-man.

Petriglieri, Gianpiero, Jennifer Louise Petriglieri, and Jack Denfeld Wood. "Fast Tracks and Inner Journeys: Crafting Portable Selves for Contemporary Careers." *Administrative Science Quarterly* (July 12, 2017). doi:10.1177/0001839217720930.

Pimentel, Joseph. "College Students, Boomers Now Neighbors as Senior Housing Goes Up near Universities." Bisnow (January 3, 2018). https://www.bisnow.com/national/news/senior-housing/is-building-senior-housing-next-to-universities-the-next-big-housing-trend-in-the-us-83208.

"Political Polarization in the American Public: How Increasing Ideological Uniformity and Partisan Antipathy Affect Politics, Compromise and Everyday Life." Pew Research Center (June 12, 2014). http://www.people-press.org/2014/06/12/political-polarization-in-the-american-public/.

Prinstein, Mitch. "Popular People Live Longer." *New York Times* (June 1, 2017). https://www.nytimes.com/2017/06/01/opinion/sunday/popular-people-live-longer.html?mcubz=0&_r=0.

Project for Public Spaces. "Ray Oldenburg." Last modified December 31, 2008. Accessed July 19, 2018. https://www.pps.org/article/roldenburg.

Putnam, Robert D. *Bowling Alone: The Collapse and Revival of American Community.* New York: Simon & Schuster, 2001.

Redford, Patrick. "Vikings Hire Teen Consultant to Teach Them How to Be Cool." *Deadspin* (September 13, 2017). https://deadspin.com/vikings-hire-teen-consultant-to-teach-them-how-to-be-co-1806527641.

Remnick, David. "Leonard Cohen Makes It Darker." *New Yorker* (October 17, 2016). https://www.newyorker.com/magazine/2016/10/17/leonard-cohen-makes-it-darker.

Rideout, Victoria. *The Common Sense Census: Media Use by Kids Age Zero to Eight.* San Francisco: Common Sense Media, 2017. https://www.commonsensemedia.org/sites/default/files/uploads/research/0-8_executivesummary_release_final_1.pdf.

"Rising Student Debt Weighs Heavily on Millennials: Student Debt Jumps 150 Percent." The Center for Generational Kinetics (September 18, 2017). http://genhq.com/rising-student-debt-weighs-heavily-millennials/.

Riess, Jana. "The Bible in Emojis? Terrific Idea, Sloppy Execution." *Religion News Service* (June 1, 2016). https://religionnews.com/2016/06/01/the-bible-in-emojis-terrific-idea-sloppy-execution/.

Rigoni, Brandon, and Bailey Nelson, "Few Millennials Are Engaged at Work," Gallup Business Journal (August 30, 2016), https://news.gallup.com/businessjournal/195209/few-millennials-engaged-work.aspx?utm_source=link_newsv9&utm_campaign=item_211799&utm_medium=copy.

Ritholtz, Barry. "Millennials Are Out of the Basement and Into Buying Homes." *Bloomberg Opinion* (February 2, 2018). https://www.bloomberg.com/view/articles/2018-02-02/millennials-are-out-of-the-basement-and-into-buying-homes.

Roehlkepartain, Eugene, Kent Pekel, Amy Syvertsen, Jenna Sethi, Theresa Sullivan, and Peter Scales. *Relationships First: Creating Connections That Help Young People Thrive* (Minneapolis, MN: Search Institute, 2017). http://page.search-institute org/relationships-first-020217a.

Sander, Thomas H., and Robert D. Putnam. "Still Bowling Alone? The Post-9/11 Split." *Journal of Democracy* 21, no. 1 (2010): 9–16. doi: 10.1353/jod.0.0153.

Saporito, Thomas J. "It's Time to Acknowledge CEO Loneliness." *Harvard Business Review* (February 15, 2012). https://hbr.org/2012/02/its-time-to-acknowledge-ceo-lo.

Scheiber, Noam. "The Pop Up Employer: Build a Team, Do the Job, Say Goodbye." *New York Times* (July 12, 2017). https://www.nytimes.com/2017/07/12/business/economy/flash-organizations-labor.html?emc=eta1.

Schwartz, Barry. *The Paradox of Choice: Why More Is Less.* New York: HarperCollins Publishers Inc., 2003.

Search Institute. Accessed July 27, 2018. https://www.search-institute.org/.

Search Institute. "The Developmental Relationships Framework." Accessed July 27, 2018. https://www.search-institute.org/wp-content/uploads/2018/05/Developmental-Relationships-Framework_English.pdf.

Search Institute. "Leadership Team." Accessed July 27, 2018. https://www.search-institute.org/.

Seinfeld, Jerry. "The Old Man," *Seinfeld.* Season 4. Episode 17. Directed by Tom Cherones. Aired February 18, 1993. Los Angeles, CA: Castle Rock Entertainment, 1993.

Seppala, Emma, and Peter Sims, "The Average American Has Only One Close Friend—Here's How We Got to This Point," *Business Insider* (July 16, 2017), http://www.businessinsider.com/emma-seppala-the-average-american-has-only-one-close-friend-2017-7.

Sherman, Erik. "Why Millennials Boomerang Home: It's Not Student Loans. It's Worse," *Forbes* (January 11, 2017). https://www.forbes.com/sites/eriksherman/2017/01/11/why-millennials-boomerang-home-its-not-student-loans-its-worse/#5677e5a45d86.

Spayd, Liz. "As Recession Forces Layoffs, Older Workers Feel Targeted; Area, Nation Have Rise in Bias Complaints." *Washington Post* (September 29, 1992). https://www.highbeam.com/doc/1P2-1027461.html.

Stillman, David, and Jonah Stillman. *Gen Z @ Work: How the Next Generation Is Transforming the Workplace*. New York: Harper Business, 2017.

Stillman, David. *GenZGuru* (blog). Accessed July 27, 2018. http://genzguru.com/blog.

Stratasys. "4D Printing: Revolutionizing Material Form and Control." Accessed February 13, 2018. http://www.stratasys.com/industries/education/research/4d-printing-project.

Sutter Health: Palo Alto Medical Foundation. *Highlights from the linkAges Community Evaluation* (2016). http://www.mitimebanks.org/wp-content/uploads/2011/12/linkAges-Community-Evaluation-Highlights.pdf.

Tavernise, Sabrina. "U.S. Suicide Rate Surges to a 30-Year High." *New York Times* (April 22, 2016). https://www.nytimes.com/2016/04/22/health/us-suicide-rate-surges-to-a-30-year-high.html.

Turkle, Sherry. *Reclaiming Conversation: The Power of Talk in a Digital Age*. New York: Penguin Press, 2015.

Twenge, Jean M. "Have Smartphones Destroyed a Generation?" *The Atlantic* (September 2017). https://www.theatlantic.com/magazine/archive/2017/09/has-the-smartphone-destroyed-a-generation/534198/.

U.S. Census Bureau. "Sixty-Five Plus in the United States." U.S. Department of Commerce. Last modified October 31, 2011. https://www.census.gov/population/socdemo/statbriefs/agebrief.html.

United Hospital Fund. "NORC Blueprint: A Guide to Community Action." 2015. http://www.norcblueprint.org/faq/.

Wai, Jonathan. "The Myth of the College Dropout." *CBS News* (April 21, 2017). https://www.cbsnews.com/news/the-myth-of-the-college-dropout/.

Werde, Skylar. "Early Boomers + Generation Jones: Meet the Two Boomer Subgroups." *Bridgeworks* (blog). November 9, 2015. http://www.generations.com/2015/11/09/early-boomers-generation-jones-meet-the-two-boomer-subgroups/.

"The Whys and Hows of Generations Research." Pew Research Center (September 3, 2015). http://www.people-press.org/2015/09/03/the-whys-and-hows-of-generations-research/.

Whyte, William Hollingsworth. *The Organization Man*. Garden City, NY: Doubleday, 1956.

"Wills For Heroes." Minnesota State Bar Association. Accessed June 21, 2018. https://www.mnbar.org/about-msba/related-organizations/wills-for-heroes#.WyJzSadKg2w.

World Health Organization. "Age-Friendly Cities and Communities." Accessed July 19, 2018. http://www.who.int/ageing/projects/age-friendly-cities-communities/en/.

World Trade Organization. "The WTO." Accessed February 11, 2018. https://www.wto.org/english/thewto_e/thewto_e.htm.

WP Master. "99Designs x WP Master." 2018. https://wpmaster.com/99designs-x-wp-master/.

Wright. "8 Modern In-Law Units." *Dwell* (May 13, 2017). https://www.dwell.com/article/8-modern-in-law-units-12c75f54.

"Your Eyes Really Are the Window to Your Soul." *Psychology Today* (December 31, 2015). https://www.psychologytoday.com/blog/talking-apes/201512/your-eyes-really-are-the-window-your-soul.

~

Index